FOREVER 22

FOREVER 22

CARSON GEORGE

Library of Congress Control Number:		2014912350
ISBN:	Hardcover	978-1-4990-4870-4
	Softcover	978-1-4990-4871-1
	eBook	978-1-4990-4869-8

This book was printed in the United States of America.

Rev. date: 07/09/2014

To order additional copies of this book, contact:
Xlibris LLC
1-888-795-4274
www.Xlibris.com
Orders@Xlibris.com
552164

FOREWORD

When one meets Carson George for the first time, one immediately comes away with a smile and the sense of a happy man who has a genuine and real love of life and the positive outlook of someone being blessed. Yet the real story that unfolds each and every day is that of a man from the hills of Kentucky who has witnessed and experienced firsthand the pain and heartache that comes from war.

First, Carson served in the army during Vietnam, then as a civilian contractor in support of American troops in Iraq. While working in Iraq, Carson and his family suffered the ultimate fate of a phone call and a knock on the door with the words "We regret to inform you." A loving father lost his marine son, Lance Corporal Phillip C. George, who was serving in Afghanistan in 2005. Carson was given the honor of accompanying Phillip's body home to Texas. Carson's life was changed forever.

Carson knew when he hung up the phone what he had to do. The journey he was to begin would eventually have him travel all over the state of Texas honoring all the Texas military fallen heroes since September 11, 2001, and their families. His story is of one man who has come to know that with God all things are possible, and that each of us can make a positive difference in other people's lives. By focusing on others and giving honor where honor is due, an army of one can move hearts, inspire others, and change lives in ways that are unimaginable. It is in giving that one truly receives the full blessings of life.

Through his writing, Carson shares his most intimate thoughts and feelings that have given him the strength he never knew was his but came to him through the Grace of God. Through this book's pages, he shares stories of many of the amazing places and people he has met in his travels. You will discover, as I have, that Carson's son Phillip is very much alive and lives through his father's unselfish desire to serve others and to be a part of something much greater than himself—the fellowship of men.

You will undoubtedly be inspired as I have been in getting to know Carson George on an intimate level. In *Forever 22*, Carson shares a powerful message and his personal testimony of his healing transformation. Even through the loss of a son, Carson is living proof that you can still have and share a spiritual and physical happiness beyond all understanding, while sharing the joy that comes from the love of God.

Forever 22 is the story and journey of a Gold Star father who has endured the loss of his son in battle and has come to discover a higher understanding and appreciation of his faith in God, and the life lessons learned that have revealed the real power and purpose of God's love and the victory that comes from it.

Roy A. James
Texas State Director
Honor and Remember of Texas

INTRODUCTION

Need for Change

August 18, 2005, was a day that changed my life forever. I want to thank you for giving me this opportunity to share this life-changing experience with you. My intent is to have you feel as though you are right beside me every step of the way. A chance to walk that mile in my boots, if you will. A chance to walk with me from the starting point and beyond. Forever 22 will grab your heart during the lighter times of life, especially those that we can laugh about because they were laughable. Then there are those times when you will try to feel my pain but cannot even begin to get there. Your walk with me will give you a chance to see how a solid foundation at times is the only rock solid enough to stand against the storm that comes into one's life. Walking with me, you will see that God walks with you during the good, the bad, and the ugly of life. You will see that God, as some believe, is not safely tucked away, far out in the heavens somewhere. As you walk with me, you will see that He answers ordinary, everyday prayers. You and I walking side by side will learn that while we cannot always prevent bad things from happening, we can build a strong foundation on which we can stand against them. Facing into the storm and coming out the other side of it, standing on our solid rock. As you and I walk through this story, we will face all that comes our way. We can control the way we deal with whatever we have to face.

To start the walk beside me you should probably, in your mind, put on a pair of steel-toed work boots. Steel toes are required where we are going. We will begin this story with a kind of meet-and-greet. Probably one of the first things you need to know about me is that I am an early riser. Most mornings start for me around O dark thirty—that is a military phrase used for long before the sun rises. Very few mornings do I start my day without a cup of black joe—that is, my morning coffee without cream or sugar. My thought here is do not ruin a good cup of joe. If you are an early riser, then we already have something in common. This is a special time of my day: while sipping my joe, I search my heart for the answer God has given it, from "when I lay my head down" the night before. So now that you have your hypothetical boots on, you are ready to have your morning cup of joe with me. This is most likely a bit earlier than you are used to getting up. It is during these early morning hours you will learn about this concept God introduced to my heart. The introduction to "When I lay my head down" to my heart happened sometime before the start of this story. That is kind of the way God has been throughout my life. I rather allowed Him to be there. I had reached the point in life where I had no idea which way to go but continued on the path I was on anyway, and that just was not an attractive option.

The month of May 2004 has just started when we start our journey. It's an ordinary night. At fifty-six years old, I have been giving a lot of thought to the last third of my life. I think it might be safe for us to assume that at around sixty, most of us understand that we are at least close to entering into the years fondly referred to as the golden years. Assuming that a point well taken as being close to a given fact, then try to imagine being at this point in life and having no idea how you are going to get through them and with what you will go through them with. At this point, I am a man, like so many, with more life left than the means to live it. While money does not have to be the number one priority in life—in fact, I believe that if it is, then you might go through the last part of your life with your money being the only thing you have—I do believe that it is a necessity, and I was coming up short in this department.

I think we can fairly divide our life into three segments. The first third is that time from birth until it is time for you to leave the nest of home. The second third is that period from leaving the nest to the time before retirement from the work world, not retirement from life. The third is that part of life that takes you into those final chapters of your life to your final sunset.

It is that last third that I welcome you to join me for this walk. You are going to be walking into the front edge of those sunset years with me. From where we stand right now, I do not see much of a sunset, nor do I see anything golden in them. I am about to turn fifty-six years old in a few days. Now if you are a much younger reader, do not go away. You really need to pay attention, so you do not make the same mistakes I have made. I wrote *Forever 22* with the purpose of making a difference in other people's lives. From the experiences of others, we'll learn that the wise live their lives the way God intended them to live.

The intent here is to encourage and inspire you no matter what point you happen to be on at this time. We are now ready to start walking through this story together. If you have some years on you and reading this book, then most likely, you know what I am talking about in the first few pages of this chapter. You probably identify with the dilemma I find myself at the time; either way, I had you in mind.

We will start our walk out with a very short and to-the-point introduction. We will start with the concept of "when I lay my head down"—a very simple and most powerful concept. If you know that God is always with us, then stick around. If you are uncertain, stick around and you will find out that He is. As I share how God changed my life through a tragedy, walk with me from what seemed to be a doomed rest of my life through a revival of hope and then to what would seems to be a great finish to my working days when we get to the mountaintop. What an experience: just when everything seems to be working against you. One morning, while on that mountaintop, within minutes, life would change forever. Come and walk beside me as I find myself in a lonesome valley, knocked off that mountaintop in a flash of a moment in time. Walk with me when my heart could not comprehend anything of what had happened when I found myself in the valley of the shadow of death. Walk beside me as I relive my walk in the valley on my own; l let your heart rejoice in knowing that I did not have to walk it alone after all.

I am an eight-year Vietnam army veteran—that and a dime would not get me a cup of coffee as it would have during the WWII era. I have exactly zilch set aside for retirement. As you take that walk in my boots, you will learn that I have never blamed anyone else for my lack. It simply could never fly with me as I would know in my heart that there would not be one ounce of truth in it. I am solely responsible for being where I find myself now. I have always made a living using my hands. I am a Christian, a husband, and a father; and at this point in life, I have become a political junkie. I can argue and argue until I am blue in the face, and when I wake up the next morning, the world does not seem to have changed a whole lot by anything I might say or think one way or the other. I would stay up all night, or at least until election results are in from the polling places. I would follow the political talk shows on the radio and on television (we did not have cable then).

Since you are walking in my boots, try to imagine yourself as I described me in the preceding paragraphs. Can you feel the weight on your shoulders and the heaviness of each step you try to take, knowing you might have been in a better place, at least financially, had you been a little wiser about your choices? As you walk on in my shoes, can you feel the slump in my shoulders as I grasp a full understanding of the fact that I would have to continue for as long as I can in the direction I have been traveling? I simply saw no option I could reach for; everything was beyond my reach.

I will never forget the evening that would change my life come the following morning. My wife and I sat down in front of the television; it was time for the local news. We were the only ones at home. Sara, our youngest daughter and the only one of our children left living at home, was out for the evening. We were ready to eat supper, and since the kids for the most part were out of the house now, it had become our habit to eat in the living room while watching the local and world news.

One segment would catch my attention briefly. A reporter interviewed a woman who was about to go to Iraq to work. She was at a processing center for Kellogg, Brown & Root (KBR). When the reporter asked the woman why she would take a job that would take her to a war zone, her answer was simple and to the point. She explained that she had no retirement fund, and this gave her a chance to change that.

As we watched the report, I did not think anything of it one way or the other. I was ready for the political stuff to come up next. My wife, Penny, was apparently paying attention, and she connected our situation at hand with the reasoning of the woman leaving for Iraq. Penny, almost in a simple passing statement, made a remark after the reporter was finished. "Maybe that's what you ought to do." If I had given it a half thought, I would have realized it was a better solution than any thoughts I had been having.

I found myself in a situation that so many Americans find themselves. Life was coming to the last chapters. The length of time of those last chapters of life would not be the important question; having the means to make it through those years would be. It was getting close to the time to hang up the tool belt, so to speak. The problem with that idea is I would still need to work; I could not afford to hang anything up. I had nothing to retire on, and social security was about eight years out and would not be enough to be able to quit working anyhow. With no idea of what I could do differently, I could not even afford to think about where I would like to be. If I had a choice in changing directions, I would certainly do it. I have always been able to think outside the box, but this box was about to collapse on me. I had not a clue as to how to change any of it. I had worked the last thirty years for myself, and with a lot of hard work, long hours, and long weeks, I manage to eke out a living for my family. When I think of my life in this sense, I am reminded of the television show *The Beverly Hillbillies*. I barely keep my family in a home and put food on the table. However, when I look back on those times in the past, I see that God's hand had been there, and I could not deny it. He had blessed me with so much more than anything money could buy. Do not get me wrong here: if I had a choice of more or less money, I would take more. However, we know that money in itself does not define who we are or who we will be in the end. If I had a chance to do things in a more prudent manner, making wiser choices, then I would do it. Hindsight, as they say, is often 20/20; financial situation, good or bad, does not produce the blessings of life.

If walking beside me sounds familiar, welcome to a point so many Americans are in today. We work hard all of our lives, we raise our families, and at the end of that road, there is more life left than money needed to live on. Can you begin to feel the weight of the situation I find myself in?

All my life, I have believed firmly in God and believed without doubt that Christ died on the cross for my sake. I have no problem believing that God created all that is, and that includes me. When it came to the immediate problems of life, I believed that God gave us a mind to use; and if we did not, we lived the consequences of our choices.

I guess I rather felt that while God was a God that loved us—after all, His Son died for us—He just did not manipulate our lives. Therefore, I did things my way. Now looking at fifty-seven years of life, I see that I did not do such a grand job in preparing for my so-called golden years.

Sometime Ago God Taught My Heart

We will notice the current situation in just a little bit. To get a clear understanding of how yesterday, today, and tomorrow connect, you need to now just a tad about a time earlier in my life—the time I cannot even remember. God blessed me with a grateful heart. This heart would serve me well throughout my life. As you walk with me, I hope that you will be able to understand and adopt this for yourself.

Everything else was normal the rest of the evening. When I went to bed that night, I simply prayed, "Lord, I need your wisdom for tomorrow." I had no idea what tomorrow would bring. I did know I needed something other than the same old thing. I was beginning to understand that whatever it might be, I needed more of it. There was nothing more I needed at this point than wisdom greater than my own. That fact was obvious by where my life was right now. God had always been faithful from the time I start to ask Him for His wisdom to answer my prayer. The scripture teaches us that we have to ask according to His will and not our own. Let us just say, without getting theological, that that makes sense. If I ask in a foolish manner, He is faithful not to answer. I am not sure exactly when I started doing this, but I still do it to this day.

What has happened made me learn to reach beyond myself. I reach out to God, and He is capable of reaching to infinity. When I talk to others, I refer to laying my head down as a solution to that sense we get of not being wise enough, which is more often than not. Trust me, all these things will connect to Forever 22.

I hope I am beginning to create a picture for you as you walk in the boots of a man about to turn fifty-six, a man who is also at a loss as to what to do to prepare for the next phase of life. I was coming to the end of my rope with nowhere to go but down the path I was on, and that was a really a bleak option. With my body wearing out, I would not be able to do the work I had done for the past thirty years. I knew I would have to continue doing the only thing I knew how to do. I would have to work until I could no longer do it.

Keep in mind, I was at the end of my rope, doing things my way. I laid my head down that night, with the full expectation that God would answer my prayer. "Lord, I need your wisdom because my wisdom has fallen very short and shallow for the answers I need. Why ask God for His wisdom, which is beyond anything I might possess, and then stay awake to make sure He did not forget him or maybe He might need help finding His answers to my needs? That is ridiculous, if He is God and I believe He has all that I need coming from far beyond myself, then why in the world would I stay awake. God does not need my help. He needs me to be ready to act on His answer to my prayer. I learned that God is always faithful to answer; I would go to sleep and rest so I would be ready when I needed to be.

With your boots laced up and the morning's fresh pot of joe ready for that first cup, it's time to ponder what the day holds in store for us. The cup of joe is sipped, and the serious pondering begins. Things are about to change as I can feel them in my heart with each sip from the cup. I know without a doubt, because I have done it before. I know I can function without my morning cup of joe, but I would rather not, though. What happens next will be the beginning of this story through the next fifteen months. A direct

result of when I came to the point where I threw my hands up and cried out to the Lord: "I am at the end of my reach, and I can reach no farther." It was at that point, humbling my heart before God, that you and I will start making our walk toward the direction we need to go. It is amazing how stubborn we tend to become. Most of the time, gritting our teeth and with our heads lowered, we charge forward, only to run that hard head of ours into something much more solid.

It is after the second cup of "Joe" is just about finished that I could hear the words from Penny's lips from the night before, loud and clear: *Maybe that is what you ought to do.* Then the words of the woman's answer from the interview came back as a clear answer to my prayer for wisdom. These two thoughts did not come from the result of some deep, analytical process of my current situation and the weighing of options available to me that would result in an extremely methodical search for an answer to the problem at hand. No, it was the result of the simple prayer when I laid my head down the night before. "Lord I need your wisdom." God would meet me where I was. These two thoughts originated from deep within my heart and answered me as I petitioned God through prayer.

CHAPTER 1

You have my personal invitation to put your boots on, lace them up, and step into my world. Walk with me through my forty-four months in Iraq. To know what another person is experiencing, you have to walk a mile in his or her shoes, it is said. Well, are you willing to walking that mile or more with me through the good, the bad, and the downright ugly from chapter to chapter?

The mission Forever 22 found its inception one night, sometime during the first days of May 2004. Walk with me from that time forward and see how God met me where I was in life. He heard the call from my humbled heart saying, "Lord, I have no idea where or how to go from here." Have that early cup of joe with me as I ponder the depths of my heart searching for wisdom and finding one that only God could have put there.

Walk with me as we travel from Houston, Texas, and land at the Baghdad International Airport controlled by American forces. Iraq in June of 2004 was still a war zone and not a safe place to be.

Walk with me as we climb to the mountaintop, being blessed all the way, when a storm will come to my shore that will have us walking that lonesome valley of the shadow of death. I have to walk that valley on my own, but you can walk it with me. This will be that one spot you cannot possibly walk in my boots. You can walk beside me and honestly try to understand, as you will come out on the other end of that valley with me.

Face with me the aftermath of that storm as we attempt to understand what has happened. Walk beside me and discover what a difference a solid foundation makes in dealing with what is left. How I deal with it is entirely up to me. Walk with me and come to understand that while we cannot prevent the storm from coming and cannot prevent it from taking from us, we can, and must, decide how we are going to react to what it did take and what it did not take. Walk with me in courage, hope, and inspiration as they all come together at the right times.

Walk with me as only God can connect the dots of the past to the present. The dots of the past connect to the dots of tomorrow. Walk beside me as faith continues to serve me, as it did from the start, and through that lonesome valley we walked. In the end, when we turn the last page and look back, we will ask, Did we make a difference in life? Will we say "All is well with my soul" at the end of the day?

For those who have not had to walk that lonesome valley, this book is for you. That in your walk with me, you will at the end of the day understand your need for a solid foundation to stand on when the time comes. This book is for you if you have walked through that lonesome valley. This book is for you if you are in the lonesome valley now. You have to walk it on your own, but you do not have to walk that valley alone.

Answered Prayer for Wisdom

You understand this "lay my head down" thing was a new concept to me. I did trust it because it proved to be better than anything else I was doing. Believing in what you cannot touch, hear, or feel is faith; it is of the spirit. I had learned to pay attention to the answers God gave my heart, as they were always on target. Just one other thing before we start toward an answered prayer: if anyone were ever of the mind that this prayer thing is for wimps, get rid of that notion. At fifty, I started working out with weights at the local Y. At fifty-two, I was in a Shotokan karate class and bench-pressing 385 pounds most any day I wanted to. I just felt that need to dispel any notion that should not be there. In case anyone might feel too tough or strong to cry for help to God, that would be a mistake. I made the same one when I was young and thought I knew better. I thought God might need my help.

With that in mind, perhaps now you have a better picture of me. If you have your boots on, we are about to do our part to activate, if you will, the answered prayer. Many times, we can have our boots on, our finish our coffee, and yet just sit waiting, long after the necessary pondering is over, for God to make our prayer come to life. I think sometimes we conjure up a notion that God is like a genie in heaven. All we have to do is find a way to rub His mystical lamp where He dwells. God is too great. There is no containing God. He does not need to be rubbed in any way for an answer to our prayers. He simple needs, as I found out, a simple prayer from a humbled heart.

We will start early, sitting in front of the computer. I don't know about you, but when I sit down in front of the computer, I need to have a fresh cup of joe on the desk. Sitting in front of the computer screen, I sip on the black cup of joe; and as I do, I can feel the wheels turning. As we sit stroking the keys on the keyboard, as my mind runs ahead in thought, I feel my heart growing grateful for having learned to type in high school. I cannot imagine doing this from the hunt-and-peck method poking at the keyboard.

We find the KBR website quickly. Next, we need to do an online job search from their website. At this point in my life, I am not very computer savvy. But I have confidence in my heart, that I know this is an answer from God. I knew in my heart as I sat there sipping on my second or third cup of joe that God had a door open just waiting for us to step through it. Knowing this in my heart, then I knew the job had to be there. Really, believing that God is in your life doesn't mean that you get out of having to do the things you don't want to do; in fact, it means you get into more of what you don't want to do. It is our nature to take the path of least resistance. I learned that little jewel while in the army studying electronics. After spending a good bit of time on the KBR website, I realized I could not get beyond the KBR home page. We could not find the job listing; we needed that panel to get this mission under way.

During this part of the early morning hours after the "Joe", you probably have experienced a number of these things already. Out of frustration, I allowed my focus to veer off searching the KBR site to other sites that offered overseas jobs. I even took the time and energy and called some of them, and two guesses as to what happened. With no satisfaction, we would return our search to where God wanted me the first place. You walk with me through the morning in frustration, only to come to the point in the afternoon when the hands go up the air in surrender and the following declaration is made to God that I am ready to do it His way. I should have come to that point much earlier after the first couple of times chasing the rabbit, only for it to go down a hole. You are probably thinking, I should have come to this conclusion a lot sooner, and you would be right. Old habits are hard to break and change. Good grief, no wonder I am in the state I am. I turned to God and asked for help, admitting that this was beyond me. I was just whistling in the wind. Can you feel the frustration? Have you ever just whistled in the wind? As soon as we turn the focus back on the answer to my prayer, you guessed it—lo and behold, that missing jobs-listing page popped right up in front of my face. The web page that was needed for the job listings now in plain view on the monitor; I do not remember when I had seen such a welcome sight. Now we can do what we need to do for this mission to begin. Have you noticed it behooves us to follow God's instructions without adding our modifications to make them easier or better? It is worth noting that after many hours of taking charge and fixin' to do it my way, my way zeroed out. Just a humbling of the heart and a cry to God for help resulted in prayer heard. We are ready to search for that job God has for me. I am grateful you are here.

Can you feel the relief at last when we see the job listings page pop up? Simply finding the jobs posting page was cause for a grateful heart. As we search the list for the job that God has for me, we will see many jobs that I qualified for, but at this point, I was not interested in just any job but the job God wanted for me. OK, can you maybe get a sense that I have learned a lesson here, one of many to come? I will do it God's way. Simply because I qualified did not equate to the door God had opened for me and that is exactly what that job would be. Are you ready for that to become a part of your walk with me through these next chapters and beyond? Time after time, from chapter to chapter, throughout this story, God will open doors, and you and I will step through them boots first together. Learning from our missteps throughout life is a sign of wisdom, and with wisdom comes hope.

I filled out the online application and then added my résumé—the first one in my entire life. I was not concerned about my lack of experience because I knew deep down in my heart that if I did my best, God had my back on the rest. When God opens a door, no man can close it; and a door He closes, no man can open it. So, with confidence, we can push the Submit button, sending the application well into the deep parts of hyperspace to KBR.

At the end of the day, we could be satisfied with what we had produced. We started out to do what God would have us do, and after so meandering in the wrong direction, we did it. Looking back, I wish there had been someone there to poke me when I tended to go off on some tangent I did not need to be. This would have to change, and it can. The old adage that goes "The height of stupidity is doing the same wrong things and expecting a different result." Well, I had been there enough times, and long enough each time, that I was beginning to learn that what I needed was beyond my reach, but not beyond God's.

I can't remember how long it was before I received my first phone call from KBR's HR department. Three days most likely. At this point, you will see that I was through with doing it my way. When the phone call came, the HR personnel explained what would happen next. I would be getting a call from an assigned recruiter within a couple of days. Wow, can you imagine the surge of excitement that ran through my heart? I did it God's way. We can know at this point that God had opened the door. We stepped though it with both feet, as we did earlier, and with a very grateful heart. Can you get a feel for a grateful heart in this situation?

The only thing I could think about at this point was that God had answered my prayers to the condition I found myself in at the time. I was at the point where I needed to start lining jobs up to carry me through the summer. To this point, I had none. I knew they would be there when I needed them. I had one job at this time, and I would finish it soon.

The neat thing about deciding to trust God is He will join your life in progress. He will meet you where you are. Trusting God allows you to make the necessary changes that you need to make in your heart. Which in turn changes the commands your mind receives. Doing it may way, I have determined, is now nonoperational, and with good reason. You and I will not walk that road again.

The call we will get from the recruiter assigned to me would be a forty-minute conversation. With about fifteen minutes talking about the job, I had applied for and thirty minutes of the forty-five-minute-phone call about the military. The balance of the time was an exchange of military experiences as he was a veteran of WWII. It was a very pleasant conversation. At the end, he told me he would send me forms that needed to be completed, and I should end it back as soon as possible. He informed me that it would take a while to do the background check before anything else could more forward to the next level. Not a problem, I was working on God's schedule and according to God's plan.

God's Timing and Plan

With the necessary forms completed, I think it took about four days: the birth certificate was the document that would take the longest time. Now, you should understand that at this point in my life, going online to do anything was new to me, so I was never sure that what I did online really happened the way I intended it to.

Can you imagine the jubilance I felt in my heart when I got a call from my recruiter informing me that all the paperwork had come back and that I would need to report to the KBR processing center? A sense of peace flooded every inch of my being, something I had not felt in years. My recruiter told me a package would be coming within the next few days with all the information I would need to check into the hotel listed in the packet information first. Once again, we talked about the process for about fifteen minutes; then it was another thirty minutes about the military.

KBR would pay this to have people near the processing center avoiding a logistical nightmare for them and the applicant. They would, in fact, take care of the cost of meals three times a day. They had meals catered in for a cafeteria-style service.

I did not realize at the time just how much God was out ahead of me. What I did not understand was that the extra thirty minutes really was about the job. The recruiter was probing to understand my military background. He wanted to know how I felt about the military. Now that you and I are walking through this, my heart grew especially grateful for the way things happened. What life boiled down to at this time pointed to how God sometimes quietly molded our hearts in a way that we did not understand. This is how all of what we have walked through up to this point will connect with Forever 22.

It took five weeks to go through the process normally. My time would be six weeks. You might think I would have had an "Oh no" moment here. I did not. I just knew that God was in control and I needed to trust Him. My medical exam showed my blood pressure was high, and I was not in a boat by myself. It had been high for a long time, but for the hiring process to move forward, I needed to get it down to normal. Not a problem. I was under God's care, and I was beginning to realize we were doing things His way. I had my blood pressure medicine and was taking the dosage as prescribed, given the fact that my blood pressure was taken early in the morning. I decided that I needed to take the medicine earlier in the morning so my blood pressure would be in the acceptable range at the time of the blood pressure test. On the morning of the next blood pressure check, I took twice the number of pills prescribed. I wanted to make sure the blood pressure would be acceptable. I had laid my head down the night before and would not worry about the outcome.

The next morning, I just knew that the right thing to do was to double the dose. It made sense to me; does it make sense to you? I passed the balance of the medical screening with one minor glitch; everyone over the age fifty-five was required to have an EKG done. The company doctor called me for a consultation; he explained that he was concerned about a spike on my EKG. I responded that I had always been there, and he was fine with that explanation, and that was virtually the end to anything that could stop me medically. I knew without a doubt that my blood test results would return good. They were mainly looking for potential drug problems, and they did not need any chance of them popping up in a war zone. I did not even smoke, even just to inhale.

The weeklong delay due to the medical hold still did not bother me in the least bit. All I knew was that God had opened a door for me and I had stepped through it. The weeklong delay had to have a reason; stay with me to walk beside me to see how God uses circumstances in our lives for good. I hope you are seeing how all things work according to His perfect will and timing for our lives, as we trust Him more and more with them.

Leaving Is Hard to Do

The time had come to start the next phase of this mission. We had stepped through the door God had opened and could not in good conscience turn back now.

We started our morning at zero dark thirty—that is, several hours before sunrise. With all the necessary final paperwork out of the way, we were issued our steel-plated protection vest and a Kevlar helmet along with chemical and biological equipment, all tucked away in a black duffle bag, along with a new roll of gray duct tape.

My wife and my daughter showed up just as we had finished the last of the processing. I spent about three hours with Penny and Sara; we had lunch at the food court in the mall. All was well up to the point when we had to board the bus. That was when it got difficult. Penny gave me a hug, with the understanding look in her eyes that told me she knew I had to do this and then Sara. When she backed away, the tears were flowing as though from a spigot. It did a number on my heart to see my seventeen-year-old daughter in tears. I knew that I had to turn and board the bus to avoid a meltdown of my own. I wish I could pass on the peace I had while sitting on the bus knowing that all was going to be OK because God had set all of this in motion. Once on the bus and seated, my heart went to that place where I could know how blessed I had been to have the family God blessed me with. My heart was very grateful. I will never forget those tears and the sobs that came from Sara's heart that day.

The chartered bus would depart the processing center for Bush Intercontinental Airport, where we would catch a flight to Iraq by way of Gatwick, England, to Dubai and finally to Baghdad.

It is time to give God the credit for getting us to this point. I would have never been able to predict such a turn in my life.

CHAPTER 2

On the Ground in Iraq

As I reflect back with close to 20/20 vision, I realize that God, from the beginning of time, preordained God's mission in my life. Can you imagine God thinking of you that far ahead of time? That is awesome. Just goes to show us how significant your life is in the grand design of things? Can you begin to imagine what would happen if you were to ignore that mission throughout your life to the end and then it would be too late. God's plans would go on; they would go on without you, though. I can tell you that had my heart not been in a very humbled state at that time, I would not be recounting this story as it happened. That one time, my heart said, "OK, God, I give up. My way does not work, and I don't know where to go." If it had not been for that one simple act, there would be no need for this book to exist.

Because of what happened in chapter 1, you and I find ourselves landing at the Baghdad International Airport in mid-June of 2004. The United States and its coalition forces invaded Iraq on March 20, 2003. We had been in Iraq for fifteen months at that time.

With an immediate greeting of about 135 degrees in temperature and zero humidity, we deplaned. With about thirty new hires, we formed a firefighter's line to unload the luggage from the plane to a truck. Oh my stars, you should have heard the moaning and groaning. Unbelievable would be a mild way to describe these folks; you would have thought they were being asked to do the most despicable thing ever.

My mind will take me back to Nam for just a nanosecond for a quick flashback for comparison. Once you're in a war zone, it does not take much to trigger memories. Baghdad was hot and dry, and when I landed in Nam as a twenty-year-old soldier, it was hot and muggy, and the monsoon season was just winding down. There was little doubt when I looked around that there had been a war, as the remnants of the war were very visible. The threat level was very high, as evidenced by military presence everywhere.

The manifest had to be verified with a roll call. When my name was called, I answered. I approached the man holding the clipboard and flashlight (the power was out in the airport). He said he was told to keep an eye on me.

We will not think a whole lot of it. If I do not know something, worrying about it will not help. Besides, we are now most definitely on God's mission and God's time, so how can we worry?

On the Move

We will spend a short few days at Camp Anaconda. More paperwork and time spent not knowing one iota of anything about anything. I think there are times when even a thumbnail of information can keep the natives quiet. The first trip to the mess hall would absolutely blow my mind; it was like walking into a top-notch cafeteria at home.

A couple of days into our stay at Camp Anaconda, the war made its presence known on the base. A 122mm rocket and a couple of mortar rounds fired onto the base landed in the mess hall PX area during the noon mealtime. The result was three warriors killed and a KBR carpenter. I had contemplated going but at the last minute did not go; I have no idea why I did not go. It was one of those times that later on you cannot find words to explain your actions. You tell me, was this God's hedge of protection around my life that the Bible talks about, or was it mere coincidence that I did not go? Personally, I prefer, knowing what I do in my heart, to believe it was God's protection. I cannot answer the question that would naturally rise; what about protection for those killed and wounded? All I know is an answer to that thought, and it certainly is valid to ask, and I honestly do not know the answer. I can only know that when God keeps one person from harm while others are dying or injured, the answer is far beyond my wisdom, and I am not sure I could comprehend it if it were given to me. I believe God had his hand and, certainly, His heart with those souls. That question is worth a lot of consideration; however, it is beyond the scope of my intentions here.

We find ourselves spending three days at Camp Speicher. Those days would pass with no issues. I was nevertheless grateful for God sustaining me through this experience. My heart and mind still dwelt on those killed and injured at Camp Anaconda. My heart went out to their families.

Now we are on our way to Camp Warhorse, located in the Sunni Triangle. Just outside the camp is the town of BaQuba (depending on which Iraqi is spelling the name, there are three ways to spell it). At this point, we are ready to settle in so we can think of some place as home and start to work, in addition to the mission we know we are on.

As we departed Camp Anaconda and Camp Speicher, the smell of the army canvas tents still occupied a section of our memory; it's rather hard to forget the almost-unbearable heat, especially when one was in the tents with air-conditioning units that worked as close to never as they could get. However, it is no problem to me, being a Vietnam vet; I had been through worse and seen worse. The one thing I could appreciate being from Houston and the Gulf Coast was the near-zero humidity. The summers in Houston would have absolutely drain me by the end of the day.

Last Move Would Be Camp Warhorse

We spent about two hours at the flight line waiting for the Black Hawks to show up. Not a problem. We had nothing else to do or anywhere we could go. It is a fascinating sight; at least it is to me, watching the Black Hawks in the night sky. There is just something very special about that sight. I will never forget the Black Hawk trip to Camp Warhorse.

We left Camp Speicher with a full helicopter. The night air was hot and very dry even at around 2200 hours, and 175 feet or so off the desert floor did not make a difference. The sky was pitch black; the moon was at the end of its cycle with not even a thin sliver visible in the night sky. The stars poked through the blanket of darkness like white-hot diamonds that seemed suspended in thin air; they appeared as though a web spun and anchored onto the immeasurable vastness black in the heavens had caught them. God invites us to turn our eyes heavenward and know that He is God. For me, it was an awesome assurance of God's creation. Have you ever noticed that when we are in a deep search of the soul most likely we tilt our heads backward with our face to the sky? When I gazed into those magnificent skies, it served as a reminder put there by God to allow my heart to know that all was well with my soul when my eyes returned to the earth.

As I continue to my walk with you through this chapter and others, the tugs on the strings of my heart remind me of the doors God has opened, and then I am reminded of the fact that all these things do connect to Forever 22.

We made three—possibly four—stops before getting to Camp Warhorse. Just as a crewmember of the Black Hawk led us to the helicopter, he would now lead us from it to the edge of the landing zone and then he would return to the helicopter. KBR personnel were there to pick us up. It was still a thrill to be aboard a Black Hawk, but at the end of the line, after a couple of hours, it felt good to get off.

First Night at Camp Warhorse

We had about an eight-to-ten-minute ride with no lights on. Camp Warhorse operated under blackout conditions, and lights were to be visible at night for security reasons—not a foreign concept to a Vietnam vet. The operations building was a hooch used as an office. A hooch is a prefabbed building used for the temporary housing of personnel on a remote work site, or in this case, a war zone. More of the prefabbed office buildings had not arrived yet, as KBR had only been operating at Camp Warhorse for 120 days at this time.

As soon as we walked through the door, we were relieved of the paperwork we brought with us from Camp Speicher. Call these folks a clerks or anything else other than an operations specialists, and they will promptly let you know what they are and that you will address them as such. In my humble opinion, this meant they could not do a whole lot of anything else and their egos were on the line.

We signed the personnel movement log. The rest of the paperwork would wait until morning. It was 0200 hours, and everyone, including the operations personnel, was ready to hit the hay. We were handed our room keys to our temporarily assigned hooches as quarters. These were some of the new hooches that had just been set in place; they were two single-room living units with a shared common bathroom, which was not functional at the time, although that was not a problem as the shower and toilet units were not far away. This was a step up from the huge sixty-man military tent at Camp Anaconda and the smaller thirty-man tents at Camp Speicher, even with the ¾" thick plywood wall cubicle with private entry.

At Camp Speicher, that was a step up from Camp Anaconda's, open-area tent. We were experiencing incremental improvements in our living quarters with each move to our temporary semi-permanent home in Iraq. We could probably look on this experience later on as a comparison between a one-star hotel to an at least three-star one. However, for some of the new employees, grumbling about everything seemed to be a natural reaction. They could have used a good dose of "This is a day the Lord hath made; I will rejoice and be glad in it."

Now we find ourselves at Camp Warhorse: It felt so good to lie in a bed with clean sheets instead of an army cot and lay our heads down in a room with a closed door and listen to the humming of the window air-conditioning unit—music to the ears. The grateful heart kicked in big time and as the head went to the pillow, it was surely an example of "When I lay my head down."

All my life, there has always been something to be grateful for, even during those times I would insist on doing things my way. If we take the time to examine where we have been and where we are at present, we will find that we have a lot of blessings to be grateful for. We had electricity, and that meant an air-conditioning unit to keep the room cool to sleep in; lights to read by; and let's never forget to make that fresh pot of joe in the morning and at the end of the day. What more could we ask for?

We had to be up at 0600 hours to make the mandatory safety meeting at 0700 hours—that gave us four hours of solid sleep, enough for any fella. I had never attended a safety meeting in my entire life, but that would change come the morning. How ironic that may seem—my first safety meeting was in a war zone. I was used to getting up early and just doing whatever I needed to do; and this had been my habit for years.

This Would Be Home for the Next Twenty Months

We spent the morning going from department to department of the operations offices signing paperwork. We spent a small portion of the afternoon filling out more paperwork and attending briefings by one person to another. Most of it seemed to be a waste of time. I guess I have lived long enough to know when someone is above their pay grade. Camp Warhorse had only been in existence less than six months when we got there. There were twenty KBR employees.

I will never forget the first morning at the chow hall—a term I was told was no longer used when referring to the place where the troops ate. It's an obsolete term now. For today's military, many of the traditional words find their way to the traditional word wasteland to be replaced by such words as *DFac*, short for "dining facility." Bringing the warrior into the politically correct world. I choose to call it the chow hall or the mess hall. I figure I am old enough, and a Vietnam vet to boot, so had to have earned the right. This is my time to share a personal observation: Americans, who enjoy their freedom thanks to those willing to serve, owe these men and women a debt of gratitude and demand of a hands-off policy. The warrior's world should never be within reach of stupid politicians and groups bent on making warriors fit the images of their own imaginations. The food at this small base was every bit as good as the two larger bases.

When the day ended, our time sheet would reflect eight hours' time on the job today. However, we were informed that the next day would be a twelve-hour day from the 0700 hours meeting to 1900 hours that evening. For now, at the end of this day, all was well with my soul. We had found ourselves with three square meals a day and a cool place to lay our heads down at the end of the day. I reckon this is not bad for working in a war zone. Especially when compared to my war. We sure could use a pot of coffee. We would need to make a trip to the PX at the first opportunity. A fresh pot of joe to finish the day off sure would be just right; however, as I sit in my new digs, with no one else in my space, an air conditioner that works and is under my control (in fact, with a remote control for it), I am in no shape to complain about anything. When I laid my head down that night, I asked God for His wisdom as I thought about some of the decisions I had made in the past thirty-some years, I realized that my wisdom is limited to what my mind can come up with, and that runs to its end very quickly. God's wisdom was what allowed me to lay my head down this night in Iraq.

The second morning meeting was pretty much a repeat of the day before, except the new hires were asked to raise their hand and tell folks where they were from. I claimed Texas as I had lived there close to thirty years at the time, and my wife and three of our five kids were Texans. The morning safety meetings were mandatory and limited to last no longer than an hour, as the time would reflect on the payroll clock.

All things work for the good. So goes the scripture. It's hard to describe the peace you have when you know that God is with you. I think that is because the relationship between one's self and his maker goes deep into the heart, where no one or nothing can ever reach. As I understand this relationship, it is supposed to work itself out in ways where others can see the evidence what is on the inside. I am convinced that had my relationship with God not been where it was a month ago, this story would have no reason to be told. You will hear me say this a number of times because it is important not to forget where we were and who we were at the time.

Our Guided Tour of FOB Warhorse

After the morning meeting, the fellow who opened and closed the meeting approached me with his hand out and introduced himself as Ralph. He would be my boss. It only took a couple of words from Ralph for me to know that he was from Louisiana. Ralph invited me to go with him to the mess hall for breakfast; I was ready for that since I had not had a cup of joe yet. As we ate, we made small talk. He was a very likable guy.

We drove around the base, which did not take but about fifteen minutes at the most. It was a small forward operating base (FOB). We pulled up to a hangar. It was easy enough to recognize that it was a hangar, with its huge sliding doors and a roof high enough to bring a jet through. That day was not unlike any other I had experienced in my short time in the country. We entered through the open steel doors. Ralph began to explain the plywood shacks inside the massive steel-framed structure. They were mini stores that belonged to Iraqis who brought goods in to sell to the soldiers and civilian personnel of the FOB. They would operate a couple of days a week, and sometimes not that often, depending on the security situation outside of the FOB. To the left, he pointed to two framed walls. Being a carpenter, I quick realized that they had no top plate; they were out of plumb, and certainly not squared. Ralph proceeded to tell me that what I was looking at was to be my first project.

After Ralph introduced us to the base and the immediate project, he drove us to the carpentry shop. When we were in front of it, he reached over and handed me the key to the office and the key to a conex box just outside the doors of the hangar. He simply told me the conex had all the lumber in it for the gym. The conex would have to be secured whenever we were not in the area working on the project. He was then ready to return to his office.

We walked under a camo net that was stretched and tied off to two eighty-foot conexes, with the third side tied to the office conex. The conex that faced into the work area was the supply-and-tool room that belonged to the shop. The second conex belonged to the shop next to ours. The third conex, painted a beige color and with a window on the right side and the door in the center, was converted into an office. The work area had gravel for a surface. My first thought was that it was crude but not a problem. We would work with what we had and with a grateful heart. I want you to know I have not had a designated office since my army days when I was a staff sergeant in charge of transmitter radio sites. That would be twenty-nine years ago. We unlocked the office door and walked in. The first thing I did was to turn on the air-conditioning unit. The one window was a plus. I saw an immediate change I would have to make in the office. The former carpenter foreman had the desk against the wall without a window, so that would have to change. I would move the desk in front of the window, not to keep an eye on the workers but, rather, for safety reasons in the work area and to let them know I was not hiding from them.

To this point, we had not met any of the carpentry shop's crew. That would come at around 1630 hours, when they returned from the field taking care of work orders. Their work schedule was from 0700 to 1700 hours, seven days a week. We would get to meet them briefly when they came back to the shop to put things away before their ten-hour-day ended.

I do not want to take us too far into the workings of the carpentry shop because that is not the focus of this story. It is important to get a feel for where we were going and what was coming up, though. How God answers prayers definitely will have an effect on the shop and its people. What is important is that we see how God, when allowed to take over our lives, is in all that we do and all that is around us. Based on just what we have seen God do to this point, how can we say this should not be a story that includes God? If it were not for God connecting the dots, we would not have met through this story. This is how about how God brings all things together for a purpose. Each individual event or thing has to happen for us to be where we are supposed to be, and at the time, we were supposed to be there. All the dots have to connect, and Forever 22 is ready to start its journey through life.

We will have two more hours to work to make our twelve hours. Not a problem—there was plenty that needed to be done. But the first thing to do was to get a fresh pot of joe brewing. Ralph took us to the PX, where we bought two coffeemakers—one for the hooch and one for the shop. We had a lot of pondering to do before the crew returned for work the next morning, and some fresh joe would go a long way in making that task easier.

One of the first things we needed to do was get some idea of where we were going with this project on paper. We needed this not just for our own sense of direction but for the crew to see so they could get a reference point as they proceeded with their part in the project. That would guide them from one task to the other. We could not know what we were up against if we had no idea where we were going and how we were going to get there. No one had mentioned a timetable yet, so we would not even consider that.

Time for that fresh cup of joe and some serious pondering time with a good measure of "OK, Lord, I need your wisdom here." Most of the time, I would ask for wisdom when I laid my head down at night; however, I needed it now in the broad daylight. We would start with the most detailed information we were handed; it was going to be a temporary gym. Let us see how to think outside the box and come up with a plan. With pencil in hand, I made a list of what we could do in the morning, the first day on the job; and then we work.

By the end of the first real workday, the list was completed, and there was a rough sketch as I saw it at the time. Everything was basic right now, a starting place from a plan. I knew I was working with five thousand square feet of floor space. The wall needed to be top plated, plumbed, and squared. There needed to be an entrance roughed in and some windows on the long wall. That would take us through the first day. As we locked the office door, we could look back on the day and know that all was well with our soul. Now when I lay my head down tonight, I would ask God for His wisdom for tomorrow. When I got to the job site tomorrow, I needed to be able to see this project completed. There was no doubt I would be able to do that. Before closing my eyes, I thought of my family, and I thought of how much I would love to have Phillip at my side on this project. He was a US marine now, though. How neat would that have been if he could have hired on with me? Just a passing thought.

Ralph was the lead air-conditioning man and was probably the only one who knew what he would need to do for his job. He was also responsible for corralling the other trades. The electricians may not have even known they would be a part of the project yet. How would they know where to start without at least a floor plan of the project? With a simple floor plan, they could figure the electrical needs according to code.

CHAPTER 3

The First Three Projects

If your boots are on and laced up, we are ready for the next phases of our new job and God's mission for us. As we work through the next three projects I think you are going to see a couple of things happen. The foremost important thing is that I was on the way to being weaned off the need to "do it my way." I have learned my lesson, and I never want to go back to those ways. The second important thing is the claim of "Not a problem." This will become more than just a phrase for lack of anything better to say at the time, coupled with the confidence taken from "I'll do it God's way." The phrase has meaning and the power to make a difference. After all, making a difference is what Forever 22 will be all about in the time we are in Iraq.

We would build the Captain Christopher S. Cash Fitness Center as our first project at Camp Warhorse. Then would have a theater to build. Yes, you read it right—a multipurpose theater. Our third project would be designing and building the memorial for another gym built by a Turkish firm.

Captain Christophere S. Cash Fitness Center

Remember, when we first saw this project, it was but two incomplete framed walls. They were not plumbed or squared, and they did not have a top plate. On the day Ralph introduced me to my first project, after he told me what the project would be used for, I asked him if he had a set of plans. Nope was his answer. Now, would you please tell me how you build a five-thousand-square foot gym without at least some basic plans to work on? The only response I could give him was "Not a problem," and I meant that from my heart. That would become my standard answer, and everyone would get used to it. God sent me on a mission. I did not know what it was, yet. I did know that standing idle would never lead me to God's mission.

One of the first things we needed to do was to get some idea on paper of where we were going. We needed this not just for our own sense of direction but also for the crew to see for a reference that would guide them from one task to the other. We spent the first day sorting through exactly what we were up against with this project. Can you imagine having the most detailed information handed you would be the end purpose for the project. Ralph was the lead A/C man and was probably the only one who knew what he would need to do his job. The electricians would, at a minimum, need a basic floor plan to work with. I could hear Phillip in the background: *Oh, good grief, Dad.*

Tonight, "when I lay my head down"—by then a practice that was on its way to becoming routine, I would be ready for all the wisdom God could give me. Come the next morning, we would definitely need that time with a cup of joe or two and some serious pondering time. I needed all the wisdom He could send my way. When we got to the shop that morning, I had a basic drawing, which I showed to the crew, so they could get started from that after the framing had been squared away. We had some windows drawn in and a double wide door on the drawing for them to rough frame in.

We will finally get a chance to take a look at the lumber stored in the conex. All I could think when the double doors opened was, *You got to be kidding me.* Ralph stopped by as I was looking at the lumber, and he pointed to what looked like some roughly sawn four-by-sixes. Ralph pointed out that they were supposed to be used for support. Every one of them was as crooked as a dog's hind leg. I did not say anything, but I knew we would have to be very creative here: a lot of "Not a problem," thinking outside the box, and dependence on "When I lay my head down" for that wisdom far beyond my reach. You will see just how far we would have to reach at times. Not a problem, right? This kind of reminds me of some of the jobs Phillip and I would get in, definitely outside the box but not as far outside as what we were seeing as our stash of lumber. The conex was padlocked, so I handed Phillip the key. I thought, who would want to steal this? Then it occurred to me that this was all that was available. Flashback to Nam. Memories flooded my thoughts. I remember my time as a soldier. Anything not locked up was fair game, and even under lock would be at times. Soldiers do not steal; they acquire or requisition items they need.

We went back to the office, where with a pencil and some paper we would design a two-by-six-feet three-chord support to replace the purposed use of the crooked four-by-sixes. I was satisfied that it would work and met the load-bearing requirement of a ceiling being framed. We took the drawings back to the work site and started a couple of the guys nailing the two-by-sixes together.

We saw the project moved along at a quick pace once the crew knew what they had to do and where we wanted to end up. We will see the level of motivation as we would watch our warriors work out in the extreme heat in the dusty environment that had to have the equipment cleaned each morning and the floor swept because of not only the sand that would build up but also the pigeon dropping that would build up as well. The heat did not bother me; the condition our warriors had to work out in did. They deserved better than that.

After a few days of working on the new gym project, the warriors began to come in to look around and asking what it was going to be. When they heard it was going to be a gym, the look on their faces was priceless. What a blessing—more valuable than any sum that could be reflected on a time sheet. You see, God blesses us when we are motivated to give and we are well intentioned. I did not realize at the time how much work was done on each project. God was always preparing my heart for the days and months to come. That's how He operates. He is always ahead of us, and even to the end of our days, when our lives on this earth meet that final sunset, He will have been there preparing the way.

The Cash Fitness Center had been completed sometime around August 1, 2004. It was complete with rubber-interlocking mat floor, a really cool western-style bar that the MWR staff would work from behind. Probably the most significant feature to the gym were Ralph's 80 ton A/C units. It was a classy place considering where it was located. We had to deal with challenges and material issues that were far beyond normal construction in any sense of the imagination. As we walked through the project, we found no issues or challenges that could not be met. With the wisdom that resulted from when I would lay my head down why, would there ever be a problem? At the time the gym opened for use, I had no idea. The army had a ceremony planned for dedicating the facility in honor of a Warhorse fallen warrior until about three days before the scheduled event. That was an army item and had nothing to do with the carpentry shop.

The Cash Fitness Center was my first project at Camp Warhorse, and it meant a lot to me to see it used so much by the warriors. The dedication of that facility was the beginning of our involvement as the carpentry shop with the army in dedicating certain structures in honor of a fallen hero. God has a way of steering you in the direction He wants you to go, and you don't have to always—in fact, you seldom do—know exactly all the *why*'s at the time.

The gym had been open for use only a couple of weeks. I do not remember exactly when, because keeping track of information like that did not mean a lot to me. What did mean a lot was how I felt each time I would go into the gym, either to work out or to look at something because of a submitted work order for something added to what we had already done.

Dedication of the Cash Fitness Center

Now can you imagine what a surprise it was when an army major came looking for me while I was eating lunch in the DFac one day? We received a call on my radio from our operations telling me that a major and his assistant were looking for me, and that I was not to leave. We were not to use names on the radio, so they told him where he would find me. For sure, I was found; the major stopped at the end of the table where I was sitting. He introduced himself as the command chaplain and the sergeant with him as his assistant. I recognized the major as a chaplain by the cross on his collar. He told me that the KBR office told him I might be able to help him.

He explained his dilemma with the Iraqi contractors that the military had hired to make the signs they needed for the dedication of the new gym. He explained the problem: the first contractor was murdered. They were running out of time and needed to find another way to have the sign made. He asked me if I could make it, and it would have pleased me to no end to have instantly said yes to the major, but I had to tell him I had no way to make the sign. I lacked materials most of all; mostly, we did not have access to sheet metal. The Iraqi contractors were supposed to use sheet metal, and not being a sign maker, I did not see how I could help him, though I really did want to.

He thanked me for my time and left. My heart was troubled by my inability to help him. A warrior had died and was to be honored. Before the major could get more than a couple of tables away, I happened to think of a sign the carpentry shop had made for the entrance to the KBR compound. It looked good, and I could do one like that if that would work for him. I stood up and called out to the major. I walked over to him and told him I could make a sign designed after the KBR entrance sign. He said he would go look at it and get back to me.

Folks, God cares for the smaller things in our lives, and sometimes those smaller things He knows ahead of time are bigger than they seem. The suggestion was that the major take a look at the KBR sign and call me on the radio, which was our line of communications if we were not sitting in an office, where they had phone connections to each other and to the States—or as we would have said in Nam, "back to the world." The squelch on my radio squawked, and the major said, "Carpenter One, this is the Chaplain. Are you in your shop?" I confirmed that I was, and he replied, "I will be at your location in a few minutes." He and his assistant showed up with all the information we would need to make the sign. The only problem with taking on the task was that this was about two hours before my crew was due to punch out. It was also Wednesday already, and the sign needed to be ready and sitting at the entrance to the hangar the gym was in by 1700 hours that Friday for the formal dedication ceremony. When our conversation ended, I responded with my usual "Not a problem." I drew a quick sketch of the project and gave it to my crew to give them a heads-up for the next day. They immediately started bringing in the sheets of plywood that would be needed to get the project started the next day. They did this just minutes before it was time to sign the time sheet for the day.

Now that you are walking next to me, can you feel the pressure to get this project finished in time for the dedication to honor this young captain? This was a time when I believed in "Not a problem," as others had serious doubting problems. After making the trip to the mess hall, we will return to the shop to start the project. We had a couple of hours, and that would get us down the road on the project by that much.

The next morning at the shop, we had our normal work orders to take care of, so work on the sign had to be worked in as a priority. Every person who could stay at the shop that day would have a part in the sign project. Jerry, my second, and I stayed after everyone else had gone and worked on cutting the lettering out with jigsaws. As KBR employees, we normally worked from 0700 to 1900 hours. This was a normal workday seven days a week.

We were at about 2000 hours when I heard the communication on the radio: "Carpenter One, this is the Chaplain. Are you still at your shop working on the sign?" As soon as I replied yes, he told me to stop; he would be on his way to the shop. Jerry and I just looked at each other. I supposed we were being stopped because the project did not need it any longer. Maybe they had found the Iraqi contractor. When the chaplain and his assistant arrived at the shop, he started apologizing for a mistake made in the information he had provided me. Most all the information he had given me earlier that day was wrong. Captain Cash's name was probably the only right piece of information on the paper we had. He handed me the corrected information, and I assured him it was not a problem because whatever work had gone into the sign would be used anyhow. We worked for a couple of hours longer, and then turned the lights out, and went to our hooches.

That night, when I laid my head down, I simply said, "Lord, I need your wisdom here." The next morning, at 0430 hours, I had my morning coffee and went to the shop to open up as usual with a fresh pot of joe, the first item on the list. With a cup of joe in my hand, I sat down at my desk, and after some contemplation, I knew that all was going to be OK. God has a way of answering prayers: getting this project finished on time was not about my crew or me. It was about honoring a young warrior who made the ultimate sacrifice for his country. I had the bio on Captain Cash that the chaplain provided: He was married with two sons. When I read that part of his bio, I felt a pain in my heart that I had never felt before. At the time, I accepted what I felt but did not understand why I was feeling this pain so deeply and personal. I did not know Captain Cash.

I put as many men as I could on the project the next day, and at the end of the day, I was pleased with the progress. My crew of third country nationals was still made up mostly of Filipinos and Nepalese. There was no doubt in my mind that they understood the meaning of the work they were doing. The crew worked until their punch-out time, and then the shop's expats worked on after supper. We worked again until about 2200 hours.

Friday came around, and the chaplain checked in with me for a progress report. At this point, I knew with all confidence that only God could have told me that the sign would be ready. It would be close, but ready. We worked all day on it—the ceremony was still set to start at 1700 hours—and at 1600 hours, it was almost ready. I told the chaplain that it would be there at 1700 hours. The crew was starting to have doubts, but I knew where my strength was coming from, and it was sufficient. At around 1640, I called for a forklift to be brought around in front of the carpentry shop. It showed up at 1645 hours. The sign was loaded onto the forklift, and at 1650, I was able to tell the chaplain it was on its way. The trip would take only five minutes to be in front of the hangar doors where the ceremony was to take place. It arrived right on the dot at 1655 hours, and they proceeded to place a sheet over the sign so it could be unveiled at the prescribed time. My soul felt blessed, not because of anything I did but because Captain Cash had given the ultimate honor, and the dedication of the shop's crew to make the sign ready in time to honor this young officer was truly a blessing. It just goes to show that God is always on time.

In Retrospect

It is important to believe that God is more than a concept that rests so far away in the heavens. This belief was an essential part of my life moving forward on my mission in Iraq. I suppose we could look at the way things have happened up to this point and come up with some sort of the-right-place-at-the-right-time scenario. That might be sufficient for some, but it would never satisfy my heart. Looking back now, building the Cash Fitness Center, the sign, and all that were to come after that time was God's way of preparing my heart for those things that were to come much later. You see, God knows exactly what we need before we ever need it, and he truly does prepare the way for us.

By February of 2005, the little carpentry shop where I was foreman consisted of ten American expats (that was what we were referred to as American expatriated to work abroad) and about twenty foreign nationals working as carpenters. At that time, most of them were Filipinos, with the others being either Nepalese or Sri Lankans. To have this group of craftsmen to work with, I never felt more blessed. We also had one Iraqi working with us from Al Khalis, a small city near just northwest of BaQubah. You will get to know him better as this story moves forward. His name was Addai. The men worked together extremely well, and for that, I was grateful. The other shops did not fare so well. Their problem was with the expats who could not work together. I would enjoy taking the time to tell you about these men. What it was like to work in a war zone, however, that story is for another time, and it is quite a story.

The Theater

Now you and I are going to take on a project that would become one of my most challenging for the carpentry shop. It was early November 2004, and I was called to our camp manager's office. He was the big boss of the KBR operations at Camp Warhorse. When I entered his office, he introduced me to the army officers present and then proceeded to tell me that they had decided they wanted to move forward on building a multipurpose theater. Our camp manager was Eddie Nagle, and shortly after I got to Warhorse, he called me into his office and told me about the possibility of building a theater on the base. I had not heard any more about it until the meeting in his office with the military.

As they laid out the project's objective and proposed use, Eddie asked me if I thought we could do the job. I responded with "Not a problem," and next, I was asked how much time I needed. I asked for 120 days to do it, and I was given ninety-five days. The army had enough material already on hand to get started. I did not argue; I simply replied, "Not a problem." My thinking was that under my own wisdom, I would not be able to do this; but with God's wisdom, I knew we could build it without blinking an eye, and I believed that wholeheartedly.

This would be a great testing of the idea of reaching beyond where I knew I could not reach but where God was more than capable.

One thing about trusting in God wholeheartedly is that there is a confidence that cannot come without knowing that God is with you. I knew in my heart that I could finish the project on time. It was scheduled to start sometime during the period that I was scheduled to take my R&R (rest and recreation). I told my construction foreman that it would be a wise idea to not start until I got back. Even if the go signal came the day after I left, it would be only ten days before I would be back to work at Camp Warhorse. God's wisdom, not my pride, made this a wise request because I did not have one carpenter who was qualified to lead the project. I could not get an answer from the man.

Well, it happened. The wisdom God provided me completely ignored a chance at grabbing personal satisfaction. That is not as important as what happens next. I received an e-mail from the foreman left in charge. He said that he had no idea how to get the forty-one-foot prebuilt trusses into a forty-foot opening. He asked if it would be OK if he did it his way. I replied to his e-mail, telling him, "You are a carpentry foreman and in charge." I knew in my heart that he most likely had already done his surgical magic on the trusses.

I was back at the shop in less than ten days from the time they started the project. I normally returned to Camp Warhorse almost midnight. I laid my head down that night, as I knew I would need God's wisdom, and a good dose of patience. I was up at 0430 hours, put on my fresh pot of joe on in the hooch. And as I sipped from my cup in front of me on my desk, I did a lot of pondering. I knew my heart would need it.

As I had so become accustomed to, I stepped out into the still darkness and took time to stare up into the starry heavens, and knew God was with me. It was mid-November, and the mornings were turning pleasantly crisp, with temperatures in the upper forties. I was definitely back at Warhorse and my routine. I was on my way to the phone room.

As I walked to the shop, I thought of my family. I thought of Phillip, and for as often as I would probably say "Not a problem," he would reply with "Oh, good grief." I was looking forward to another couple of cups of joe; and instead of going to the mess hall, I would use the time before the safety meeting to do more pondering.

After the safety meeting, I would find a total mess of the trusses leaning against the two long walls that were totally framed wrong. I left them with drawings of each detail. When I saw the forty-one-foot trusses against the walls cut into three individual sections, I could not believe it. My foreman said it can't be done the way I had them designed, and yet he had no idea how to make the now three sections work spanning a forty-foot opening. I think the important thing at this point is that I knew God would give me the wisdom I would need to solve this debacle. Not a problem—God always has a solution when we think all is beyond our reach. This was certainly beyond my reach. For the life of me, I could not understand why they did not wait. My ability to get things done was a given, as evidenced by the projects the shop had completed. By this time, Eddie was no longer the camp manager; he had been moved up the ladder to project manager at Camp Speicher. We had a new camp manager to take his place. What the camp manager could or could not do at this point would not get the theater trusses issue solved and keep the project on schedule. The problem was with us, and it needed to be solved. The deed had been done. In addition, what to do about the situation was the question that needed answers. That night, when I laid my head down, I knew with confidence—and that point is important, as you will see throughout this recount—that God would not fail to answer my prayer

Sure enough, the next morning, I was up at 0400 hours. I had a couple of cups of coffee before exiting my hooch and heading for the phone room to make my normal morning call home with this assurance in my heart: "This is a day the Lord hath made; I will rejoice and be glad in it." Once I was sitting at my desk in the office of the shop, I could see those trusses leaning against the wall in three pieces. Then I thought about solutions. I did not have the option or the luxury of starting over; time and material not being available ruled that out. I had to make what I had work. Then it became as clear as the summer skies over Iraq what the solution to the truss situation was. We would simply put them back together with long pieces of like lumber on the bottom main pieces and run supporting pieces on both sides of the upper third of the truss. This would require lumber that we really did not have to spare, but it was the only way that we could still stay on schedule. The fix would be structurally sound. I had to be confident of this fact, or I would not allow it to proceed. When the guys came in to work that morning, I told them how we were going to solve the problem. They went straight to work, getting the solution on track. The walls had to be corrected in order for them to function with the intended purpose. I think the thing we take away from this is that when things do not go the way they should and no answers seem to be at hand, then it is time to go beyond one's self. I had come to rely on my "when I lay my head down" times. God has always been faithful when I ask in earnest.

I had never built a theater before, but I was confident in the awesome God I served. The project was probably one of the most challenging of my time in Iraq. We were on schedule to meet the completion date of February 25. There is an old saying that goes, "There but for the grace of God go I."

As soon as this project was finished, there would be a ceremony to dedicate the theater in honor of a fallen warrior. On January 25, 2005, the Faulkenburg Theater was dedicated in honor of Command Sergeant Major Steven Faulkenburg. The final touches to the theater consisted of handcrafted bio board on one side of the concession area and unit patches on another board on the opposite side. A large Red One unit patch was mounted on the wall in the lobby to the row of other big handmade unit patches. The patches would be one of the first things to meet the eyes upon entering the lobby of the new theater. Once again, during the ceremony my heart felt the heaviness of this loss. As I knew, CSM Faulkenburg left behind a wife and three daughters. Again, I did not understand why these dedications caused me to feel more than just compassion or sympathy for the families. It was deeper than that. I looked CSM Faulkenburg up on the web. To this day, when I think about our nation's heroes, my heart still tightens. What a price, indeed, they and their families have paid.

The David J. Salie Gym

The David J. Salie Gym was a large metal building built specifically as a gym. It was nice. This project was started sometime around the same time as we were dedicating the Cash Fitness Center. By the time we got to the dedication of the theater, the red iron was in place, and the roof and the skin was on the structure. A lot was going on for such a small fob.

The carpentry shop and its crew had very little interaction with the building project. A Turkish construction company constructed it. We helped in a couple of areas, one of which was when they had a problem with the hardwood floor, buckling from moisture was one such time. They thought the roof was leaking but could never find the source of the leak. I believe it was Ralph, who finally pointed out to them that their problem was a matter of condensation created by the slab of wood. Consequently, the wood would buckle. He suggested that they had their flooring cut too close to the walls, and the wood could not naturally swell and expand without buckling. One other time I sent some of my crew to the gym to help with the interlocking rubber mat in the weight room. We had experience with this from building the Cash Fitness Center. You see, when God causes you to have a grateful and glad heart, it is always a joy to help someone else.

I was given the work order to create a memorial sign for the Salie Fitness Center about forty-five days, give or take a few, before it needed to be ready for the Memorial Day Service, which would include the dedication of the building. Once again, I would have to rely on when I lay my head down for the answers I needed.

I want you to have a better feel for how this works, so if you could pretend your eyes are closed as you read this paragraph, I will try my best to write in a way that you can feel how when I lay my head down works. OK, I am ready if you are. We had just put on a fresh pot of brew. We were ready to sit down with the first cup in our hand. As we sat drinking coffee, we pondered the task we had at hand. This had to be something worthy of the price this warrior, and his family, paid. Whatever we came up with had to come from deep in the heart. Sip after sip of the black joe in my cup, my heart was beginning to bring up from where only God could show me the beginnings of an answer. Can you feel that happening? You reaching beyond your reach to where only God could go?

By the time I had sipped the last cup of joe, the image of the memorial to honor this hero was clear in my mind. This is such a sensational feeling when this happens that you can almost feel the flow of energy from the heart to the mind. This has nothing to do with thinking you are physic, it has everything to do with the way God works with the Holy Spirit within the Christian. By the time we reach the three-quarter mark of coffee being sipped, the visual in the mind is clear. There is a sense of relief because you know God has given you the answers you sought. Now we can finish off that cup of somewhat cooler joe. I have to ask you, isn't God awesome?

We get a refill, and now is the time to lay the vision out on paper. We know what materials we have to work with, so we have to design our vision from what we have available. This was the part of my job I enjoyed doing each day, meeting the challenges as they came with a glad and grateful heart. Therefore, now we know that whatever we came up with, we had to start with a four-by-eight sheet of plywood. The only specific on the work order was that it was to be a memorial, period. In most cases, this makes the task much easier, as it allows us to work according to the vision given to us. OK, we have a blank piece of plywood. Now is the time. I am so grateful for the gift God has given me to be able to see most of my projects completed. Can you feel the heart working here? Can you feel the help that cup of coffee in our hands is giving us as we sip away at it?

My heart goes back to the Cash and Faulkenberg project as I am reminded of the pain I felt at the time for the warrior and his family. As I pondered this, my heart put things together with an image that slowly came together. When you close your eyes, can you see Sergeant Salie, the soldier; Sergeant Salie, the father and husband; and then finally Sergeant Salie in the line of duty? That would be our memorial to Sergeant Salie. Can you see as I see a larger handpainted portrait of Sergeant Salie the soldier in full battle rattle, then to the left Sergeant Salie, the family man and to the right Sergeant Salie in the line of duty? The next line, the handpainted text containing his bio. Unit patches, one at each edge. Can you see that God moves the heart beyond what it is capable of on its own? Now we need to address the next need: I could not visualize this memorial with a simple border, not for what it would represent. Again, it was time for us to turn to God.

The next morning, we found that God had been faithful. As I sipped my morning cups of joe, one thought continued to recur: this has to be worthy of the cause and cost to the warrior and his family. As we sat down with our cup of joe and sip at it with our hearts free to ponder and reveal the answer we needed, you know about the recurring thought as I told you while making the fresh pot. That thought has become rather etched in my heart now. Therefore, we need to allow ourselves to be open in that direction. When I was a senior in high school, my heart yielded the answer by way of my industrial arts class. I clearly recall studying the different Greek architectural designs. The Corinthian style immediately came to the forefront of the images available, and my mind rolled past a number of them. The Corinthian style struck me as the perfect answer to crown the honor that would be below it. Can you see it, crowning the precious images and text below it?

Now for the rest of the trim and the base, with the Corinthian style cap, the rest of the memorial had to complement it. After another "when I lay my head down" time and the morning coffee to start the next day once again, the answer was there. Is this becoming a part of your routine now? Do you when you lay your head down expect the Lord to answer your prayers given in earnest and according to his will? I could see the full fluted columns that would claim each side with a half bullnose piece between them. All of this would rest on a two-by-six with a bullnose edge on the front side. Then the memorial would rest on two half-round fluted columns, which would rest on three-tiered semicircles two inches thick and rounded at the edges. I could see it finished.

The crew would take the drawings and do their gifted work on it. When the construction phase of the project was finished, bright white paint was applied to the trim. The three bases below the columns would look like granite. The sign painter from Sri Lanka would paint the art portion of the project. It is in my heart that I tell you how special this man is. I gave him a photo of Sergeant Salie in his full battle rattle . The photo we would use for the family man depiction was a priceless black-and-white of Sergeant Salie walking away from the camera with two of his kids holding his hand as they walked. The other side of Sergeant Salie in full battle rattle would be a photo I took when the battalion sergeant major sent me his Humvee with driver and gunner to take photos below the guard tower. Now with those three images, my painter, hired by a Kuwaiti subcontractor to KBR as a sign painter, did that. But he was much more. I think the best way to sum it up is with the story of what happened one day. One day an expat happened by him while he was working on a project outside. The expat stopped for a moment and then asked him how he learned to paint like that. He simply and honestly replied, "God. God taught me." He explained that he was too poor in his country to go to school; he also explained that both his parents were artists.

This is one of the reasons I have taken so much effort to explain how this project came about and how the unknown details had answers far beyond our reach. Can you see and feel beyond yourself to reach a point where is the only thing impossible was to touch God. This is the way it is. I believe God made it possible for this artist from a different land and culture to be where he needed to be, when he need to be, and what I needed to be as a painter. He was a Christian Sri Lankan. As you have already read, all of this will connect and be even more visible, and you walk with me in my boots. What this young artist did most likely without ever realizing it was to give witness to God's power and glory.

The memorial was finished ahead of time, and that was a good feeling, I never had any doubt; not a problem, right? The warriors were already using the weight room, which had opened for use about three weeks before the ceremony was set for Memorial Day. The date the army chose for the dedication was Memorial Day 2005. It would be the first time, I believe. This is the way I heard it—as a fact, the army would combine the traditional Memorial Day observation with a dedication ceremony. The ceremony was held at 1700 hours, a time that would coincide with the Memorial Day service being held at Fort Steward, Georgia, home of the Infantry Three Division.

After three dedications, I could not stop the memories from Vietnam and the thoughts of the moment with my son in the Marine Corps. I simply took one day at a time and fully humbled my heart to the fact that God was in control of my life in Iraq and that He was in control of Phillip's life as a marine. Again, my heart felt the pain for the family and friends left by this warrior. At the end of the ceremony, this one weighed even heavier on my heart, and I still had no idea why. My family was all safe, Aaron was working as a police dispatcher at the time, and Phillip was still at K-Bay. I only knew what I was feeling was what God wanted me to feel and that the answer would come later.

I had come to know that God was the author of my heart being capable of feeling these things beyond what was normal, which was part of trusting God. Trusting in God's knowledge of the road ahead and His ability to prepare us for it made good sense to me only at this point in my life. We often heard the expression "Only God knows. Then there's also the statement often uttered: "How could anyone ever have been ready for that?" That is in part what is at the root of my writing this book. If we can accept that "only God knows" and that we cannot possibly know most of the time. What you and I can do is if we believe God to be who we really know He is and not what we think He is, then we can trust that His knowing is sufficient. We can accept that we do not have to know all of what tomorrow holds. God knows our needs. He has already been there in our tomorrow, and at the same time, He stands beside us, ready to walk into tomorrow with us.

At the end of the ceremony, all was well with my soul, even in the time of pain for the fallen warrior and his family. There was a sense of peace from the feeling that God was at the ceremony. I can know this because if I could feel Him in my heart, then He was there. At this point in my life on FOB Warhorse, I had come to have a much better understand and appreciation for our men and women in uniform, perhaps in part because of the memories being around them brought back of my own eight years of serving in uniform along with a tour in Nam. With another part being the fact that my son Phillip was wearing a marine uniform now and proud that he was. The grateful heart would help me, as I was ready to move on to the next moment of life and into the tomorrows that waited for me.

Another one of those times had occurred while I was writing this manuscript. I just thought about the saying "Time waits for no man." I don't feel that is quite true. While time may stop for no man, your tomorrows will wait in time for you to get there. How we get there and the shape we are in when we get there is dependent upon how we have dealt with our yesterdays.

As you walk beside me can you get a better feel for how the mission is being set up? Can you feel the dots from years ago connecting? Can you feel the dots from different areas of the world coming together to fulfill God's purpose. Are you ready for many more early mornings and more cups of joe?

CHAPTER 4

As Time and Mission Move On

Thank you for sticking with me on this journey as it moves forward. At the time I was writing this book, "when I lay my head down" has become not just a routine part of my life but an essential one as I move forward in the direction God has chosen for me. As we have seen in the projects that have crossed our path to this point, I have never done a lot of the things I was called to do in Iraq. God's wisdom never failed, as you will see in the pages and chapters ahead. The dots would connect as the situation required them to be connected. I have never written a book before, and trust me, I would not be doing it now without "when lay my head down" and knowing that God would answer my prayers.

I hope that as we move forward, you will begin to feel God writing on your own heart. Just as getting the Cash Fitness Center built, the Faulkenberg Theater, the Salie Fitness Center, and many more projects in between those, reaching beyond myself to that point where only God can reach, made what I could not do on my own doable. As you walk with me, it is my sincere hope you will be able to clearly see and feel how God truly tends to the details of the missions he sets us on. We have to set about doing our part to move that mission forward. It is my prayer that I can articulate how God, from the beginning, connected those unseen or forgotten dots available to be used later to fulfill parts of the mission we are on.

We are moving into June 2005 of our walk together, the temperatures are soaring well above one hundred degrees, and will go much higher.

You and I are going into our second summer at Camp Warhorse, how just a few days from one year, we have accomplished much. We have taken this journey one step and one day at a time, just as God would have us to do no matter where or what we are doing.

Since I was not into video games or online anything else, did I get no satisfaction out of surfing the web, as they say? Therefore, you and I are going discover what we need to be doing with our time. We are on a mission.

Once we decide on what we are supposed to be doing, we most likely will have no idea where to start. Most definitely, at this point, we certainly know where to start looking for answers. In addition, we both know what we can count on. That is right—"when I lay my head down" is the solution. We are in the carpentry shop office, after the short walk from the hooch and the phone room. Are you ready for your first cup of joe to start this new chapter? As we sit and sip the first few swallows of fresh brew, I can tell you God has an answer for what to do with the spare time. We just need a few more sips of the hot joe in our cups, coupled with a little more pondering time.

This morning, as I was lacing up my boots and taking time between boots to sip a bit of the black brew in my cup, the strings of my heart were stirred as I thought about the two years I had spent with my church, Alta Vista in Pasadena, Texas. I spent two years at church learning how to make stained-glass windows in a class conducted twice a week. I sure did enjoy it and missed it at times.

We are sitting in the carpentry shop office with that morning cup of joe in hand, using our time wisely in pondering for an answer to our need.

The more I thought about the glass class I took back home, the more I began to see a vision of a glass class in the shop as I looked out the window in front of my desk. I can see a class in the shop after KBR work hours. The longer I looked out the window, the more I was convinced God had given my heart the solution to another part of our mission. As my eyes surveyed the shop through the window, I could visualize a stained-glass class with our warriors and KBR people enjoying what they were doing, just as I did at church back home after work hours. By the time we had finished our cup of joe, were ready to map out the details of our plan on paper, ready to be set in motion. In my mind and my heart, the glass class had already started. God has done His part in stirring the strings of my heart. I just needed to do my part.

Are you ready now? More dots are about to connect to the many other dots already connected and connecting now that we are in Iraq with our mission not yet fully in gear but getting out of first.

The more the memories would come to mind, the more I began to see the answer to my quandary as to what to do with my time off. This is why making those memories is so important. Can you even begin to imagine being in this spot and not having any significant memories come to mind that you can use as examples? By the time the third cup of joe was down the tube, the answer became clearer.

I am not a trained teacher, but just like what happened with the answer given by the shop painter earlier, God has taught my heart and given me the vision of part of the mission we are here on, and ended the argument against doing it, if there were any thoughts of going there. Who could match the teachings that come from God? That brings to mind an important point: I have never built a gym before, never built a theater or memorial projects, yet you and I have seen how God connects the experiences of the past to the needs of the future. For the glass class, I would draw on the experience of the glass class at home, using the teaching method that impressed me enough. I thought that God would use it now for the method of instruction in proceeding with this mission. I had taught an electronics classes while in the army at Fort Ritchie, Maryland, and a black-and-white photography class at my first church in Houston, hence the teaching experience, as was needed for the class to start.

Continue to walk with me and see how God will use these experiences to help me teach the glass class at the carpentry shop in Iraq. God had prepared the way a long time ago for this chapter in my life. He is standing by to do this in your life right now. As a reminder, you are the reason this book exists as *Forever 22*.

God Will Never Set You on a Mission You Cannot Do

As we sit in the carpentry shop office with our morning cup of joe, we can be sure in our hearts that the glass class will start. That is all of the detail I have for the moment; however, it is all I need to know that

I need to pay attention to, because the details will follow. Can you feel once again the excitement over what God is about to do? It feels good, does it not? We can start sorting things out as they arrive. There has to be an order—something I have so badly needed in my life for so long, for what is coming down the pike. We can put action to work against the instructions for the vision we now have.

A quick question for you: can you see, when we pray to God to answer a prayer we should not be surprised, when that answer shows up on our doorstep we had better be ready for it to keep from being behind the proverbial eight ball, so to speak? The closer our time comes to actually starting the class, my thoughts will focus on the teacher I had and how she taught the stained glass class at church that I admired so much and how she taught that class. This was beyond any doubt that God brought her to our church as an answer to a prayer. We can see now that her being there would be far beyond just teaching glass classes. Her mission during this time would reach far beyond the classroom walls of the Alta Vista church and her people who attended the class. Brenda taught for over two years at the church. She probably does not know the impact she has had by answering God's call to her heart. We will learn as we go through our journey together that answering the call is far more important than knowing its outcome.

As my thoughts began to click together, I could see us in the shop after hours teaching glass classes. I would teach in the same style that my stained-glass teacher taught me. In addition, as the thoughts came to mind, I saw each detail that needed attention ahead of the opening class. I could see everything from equipping the class to outlining the benefits. The plan would be submitted to my boss as a plan that would be good not only for those who cared to attend the class. The plan needed to include the fact that it would be beneficial for KBR and its camp manager with the army. I knew in my heart that the logistics of the project would not be a problem.

I had already determined the fact that any military in the class would not have to pay for anything. I would do this because it would be a blessing to my heart. In addition, to keep any future conflicts of interest from arising, there would be no charge at all to the KBR folks. All they had to do was pay for their one glass that would be ordered for them. The KBR folks would only have to pay for the cost of the glass they used for their personal projects. This would eliminate any notion of profit. We had come to the point of presenting the idea to the boss. We did just that, and all went well. He liked the idea.

Now with the project approved, it was time to step through that door that swung wide for us. When we take a close look at the doors we have already stepped through and what we have already achieved, we will see it is an amazing record. We have a ready-made classroom in the carpentry shop for use after hours. We have access to the Internet to order tools and glass supplies. I have the funds available because God opened the doors to this job. I felt from the time that first paycheck was deposited that there was more to my being in Iraq than just a paycheck earned. We can now understand how God provides for our physical personal needs and prayers said for those needs for the mission given us. God understands the need for a balance between who we are physically and who we are spiritually—bringing those two in harmony is where we are the happiest and living according to who we were created to be. The old song "I've Gotta Be Me" comes to mind.

Funding for this mission, as long as prudence is the order of the day when it comes to spending, I could do this totally on my own without soliciting help. God had shown my heart that this was the best route to take. Who are we to argue with that agreement? That being the fact, the issue was settled. A quick search of stained-glass websites yielded one name that jumped out of all others: I fund the homepage for Sunshine Glass Works. They were located in Buffalo, and I felt at ease with them right away. Sunshine Glass was just a few miles from the Army Post Office (APO). I would only need to pay for shipping cost from Buffalo to the APO. They would become real partners in my effort to teach working with stained glass at Camp Warhorse in Iraq.

I returned to Sunshine Glass's website to get a phone number. I needed to talk to someone to make sure I could get my orders mailed to Iraq. With the phone call made, the question answered, there would be no problem shipping as they shipped all over the world. I talked to Scott, their salesman, and at the end of the question, I made my first order. That would be an order of tools only since I did not know at the time what type of glass I would need. This was great because I would order plain glass through Addai, and he would bring it in from the local economy. I would use this to teach glass cutting techniques. Grinding the cut edges would be a part of the first few classes, as we would have a grinder coming in with the first order of tools.

With the first class set to start the first week in June, I was only three days from the first class starting. As we walked through the shop, each morning, we knew at this point that everything was in place except a project and its drawing. I knew I would have to rely on God because I had no ideas. I drew a blank each time I thought about the first class. In addition, no matter how hard I tried, I just flat out could not think of anything. You would think that would not be such a hard thing. I reckon the fact that I knew the project had to be unique helped create the roadblock to coming up with an idea. The project had to satisfy a number of points to qualify. Whatever we chose had to contain a lot of meaning and symbolism because of where we were and the time we were going to be during this mission with the stained glass windows. After all, we were setting out on a first in Iraq—Americans making a stained glass window with the image of a Christian soldier kneeling before a stained glass window praying. What a powerful scene and undertaking.

When I needed answers, I turned to "when I lay my head down." We have learned not to wait until we have exhausted everything within us. Operating our lives from this point of depending on God just seemed to be the right thing for us to do now. It is for that reason I hope your walk with me will help persuade you to look at your own "when I lay my head down," allowing it to become a part of your daily routine, putting it in front of what comes naturally for you.

Without exception, we have learned the best option for a solution to a problem is to seek God's wisdom first. As we have seen time after time, God's wisdom comes to the rescue. When we thought we had the issues taken care of, there was one left that needed to be dealt with. I needed to find someone to draw a pattern for the kneeling soldier.

As we walked through the process of getting ready for the first class, I think you will admit that by the grace of God we have arrived to the point where we are. We are finding that those early-morning hours and a hot cup of black "oe, black for me, becomes an invaluable tool to finding answers in places our own knowledge and wisdom cannot go, because it simply does not exist.

Waking up with less than three days before I needed the teaching project, I knew as I sipped my morning cup of joe that God would not leave me high and dry at this point. We have learned in our walk together that being in this spot is no reason for us to panic when we have the power of "when I lay my head down" and three days left.

On the first of the three mornings left, I established my routine of walking from the hooch, started with "This is a day the Lord hath made; I will rejoice and be glad in it" firmly planted in my heart. This really was the state of my heart now on most mornings. I unlocked the carpentry shop after having finished the phone room routine. Being able to check in with the folks back home was a real boost to getting the day started. After all, being in Iraq with the ability to earn more money than I had ever earned in my life was God's way of supplying my need to provide for my family. There were times when some of the other expats would show up to join us for a cup of joe; this was one of those mornings. I had no objection to this because it would give me a chance to run by them what God had told me through my heart. Once inside, I paused as I had become accustomed to doing now. This had become an addition to my morning routine once I arrived at the shop, to allow my heart to take in a feel for the day. I do not know what else to call it. I would do a quick survey of the shop; I could see the glass class happening in my mind and heart. I never spent an excessive time doing this unless God was working on my heart.

The door to the shop was unlocked, and thoughts of the glass class would occupy my mind as we walked to the locked door of the office. Like regular clockwork, a fresh pot of joe would be the first order of this part of the morning. We had an extra cup to fill and share with this morning, and that was a good thing. Once the brew was finished, ah, ya gotta love the smell of fresh-brewed joe. This would be one of those mornings where we would sit quietly for a spell just sipping and pondering until time for breakfast. The lack of conversation at this point meant this was time spent with a humbled heart taking in what God had for us from the night before—"when I laid my head down"—for the day and the challenges of that day ahead of us.

But before we started on the day's work, we would go to the mess hall to have breakfast, the most important meal of a busy day—something I learned growing up in a farm.

As we leave, the shop there was no doubt the answer we needed would come during the course of the day, I could feel this in my heart. I was just used to so many answers coming with the morning cup of joe. Sometimes, however, the answers simply were not there while we were sitting in the office pondering. After the morning safety meeting, it was back to the shop, where we would start the day. New work orders where picked up from cubbyholes for each section by that section's foreman. The outstanding work orders were considered first to determine if they could be filled and then given priority. We would look at the new work orders, assign them a priority, and then assign tasks to a carpenter or a crew depending on the nature of the work order.

We had no special projects going for the moment. That would be a blessing for the short time that it lasted; even if it lasted for just half a day or fewer hours, we knew that this temporary condition had to be enjoyed for its duration. After the crew departed with work orders in their hands and went their ways, we would sit down at the desk to get what little paperwork that needed to be attended to out of the way. This was a real problem for me as I did not like paperwork—not even the smallest amount. God was working on me in this area. It is a sore spot that to this day I need God's wisdom to overcome. You may be wondering again, how does this connect with *Forever22*? It will, by many dots, and God will connect them all. I suppose the best thing I can say at this point is that everything in our life is related to the whole.

With the paperwork completed, we were ready to make our trip around the base and check on the work progress of each work order. For most mornings, this was our routine. Now, are you ready to see why I do not stress out? We drive from one location to the other, checking and finding out if the crew needed anything to finish the tasks assigned to them. I am not a micromanager. I cannot stand being micromanaged, and I certainly am not going to do it to someone else. I do feel it to be an obligation to manage the project efficiently and stay on top of how my crew was doing in the field. After all, our client was the most valuable asset our country has. This style helped the carpentry shop operate as smoothly as it did. There was never a job we could not take on and complete. As a shop, we would perform our task without complaining; this attitude would also be my attitude for the rest of my life.

As we stopped at one work location after another, the carpentry shop would have five or six work orders taken care of most days. We would check in with the crew, and there were times when they would have to leave the site to return to the shop for items.

On this second morning of the three days left to find a teaching project, the day was already heating up, and it was only around 1000 hours, with the temperature already above one hundred degrees. It seemed the talcum-like sand was deeper this season than it was the year before and at an earlier time. We would be passing by a spot that was always a point of respect for me. It was an area just off the road—a combination of concrete T-walls and plates of steel that would serve as a memorial for the warriors lost at Camp Warhorse. This point was hallowed ground in honor of those who gave the ultimate sacrifice. On this particular morning, we would find a sight we would never forget. As we passed the memorial, we pulled the truck to a stop off the side of the road to take a photo of the lone female soldier stand at the wall in silent reverence. You can see that photo on my website pages set aside for this book. I can see an image today as clear as if we had just pulled over to take the photo. This sight struck a chord in my heart that spoke volumes about our warriors.

We will continue our drive. It will take us by the base chapel. There had been a female specialist under the cover of a camo-net; she was painting religious depiction on the concrete, requiring protection barriers. She had completed at least three the last trip by the chapel. I was looking forward to see any new paintings she might have finished. As we drove closer, we could see the camo and the specialist, busy painting.

As we approached the chapel, my eyes rested squarely on a painting I had never seen before. My heart about stopped. I could not believe what I was seeing. It was a new painting depicting a warrior kneeling on one knee in front of a stained glass window. He was holding his rifle by the side of his knee. Across the other knee, with his arm resting on the bent knee, his helmet dangled loosely at the side of his leg. The one thing that caused my heart to know this was the image I was looking for was the stained glass window painted in the background. We stopped to take a photo of the painting. My day made, my prayer answered—what more could I ask for? There was no doubt in my mind that God had inspired this young specialist. We need to understand a little more about trusting God and waiting for His answers, if waiting is what we needs to be done. We need to pass on a fact seen here—that faith gives us the strength not to give up when all seems contrary to where we need them to be. My heart was truly blessed and full of gratefulness to this artist.

We took the photo and proceeded to finish checking on the men in the field. At this point, I have to ask you if you have ever experienced an overjoyed heart. It is an awesome feeling. It is a feeling that all is right in your world. This image made everything complete for me. I was ready to start my classes, with only one thing left to do, and that was to draw the cartoon, as the pattern is referred to in the stained glass world.

Now we had only one problem left to solve: I was not an artist by any stretch of the imagination. How in the world was I going to get around this fact? We would need to find someone to draw the pattern of the kneeling soldier. We were two days from the first class, and I still needed one more item taken care of. I did not hesitate that night when I laid my head down to petition God for the wisdom to find a solution to my problem. I was sure God would have the answer for us the next day. I had no doubt about that fact when I laid my head down that night. I just did not know God would answer that prayer in the fashion He would the next morning. That is probably the best reason I can think of for not trying to get ahead of God. Take one step at a time on the path He lit before each step.

God's wisdom is certainly not our wisdom, so forever be grateful for that fact of life. The next morning, without doubt, He had answered my prayer. I was sipping on my zero dark thirty cup of joe when I realized that not only had God already provided the answer on this particular morning, but He had filled the need years ago. You are probably going to think *Now that is a stretch* after reading this. Trust me with God—it is not a stretch of the imagination, as you have seen repeatedly with God. When I was in high school, I needed to take four courses to complete the minimum credits required for the year. I had enough to graduate with only three. However, state law required three classes, so I took a class that I thought I would like most. I took an industrial arts class—it was the most appealing of all the classes from which I could choose. The class consisted of a number of topics within the course of study, and one happened to be mechanical drawing. I was good with math, so it should not be a problem. As the year started, I found that I could do well in the class, and I had no problem understanding the concepts well in all of the sections of study. Once I graduated, I never thought I would ever use what I had learned. I had no idea what I wanted to do after high school. My self-confidence level was extremely low; I would take whatever came my way. I would for a long time underestimate who God had created me to be.

When I look back now, I see that all the dots from the past to the present connect according to God's will and His time. These dots of life connect at the right time and place. I have used what I learned in the industrial arts class in my work more than a few times over the past forty-some years. Those skills have served me well for those many years. Now they were about to serve me well once again in Iraq. The skills I learned from the high school industrial arts class would prove useful. What I learned in high school served me well throughout my working years before Iraq.

During my morning, routine at the carpentry shop in the morning, the new glass class was to kick off. I sat at my desk sipping my morning joe, and it is probably clear to you that the wheels were turning in my head. I realized how God had prepared me for this a long time ago. All I had to do was overlay a 1:1 grid on an 8x11 ½" print of the kneeling soldier. With a ratio of 4:1 on a blank sheet, it then became just a matter of connecting the grid points on the larger paper that would correspond to the smaller grid to corresponding points on the larger grid. Are you with me? That did not take long; now it was a matter of just getting it done. The onus was on me and not on someone else to get the drawing done. I got busy and got the drawing done. We will see that once God gives us an answer; we no longer have the right to sit around waiting for God. He has done His part.

Now we can go online and order the glass we needed. Sunshine Glass was awesome; I was very sure about my choices of glass, so when I talked to Scott, he asked me to send him a copy of the project. Problem solved: he chose the glass, I paid for it, and my first shipment of stained glass was on its way to Iraq. That was exciting in itself. The first couple of classes started with some very basic things about glass—how to cut it and break it. The use of the wire saw and grinder was next. Then we moved to the kneeling soldier. I had them practice cutting clear glass to fit the pattern. The stained glass had not come in yet, and they were not quite ready for that, did not want to practice on that, especially since we had to order it and have it shipped to Iraq. When the stained glass did come in, they were ready for it. The first night of cutting stained glass was a real blessing.

God Will Lead the Way

The first class was a real joy. Everything went according to Hoyle. (That is an old saying that came from the rules of the game that accompanied new decks of playing cards made by the Hoyle company. Just had to throw that tidbit in for clarification.) We saw with each passing class a growth in the number of folks showing up. Good things began to happen beyond cutting and grinding glass. Eventually, the classes would become more than just about learning to cut glass to build a stained glass window. Don't get me wrong, I enjoyed teaching the art of the stained glass window. However, the most gratifying part of the class was what the folks learned in addition to stained glass art. We had started noticing that the stress level in the people who came to the class had begun to drop. We would notice how their self-confidence would get a boost in some of the folks. I saw attitude changes in others. My heart filled with joy. I thought, *OK, God, you have blessed my soul richly here.* The class became more than just a part of my weekly routine; it became a part of my life and of those who came. God was busy touching hearts. As we moved forward with the classes, I noticed the attitudes of the day would be lost somewhere just outside the door. I would hear this from them. It became a time of fellowship, and moreover, God got the glory.

You don't have to beat folks up to let them know that God cares. God used this time for me to teach a concept that He had taught my heart a long time ago. As time passed and new people would show up for the class, I would invariably hear someone say, "Carson, I have a problem." My response to them, after taking a look at their problem, would be "Not a problem." You have been with me long enough now to know that is my stock reply to situations. It does not mean that I approach problems with a cavalier attitude. It is really the antithesis to worry. In fact, worry, as opposed to concern, over a situation is a deterrent to solving the problem at hand. We have learned to simply look at the problem. Then with a level of calmness of heart and mind, we would assess the problem. It was not long before newcomers would hear someone other than me pipe up with "Not a problem." That was music to my soul.

I got a measure of the blessing from the level of satisfaction that came when people who made glass projects that they were proud of and shipped home. We saw some of the projects shown off at the morning safety meetings. As I think back, one person in particular comes to mind—a dad whose little girl loved horses. He made her a stained glass horse head, the glass was about eighteen by twenty-two inches.

We learn that by giving from the heart and out of the abundance God has given to us, we are truly blessed and have riches no amount of money could possibly purchase or replace. This one little thing would become just one item of many lessons God had in store for me to get to where I needed to be in the building of a solid foundation. Achieving a solid foundation, we accomplished this by laying one building stone at a time, one on top of the other, with the mortar of faith binding the joints. Having a solid faith and knowledge of the fact that God is in control will serve you well.

The glass class would be on my calendar twice a week for just about a year and a half. During this time, we would undergo a major change in the class hours. A few short weeks after the first class started, people began to show up right after 1900 hours, as soon as our workday ended. The class was scheduled to start at 1930 hours, but I had no problem with starting a half hour earlier. It was not long before we were going until 2200 hours. Once again, "not a problem." My soul was blessed, and my heart was in that grateful spot. As we move along, can you feel the excitement for this mission? It was truly a bright spot during the after-work hours, much better than watching pirated movies from the Iraqi vendor on base. You will notice that our hearts are the fullest with blessings when we are in the giving mode. We reap more than we ever sow—that is, experiencing an abundance of life. Then the twice-a-week scheduled glass classes morphed into just about every day of the week for most people. Once again, can you feel the joy in your soul as you think about how the class developed and what it meant to each person in the class? My soul became so tremendously blessed by this expansion. This meant that at least by the number of folks in the glass class, they were getting more than just glass-cutting skills. They most definitely were blessed most of the time without knowing God was touching their hearts by allowing them to do something creative.

It is my prayer that by now you are practicing, or at least considering, the lines "When I lay my head down" and "Not a problem." In the days before the start of this chapter in my life of doing things my way, I would have never believed I could have done the things we have done in Iraq. I might have had a fleeting thought of wanting to grab hold of a moment of a vision. That vision would always get left by the wayside and die on the vine simply as a daydream ends when it meets with reality. My reality was limited to what I could see and touch; I had no idea of reaching beyond anything I could touch to meet with God's reach even though I knew God was real.

With all that you have walked with me through over a period of about sixteen months up to this point, you have seen how God, when given the green light in one's life, changes your life. Oftentimes, what one person goes through and endures, they are only able to do so because their faith is strong and their foundation is solid. From those experiences, others benefit. You have heard how out of the ashes a new life takes shape. Life's storms and circumstances are going to come; however, when they pass, and they will, it is how we decide to react to them that will determine whether we spring back or slip into a defeated bliss. With a strong faith and a solid foundation, they will serve you well, and they will not allow you to stay beaten down by storm or circumstance.

Having you walk with me through sixteen months of an incredible journey is an honor. We have gone from despair to being on a mission that has taken us from my living room to the desert of Iraq during America's war on terror. You have seen how God connects the dots of our lives; this means He can connect the dots of your life, and all you have to do is let Him do it. Realize that yielding a humbled heart to God is the start of it all. Walking with me, you have witnessed through this story how my heart was being taught so much. God taught my heart to listen first before I could ever take that first step in the right direction.

As you and I are about to walk together through the next chapters, we are going to be faced with needing all the faith the two of us can muster together and have a foundation on which to stand that will not give way. You will be there to face this with me, and I pray that you come through it a much stronger and wiser person. As it will certainly test me as my faith is tried and my foundation chipped away at.

CHAPTER 5

The Dots Connect

Our walk through the remaining chapters together will bring us through the toughest times of the forty-four months we will spend in Iraq. As the story unfolds, there will be a part of it indelibly written in my heart, as long as I live. You will walk with me and see how the dots from an evening news cast and the humbling of my heart connect to cause a mega change in my life. You have already seen how God connected the dots from my childhood to our landing in Iraq. Now we are about to walk into the connecting of a new dot that will not be a pleasant journey, and no joy for some time. As you have walked with me, you have seen answered prayers time after time.

As we move forward in this chapter, you will experience how God makes a difference during the stormy parts of life. To this point, we have seen God answer prayers in many circumstances that have come up with an almost regular frequency. What we are going to walk through next is a major storm of epic proportions. You will come to understand while walking with me that only by the grace of God can one endure the heavy load they have placed upon themselves at times. You will walk that lonesome valley that only I could walk for myself, though you can accompany me this time. We will walk these next chapters together, where we will see all the dots of my life at this time connect by the grace of God and bring us to the creation of the point of Forever 22, even though we will not know this title exists yet. It will connect in the deepest reaches of my heart though.

On August 18, 2005, Forever 22 will begin without making itself known to my heart by way of the connecting dots you and I have been talking about to this point. I will use the phrase "given life" from this point on because at this point, this date will live in my heart for as long as my heart will pump an ounce of my life's blood through my body. Walk beside me once again as we start the second of the three sections this book seems to divide itself in. See why God's hand on my life will become crucial for survival as I recount the story for your walk with me. Walk beside me through that lonesome valley of the shadow of death, if you can imagine or feel from that walk some of the burden of my heart. On the other hand, just maybe you're like so many others and concluded that you cannot even begin to imagine this walk as your own, and that is perfectly OK. I would never want you to have to do that. There is the heaviness of the load carried out of that dark valley, and then you will have a greater understanding of the importance of a strong faith and a solid foundation on which you can stand and face the storms in your life.

I am very grateful to you for sticking with me. This next part of the story will unfold so you will understand why this is a story truly about God first. Then it really does become a story about your walk through it with me. What has happened to change my life is real, and in the end, God has blessed my family and me in a mighty way. It is a story that in end is about all of us as we walk through the days of our lives with God. There will be no end to this story as the end can only come at the end of our life. There can only be a continuing connecting of the dots by God up to that final sunset. My story is merely a vehicle to help you walk to the point in your life that you need to be To get to that point, you need to be there when the last chapter is read the book is closed for the final time. We will find that when the depth of the pain is so gripping, it becomes physical in the truest sense of the word, and you can feel your heart actually tighten in your chest. When we are unable to find any comfort in our own wisdom and we reel from the dizzying speed of the thoughts that race through our minds, we seem to slip into a never-never land of sorts. When feel as though we have lost control of reality because reality escapes us. This is when we will find that the God who supplied all our needs before this time is more than sufficient now.

If it were not for people like yourself wanting to know this story, maybe at some point in the book, realizing that you are the reason the story is in your hands at all,

I may not have finished writing this

Reading the story of Forever 22, I do know that you will not only continue this walk with but, more importantly, you will see how important it is for us to walk with God. Knowing you are here walking beside me is a great comfort to my heart. Come with me as Forever 22 becomes more than a story of my walk through the valley of the shadow of death. Walk with me as it takes on a life of its own and becomes a story of courage, inspiration, and hope. From those three items, you become a part of this book and of its desire and hope to pass them on to others that they can walk through a story about God making a difference in their lives.

It takes the courage borne of faith to face the storms of life. It becomes a story that will encourage the concept of "when I lay my head down," knowing that God is always faithful to answer our prayer. Inspiration is drawn from the trials and tribulations of others knowing that there is a God who can walk that lonesome valley with you, and you know for the story you are reading that you do not have to walk it alone and you can possess the same solid foundation to stand on when the time comes. Your storm can never be my storm, but the consequences of that storm can be the same, the reliance on God can be just as much yours as it has been and is mine. Walk the rest of the way with me and make a difference. Build your faith and solid foundation for you to stand on as we walk from chapter to chapter. There is a light to our path and a road map with instructions ahead of us. This is not my way, however. It is God's way. Remember, I am through doing it my way.

To the Mountaintop

As we take a quick look back, over the last sixteen months, we see that you and I have walked many miles together. We have started the day with a joy in our heart that was not there before. We would find ourselves rejoicing in it and being glad because it was a day the Lord hath made for us. Even at zero dark thirty, we could feel this newfound joy. This would be the condition of the heart, as our steps would lead us from the set of metal steps after locking the hooch door. You can probably put yourself in the phone room calling home since you have been through this walk so many times doing just that. The short walk to the phone room was a great time to stop for a few moments and turn your eyes heavenward, allowing the stars that seemed to burn through the black blanket that appeared to be hiding them from your eyes, only for it to end up a vain attempt. It is as though God created them for you at that time. This sight would capture your undivided attention, and you would know that God was looking over His creation; you would understand that that included you with what seemed to be just for a fleeting moment heaven being brought down for you to touch. We would see the stars above in a way they had never seen before. They seemed so unimaginably far away; yet at the same time, they seemed to bring God so close. Can you close your mind's eyes and see the awesomeness of the heavens and feel God reaching down to you?

Those early morning hours had a joy for their simplicity and being a true witness to the God who created them and made them available for us to experience. I have always enjoyed the early morning hours. They have a special meaning in my heart, even when I was doing things my way. I just realized a point that struck a string of my heart: God touches the things that are already in us and belong to Him. Here in the desert without the man-made lights and all the noise of a city these early morning hours with a fresh cup of joe made for an extra-special feeling of being closer to God more than ever.

As we walk on this morning of August 18, 2005, as I ponder the last few days, I feel I have reached that point where because of a humbled heart and no longer intent on doing things my way, I have finally taken that U-turn I'd needed to take for such a long time. Now my life finally felt that turn in direction. I felt as though I finally made the right decisions to head in the right direction for the rest of my life, and it felt good. I knew all along that I was making the wrong choices in life. I simply could not see any alternatives to those choices I made. I realize now that part of my life that could have been made much sooner than later. One thing I have understood for a long time is that crying over spilled milk does absolutely no good. I hope that walking with me during those early mornings, you will not only see the advantages of being an early riser with a fresh cup of joe in your hand, but also that you actually feel more of life's joy during those hours.

This morning would be no different from any of many mornings we have walked through over the last number of days and months. We are on our way to the phone room, where we usually went at this time. In fact, my heart is in an extra-grateful mood this morning as we look back on yesterday at this same time. We would be getting ready for a convoy that started early from Camp Warhorse to Camp Anaconda, a journey that would end at about 2200 hours that night when we made it back through the heavily guarded entrance to Camp Warhorse.

Trucks transported every item we used at Camp Warhorse on to the base. I guess you could say we were very dependent for our daily existence on the truck convoys from other hub bases. Armed escort units made the safety and completion of mission possible for the convoys. A trip in a military convoy meant leaving the relative safety of the FOB—commonly referred to as going outside the wire. We made the trip from Camp Warhorse to Camp Anaconda by crossing the Tigris River on the floating bridge the army corps of engineers had constructed. The hard bridges, as they were referred to, that crossed the Tigris were blown up during the collation's softening of the ground conditions with a bombing campaign, hence softening that area before boots were introduced on the ground.

Can you imagine walking with me and being on this convoy as being a reason for gratefulness? Counted as an opportunity, although it's OK if you cannot see it that way. For me, the opportunity to be on such mission for a Vietnam veteran was awesome beyond compare. Then you would understand my heart being grateful for this experience, especially taking the trip in an armored Humvee and being with our warriors. As we look back, maybe we can count it as an added blessing for me.

If we take the time, we can always seem to find something just a little different with each morning to be grateful for in our walk. Each morning will continue to become very special. My heart was glad, and I was determined that no one was going to steal my joy. When that phrase came to my mind, I would think of Phillip. When he and I worked together, if we were on the road, we would listen to the Mike Richards show, and Mike would sign off the air for the day with "And don't let anything steal your joy." I guess that was a point we needed to take to heart because it would come to mind a lot in the days to follow. I used the phrase "don't let anyone steal your joy" a lot when encouragement is in order when talking to others.

My second son in the Marine Corps seemed to be doing OK in Afghanistan. He was going into his third month of deployment, and Nam was never too far away in my thoughts. I would remember his reply when I told him to keep his head down. He said, "Dad, the Marine Corps has been training marines for over two hundred years. We are ready."

My reply was simply "I understand that, son. I was ready when I went to Nam, but you see, I was not a dad then. I am now." As the last couple of months passed and as I thought about him, my best comfort and peace in knowing for a fact that he was in God's hands, which did not mean that something could not go horribly wrong. It did mean that I was blessed knowing He belonged to God. Can you imagine having a son or a daughter in harm's way and not knowing this truth? When I would get an e-mail from him, he was always doing stuff and having fun, which sounded like a statement I was familiar with as a twenty-year soldier myself writing letters home from Nam. In a war zone, the truth is meted out in a very guarded manner, if at all.

Just before reaching the phone room, I remember looking into the stars above and thanking God for a job that I loved when doing it made a world of difference. We have a great crew of men to work with, and we have had some challenging projects. The real power of saying "Not a problem" and then meaning it certainly stood tested over the last year. The glass class was well under way, with folks really enjoying being there. How much more could one person ask for?

Because the KBR headquarters was in Houston, they had a direct satellite link to Houston, where the calls were downloaded to a local exchange and then routed to the local lines. Can you imagine making a phone call home and expecting everything to be as they were the day before and the days before that? Try imagining feeling on top of the world one minute, and then, with a simple phone call, the world as you knew it would end with that call.

Prepare your heart with prayer as we walk through this part of the chapter. After picking up the receiver, my fingers did the walking as I dialed 9, and then my Houston number. From Camp Warhorse or any other base that had CapRock Satellite, the call from Iraq to Houston was a direct feed. I remember not being particularly fond of all the numbers that I had to dial when calling anywhere but Houston. I needed a calling card when calling the stained glass company in New York; it seemed half of your allotted time was spent dialing numbers.

What I cannot do is tell you what happened to my heart the moment I heard the phone picked up at the other end. As soon as my wife, Penny, picked up the phone, I fully expected the usually hello from her. Instead, what I heard was the unmistakable sound of crying from the other end. From the first sobs that reached my ears, I knew instantly in my heart without anything else being said that I had lost my son in Afghanistan. To this day, as I write these sentences, the sound of her sobs creates a pain that is just as real today as it was then. That is why I asked that you pray for me earlier. My heart hurts to the core, and it has been almost nine years. She could not say a word, and she did not have to. My heart simply sank to a bottomless place, and I felt a part of it just vanish as indescribable pain rushed in at an incalculable speed to fill the spot where that part of my heart used to be. The pain was so gripping and so sharp that it became very physical instantly. I knew Penny well enough, and I knew my family well enough to know without the necessity for words that I had lost my son Phillip the marine in Afghanistan.

I needed no words to tell me that. God's grace filled my heart before I needed to speak the next words. Only by God's grace could I function now. I told Penny that I understood and to put Sara on the phone. When Sara came on the line, all she could say was, "Oh, Dad. Phillip." When I heard my eighteen-year-old daughter crying in such pain for her brother, the pain in my heart cut even deeper and wider. I told her I understood and that I would be home in a couple of days. I had to get some things in order here before I could leave. God impressed on my heart the need for me to be strong for my family, even though the pain seemed unbearable at times. Men, this is the way God designed us. Our families are our God-given responsibilities.

As we walked through this time together, it would be nine years this coming August since that sorrowful day. As I wrote the words to the paragraph above, it was as real as the day of that phone call. I saw the words I had typed, and through blurry eyes, I would continue for some time. The pain was very real now as it was then. From this phone call, Forever 22 was born, without me realizing it at the time. All I knew then was that my son would never be more than twenty-two years old for eternity. He would forever be twenty-two.

By the grace of God, I was able to understand only one thing loud and clear: I had a hard mission in front of me. Lance Corporal Phillip C. George, my son, killed by enemy fire while serving in Afghanistan was what the Marine Corps response would be in part to the press and the family. I was in Iraq, and my family was in Texas. I could not falter, and I could not fail. To this day, I thank God for two things. The first is for the solid foundation of faith, and the second was for the military training I had for eight years, with a tour in Vietnam that allowed me to understand the need to focus on a mission at hand. My faith would provide me with the solid rock on which I would face this storm head-on. The military taught me the value of mission first; this gave me the wisdom of experience to complete my mine. Before I was off the phone to Sara, that mission in my heart was well established. Hearing the indescribable pain in the hearts of my wife and my daughter caused my heart to feel as though tons of weight had been loaded onto it. Would it cave? It could not by the grace of God. I hung up the phone. There was no time for indecision, and it hurt like hell, but I knew I had to press on. I had a long trip ahead of me.

As you walk with me through this, we know the routine well for leaving Iraq. We also knew that KBR would handle this in the most expeditious manner possible. I reckon from that time forward, most of the time, I was kind of on autopilot but for the grace of God. I do not believe I could have moved at that time, much less think of the mission ahead of me. The undisputable fact that in my heart I was comforted by the understanding I had of who my God was and where He was at that very moment allowed me to function above this ground zero of my life. More importantly, I believe from the very foundation of my soul that when a Christian's immortal soul reaches the end of its journey on this earth, the final sunset for that mortal body has reached the end of its journey. The last sunset in this life has come; the soul separates from its earthly temple and goes to be with the Lord. I was sure of that in my heart. I could not imagine not believing that. I could not fathom Phillips's soul just lingering in a space of nowhere or still present in a body that was no longer alive and nonfunctioning. Being certain of this fact did not lessen the pain in my heart. That fact allowed me to deal with Phillips's body in reverence as it was hallowed ground for his eternal soul. Now, I need you to be with me on this for our walk through the events of the next week or so.

How is your walk with me now? Can you see as you walk with me farther into the time ahead of us just how much mightier God is and just how deep he is able to reach to sustain me during this time? Folks, God's grace truly becomes sufficient for all of my needs. He is able to make an immeasurable time seem so fleeting and by the same token make a fleeting moment seem to be an immeasurable amount of time. In the physically short space between the phone room and our operations building, God had gone in and put in the support beams of His Grace that shored up the hole left in my heart, He was able to reach those depths that I knew were there but could not get to on my own. Please understand that the pain continued to seem unbearable. The sorrow at this point was too deep for me to know when it would end; however, with God, He kept it from collapsing under the weight of the pain. This, in my mind, is the miracle of faith.

Time becomes boundless, with no beginning nor end. Time is irrelevant, expect in relation to the mission I knew I had to be about. My heart had been devastated; this was bone of my bone, flesh of my flesh. I understood this in a way that I could only understand before as it related to Adam reference to God's creation of Eve from the bone of his rib and his flesh. Today my heart understands this meaning in a fuller sense of the word. Not adding to or taking from God's word but understanding the extrapolation of it beyond the reach of what I could understand before. I could hear my heart scream from the pain inside of my chest cavity. So many things echoed in my heart, and trying to make some sort of sense of what was going on seemed impossible. The more my heart screamed from the pain, the more my mind heard "This is bone of my bone and flesh of my flesh as," it would reverberate from every chamber of my heart. Those words clearly had a much fuller meaning. I understand that those words Adam spoke to God were his acknowledgment of his relationship with Eve. From that, the relationship was born—sons and daughters that were borne bone of their bone, flesh of their flesh, and therein is the reason losing a child hurts much deeper than any other loss. It is for that reason a mom and a dad should go to any lengths to protect their children.

I can write of these things today only by the grace of God. As we walk through the hours, the days, and months ahead that turn into years, my prayer is that my experience will touch the lives of others, which brings us to the purpose of this book. I have heard it said that "we all have our mountains to climb, our demons to fight." But we do not have to face them and fight them alone. God's grace is the only source capable of giving us the strength and the peace we seek.

The Rock Island I Stand on for the Days Ahead

Take a walk with me as you did in the earlier chapters, when things were much brighter. See how the precepts that made my foundation strong serve as the solid rock I have to stand during this horrific storm and the walk I must make through the valley of the shadow of death. As we walk through this, the same God who answered when I laid my head down with the wisdom I needed, answers my very need now. I want you to know beyond any doubt in your mind or heart that the solid foundation I am able to stand on with an assurance that my God will never abandon me is there for everyone who seeks it. That is what this book will continue to be about to the last chapter.

Walk with me and get to know how I was certain God was undeniably with me as I stood facing the storm. I remind you to make no mistake about the pain I felt that gripped my heart; no words could describe it then, and to this day, I still have not found words that can come close to being sufficient for description. God's Grace was sufficient. The strength of God's Grace was so solid in my heart that no matter how intense the raging storm within my heart became, there would be nothing more that could be taken.

Are you ready to walk with me through that lonesome valley? Walk with me and know that my God was there with each step I take through that valley. He will be with us the entire walk. A valley filled with sorrow and pain. Walk beside me and understand that God will bring us out the other end. The pain will still be there, but I will not have to bear it alone. An old country song written by Woody Guthrie pops into my mind at this point. I can hear the words as only he could sing them: "You have to walk that lonesome valley on your own; no one can walk it for you." I hear the words in my heart even today, only now when I hear those words I know that I do not have to continue to walk in that valley. My God has walked it with me and brought me through it to the end and has given my heart the peace that told me Phillip had never been in that valley. Yet I had to walk it in order to come out of it. Now there is no longer a valid reason for me to be wandering around in it. God walked it with me, and He will not go back there for there is nothing there for me anymore. Therefore, I have no desire to go where God is not

Those Early Hours: Those Early Hours of Waiting

Walk with me and wait with me. We will make the walk to our operations office at about 0500 hours. Reading the paragraphs above this, you would think hours, and even days, had passed when in reality it had only been less than an hour. Keep in mind that time loses relevancy. As we make our way to the office, where KBR has someone on the night shift, I have no recollection of what might have been going through my head at the time we enter the operations building.

I knew my heart was in great pain from the hole left by the huge chunk yanked from it. I knew I would need a notification from the Red Cross. I also knew, within reason, that most likely there would not be a notification for at least two more hours. I guess I just needed to occupy some time with whatever I could find to do. The Marine Corps would initiate notification to the Red Cross, who in turn would notify KBR's Houston office. KBR in Houston would notify their operations in Iraq regarding the death notice from the Red Cross. Camp Warhorse operations would receive a notification from Camp Speicher, and they in turn would notify me of Phillip's death as verified by the Red Cross.

However, in these days of the Internet, cell phones, and satellite phones, news of any sort is hard to keep a lid on. Especially when there is a protocol that not only needs adhering to, but also honored as a matter of respect. In today's world, everything seems to be almost instantaneous. An official notice from the Red Cross would initiate paperwork. Once Camp Warhorse operations received official notice, KBR was very good at getting emergencies taken care of as quickly as possible.

I will never forget Don Howard's reaction when I asked him if he had gotten a Red Cross message for me. He answered no and asked if I was expecting one. I told him yes, because I had just called home to find out that I had lost my son in Afghanistan. He asked me if I was sure, I think simply because he did not know what or how to ask me anything else. I talked to him for a short time about Phillip, and then went into the break room to get myself a cup of joe. When I returned, I finished telling him about Phillip. The moisture from his eyes was a clear sign that his heart was touched.

Don said he needed to wake Stephanie, our operations lead, but I asked him not to do that as it was not even 0600 hours yet. There was no need, because there would be nothing she could do before receiving the official Red Cross notification. I left the office. I needed to go back to my hooch to pack, and I knew I would be leaving Camp Warhorse sometime during the day. When I left the office, Don went to wake Stephanie up.

When I left operations, I returned to my hooch and packed my bags, which would contain everything I would take with me. This was the only thing I used when traveling; also, it was the only thing I had to pack in. Packing kept my time occupied for a short time while waiting for the Red Cross message. I knew when I had my backpack secured that I needed to move on to another task, and that the more I could get done now, the easier it would be later on. Living on a military base in a war zone, involved a lot of uncertainties, especially when it came to the logistics of traveling. We can go to the shop to get things in order there. A fresh cup of joe would hit the spot right now. There were still instructions that needed to be left concerning both ongoing and upcoming jobs.

I finished at the carpenter's shop and was head to our morning safety meeting. My mind was a thousand miles away; trying to pay attention to anything outside the immediate mission was impossible at this point. I was standing at the outside perimeter of the group that had gathered. During the meeting, my mind was almost home at times, but just before it got there, it would somehow end up in Nam, and I think it would be fair to say I did not hear a word said at the meeting. What relevance would anything have at this point? I did hear when Ralph made the announcement to the group at the end of the meeting about Phillip's death in Afghanistan. I suppose the point here is that God allows you to hear what you need to hear.

Ralph acknowledged that they had received a Red Cross message confirming this. I cannot remember my reaction to the announcement.

I simply was not there, although my ears heard the words. My mind would go back to Vietnam, and I would recall when a soldier would receiver that Red Cross message from home. I do remember the silence that fell over the normally noisy shuffling of boots on the loose gravel and chatter from the breakup of the morning meeting. They lined up to shake my hand, and most of them had nothing to say. How could you find the words for an appropriate response to a time such as this? The expression in their eyes revealed what was on their hearts. To this day, words cannot explain how much this meant to me. I knew they could not possibly understand, and I would never want them to. It is my prayer that "all kids outlive their parents" and with long lives of their own. Life, as designed in the beginning, was supposed to work this way.

After the safety meeting, I went into the office and signed the necessary paperwork that Stephanie had prepared for me. There would be more as details came together. There would be more, because we are a world that seems to love swimming in paperwork. Stephanie was a young Texan gal in her early twenties. She always called me Mr. Carson. I can still hear that Texas drawl to this day: "Now, Mr. Carson . . ."

I finished the paperwork and went back to my shop, where I went over things with Jerry, who would be taking my place. When we finished, I received a call over my radio from Stephanie asking me to come to the office. When I got there, Stephanie came up to me and said, "Mr. Carson, Major Matthews and Major Daniels want to make it possible for you to escort your son home, if that is something you would like to do."

I remember this as though it were yesterday. I simply, and without hesitation, said, "Stephanie, make it happen."

Stephanie quickly replied, "But, Mr. Carson, I don't want you to get your hopes up, as it might not happen."

Not a problem, right? I said, "Stephanie, you don't understand. I serve an awesome God." Now you and I can connect the dots to this point, but God has been preparing my heart for this time since we left Houston for Iraq. Are you with me on this? Remember what happens from here on leaves no doubt as to whether God is an active part in our lives. Stephanie let me know that she would confirm the offer to let me escort Phillip home. I appreciated their effort at making this possible, as I knew in my heart that God had already put it on the schedule. Stephanie would give me a call when things were set into motion.

I returned to the shop, I could not think of a better place to be at the time. I had a terrific crew there, and that made things easier. All the men were out on work assignments, so I had the place to myself to finish a few odds and ends. Then the radio broke the silence that surrounded me. It was Stephanie. "Carpenter 1, can you come to the office?"

I was more than glad to reply, "Not a problem." I walked the short distance to the operations building, knowing in my heart that I was going to be able to escort Phillip home. God's Grace abounded within my soul, weaving its way around all the pain, making its presence known to my heart. This gave me the courage, strength, and the ability to be able to focus on the mission. My God was in the habit of opening impossible doors, and I was used to stepping through them.

Spirits Identify

There are parts of that morning I simply do not remember—mostly the smaller details. We will make this our last trip from the carpentry shop to the office. As we make that short walk, we will experience a spirit that binds us together as people. We meet Addai midway to the office. As a rule, if all was well with Addai's life, he would have a big smile on his face. We will see such a smile this morning. Addai has worked on the base at the carpentry shop for the best part of a year now. He has become a good friend. He would bring dates, fresh fruit, and vegetables from his home for the shop. He would also bring a special treat at times: his wife would bake bread in an open-air oven. It was like pita bread, and so good that you could eat it alone. Addai would always bring me something to take home with me when he knew I was leaving for R&R. He once brought me a prayer rug to take home. He said, "Mr. Carson, take this to your wife and tell her to hang it on the wall. I used it to pray on." He understood and respected the difference between Islam and Christianity.

Now back to meeting Addai midway on our trip to the office. We stopped and greeted each other; he had that big smile on his face and was happy. After we greeted each other, I told him about losing Phillip. He just stood there, not moving, not saying anything. Then tears came to his eyes, and all he could do was give me a hug. Without words, he went on to the carpentry shop, and I made my way to the office. Tell me that was not a blessing from God.

A Mission Comes Together

Once again, I was in front of Stephanie, and she started with "Mr. Carson, the army has made it possible for you to escort Phillip home." Then there was the predictable, "But Mr. Carson, KBR is not going to turn you over to the army. I don't want you to get your hopes up."

I replied with the certainty and peace God had given me, "Stephanie, it will happen because I serve an awesome God."

She continued with, "Also, Colonel Salazar wanted to know if you would be willing to meet with him in his office." Colonel Salazar was the Third Infantry Division's brigade commander.

My answer to her was "Not a problem." What Stephanie didn't understand yet was that I indeed served an awesome God, and while things may seem out of our reach, you and I know for certain that what may be out of our reach, there is nothing out of God's reach. There was no need for further prayer about escorting Phillip home; I knew in my heart that God had already opened all the doors. Meeting with Colonel Salazar would be an honor; he was one of those soldier's soldiers. I had talked with him many times in the seven months before this as our carpentry shop crew worked around the base.

We entered the open door to Colonel Salazar's office. He stood up and came around his desk to greet us, and then Stephanie excused herself, explaining she needed to go down the hall to the Tactical Operations Center. She needed to make a call to Camp Speicher's HR office. Camp Speicher was our area headquarters. Stephanie would need permission from the HR department at Camp Speicher. The project manager would have to sign off on the request; the army had their part in motion. The project manager would have to receive permission from HR in Houston.

I can clearly remember standing in Colonel Salazar's office, but I do not have any recollection of what he said. It is not that what he said was meaningless; it simply means that my mind could not focus on what he was saying. I simply was not there at that point. I do remember him presenting me with the Never Forget flag. The first time I ever laid eyes on that flag flashed through my mind. I had seen the flag for the first time back in February of this year at a change-of-command ceremony. The third ID was relieving the first ID, the Big Red One, Colonel Pittard's command. I remembered how impressed I was with the flag and what it stood for. My heart understood at that moment why it meant so much during the earlier change-of-command ceremony back in February.

The colonel and I had just stepped out of his office, and the first images my eyes focused on were two of my friends leaning against the opposite wall. They were both big men, both veterans and both Texans. Terry Greer was an airborne ranger, and Bill Sanders was a Vietnam veteran my age. I was in Nam a year before him. I was army, and he was a river rat for the navy.

When turned my attention down the hallway that led to the TOC, I saw Stephanie coming toward us. She was shaking her head and saying, "I don't believe it. I don't believe it." She appeared to be walking two feet above the floor. I knew all was well, because God had gone ahead and opened the doors. How's that for an awesome God?

When Stephanie reached us, she said to Colonel Salazar, "Sir, all KBR wants is for you to let them know where he is all the time."

Now we understand more about how the dots connect. I was going to escort my Marine home. This would be a very special and rare thing: a Vietnam veteran would be on an Angel Flight taking home his son who had given his life in Afghanistan for the cause of his country.

As I am writing, it is hard to keep the lumps out of my throat as the pain from my heart makes its way to the surface from that indescribable depth that only God can know. My vision becomes blurry as the pain grips my heart. I feel the warm streams run down each side of my face. The pride I felt in having served my country only amplified the pride I felt in my son. I saw the tears rolling down the cheeks of these two big men and knew their hearts were hurting in an unspeakable manner as they too were both fathers. There was also that element that is hard for most people to understand, and that is the sense of brotherhood that the military has and which veterans share as their lives go on outside their service time. There are times when only tears can express what words cannot.

I feel that it is very important to take the time at this point to make sure that I am writing in a way that makes sense to you as you walk with me. My prayer and intention for your walk with me is not for you to feel pity for me. Walking with me, I hope you will understand the design God has for your life. My son sacrificed his life on the battlefield not that my life would be rendered useless by what he has so gallantly given but, on the contrary, that I might move forward through the sorrow of that day. Phillip's sacrifice, along with all the sacrifices that made for this nation's freedom are so we can carry on with our lives. They too have their numbered days. It is my prayer that in your walk with me through the rest of this journey, you will, in the end, be encouraged, reassured, or motivated to answer God's call to your life, and your life too would be an inspiration to others.

CHAPTER 6

Leaving Iraq: Escorting My Marine Home

Are you ready to get on a Black Hawk with me for a trip to Camp Anaconda? We have been there many times before in the months that have passed in our journey to this point. There was beginning to be some doubt from operations and HR as to whether we would be able to get a chopper out of Camp Warhorse. As for me, not a problem. My heart knew God had gone before me, leaving my heart at peace. God gives us the peace in our hearts to know all is well. Sometimes, when we know that God is providing for us, it is best if we keep a thing like this to ourselves. It is human nature to say "I have given it my best. There is nothing more left for me to do." Well, that is true, and that is when we have to reach beyond ourselves to God. He can reach to infinity.

We did get on that chopper around 1300 hours, lifted off, and headed to Camp Anaconda. We were surprised when we had to go through a US customs station once arriving at Bald. The air force had a customs operation in the middle of the desert in the Iraqi war zone. This was one of those believe-it-or-not moments for me. Once inside the compound, there was no leaving it until boarding the plane. Processing in was quick and easy, especially if all you have is a backpack and a huge load of grief. Now we just had to wait for a plane to become available for the long seven-hour flight to Ramstein, Germany. I cannot remember exactly when we would find out what time we would be flying out of Balad. In a war zone, everything is subject to the changing needs of the warriors on the ground. We were used to this by now. If you don't deal with changes very well, then maybe walking beside me will help us get a handle on the use of "Not a problem."

Memories

I would spend the five-hour wait at the customs holding area remembering Phillip as boy. The memories would come to mind just as if I was looking at a photo album plugged into my mind's memory banks somehow. There were many memories of Phillip as a boy and teenager, and they were terrific. The memories of him as a young adult are few, because shortly after leaving those teen years, he was off becoming a marine. Phillip was 22.3½ years in the Marine Corps at the time; that did not leave a lot of time for us during his years as a young man just out of his teens. God once again steps in and my heart becomes very grateful for the time Phillip was with us. With that grateful heart, my mind would go back and kind of settle on the memories of Phillip being with me from the time he was a little lad. The memories brought measured amounts of relief that would ease the pain. For that reason, I feel it a part of my mission to encourage young families to make those memories today. Can you imagine sitting around waiting for a plane to arrive to carry you home to bury your son or daughter and have to struggle to find good memories? Can you imagine having to go through the "I wish I had done this" process? Memories of Phillip being so shy during his young years flooded my head and heart as I could feel that little arm wrapped around one of my legs. Phillip was never more than an arm's length away from either of my legs. Those memories brought back the knowledge that my leg was his anchoring point for safety as long as that little arm was around my leg.

Can you imagine the power those memories possess? They have the ability to help you either overcome the pain within or add to it. How those memories work depends on the condition of your heart at the time. If those memories are coming from a grateful heart for the time God has allowed you to have with your loved one. Then they will present themselves as precious memories for you to cherish forever with a grateful heart and bring a smile to bear even though the heart is in pain at that time. If, on the other hand, the memories only bring more pain and seems only to add more pain to what you are already experiencing, then most likely, your loss is more about what you have to deal with now.

I almost decided not to write that message; it was on my heart so much. I know I cannot go any further without telling it the way I see it. I have met some and have read the comments from many on the social media networks, from those who are hurting in ways that they do not have to. I can only speak for myself and not judge anyone's heart, as I cannot see it. What I can offer is a way to move forward with your pain. It will always be with us. For that reason, I do not like the term. It is as if "moving on" suggests that we can somehow move into our tomorrows, leaving all the hurt behind. Life simply does not work that way. For me, I do not have to walk this walk alone. I have God with me at all times, and His Grace is sufficient, as you have seen during your walk with me. Once again, it is impressed on my heart to tell you that my son did not die so that I would end up wandering around in that lonesome valley of the shadow of death. Once again, my heart will tell you that if that is where you are, that is not where you will find your loved one, so why are you even there? Why are you not honoring his life as he has given it in sacrifice that we can chose to live life as God designed it for us to live it? Well, I have that off my chest. Now, to move on without preaching.

Our camping trips would help me rise above the pain I felt in my heat at the time. That is what those memories we build with our loved ones is supposed to do. Memories of summer break when Phillip would work with me. I had more than enough terrific moments of memory to fill the time, playing their intended purpose out while I waited at Balad. Memories are, with intention, designed to occupy a spot in the heart, where they are stronger than the bad things on the exterior that can cause so much pain. The hole in my heart that can never be replaced will always be there as a constant reminder of the depth of my loss. What cannot be touched by any level of grief caused by this huge hole are memories I have of Phillip. What ripped that portion of my heart out cannot touch that part of my heart that houses my memories of Phillip. Can you imagine going through this time without those memories to counter the pain?

As we walk through this together, my question for you is how would you have dealt with this under similar circumstances? If your answer is "I don't know," then I am writing this book for you to encourage you to start building that faith for a foundation to stand on when the time comes when you will need it. If on the other hand you answer me saying you are not sure then this book is for inspiration, that you can build your faith with certainty. If your answer is "I hope I would do the things you have done," then this book is for you as an encouragement to hold on to what you have and make it stronger as you walk each day of life. Keep building your faith and maintain that foundation to face the storms of life. You will prevail against all that comes against you because of the foundation you have to stand on. I have been asked by people wondering if losing someone so close would be harder to deal with than if the ties had not be so close.

From my perspective, after all this time, I can tell you unequivocally, no. Based on my own experience of course. What I find the harder thing to deal with would be if I had not taken the time to make those memories. I know being faced with the questions and the guilt that come with the thoughts of wishing I had pound the mind. I am certain you can see how this would be like rubbing salt into a wound. The memories during that five hours let me know just how blessed my life was that God allowed Phillip to be that part of my life. My thoughts would turn to his brother and sisters and how much I loved and appreciated them just as much for being a part of my life.

My mind would switch gears on me without warning. Between the memories of Phillip, I would recall when I first applied for this job with KBR. With the dots connected now, I knew God had a reason for me being in Iraq. Earning a living is not God's mission for us in life; it is just a way for us to sustain ourselves while on God's mission. My heart will forever be grateful for a better-than-good salary while working for KBR. It was not only a vehicle for my being there, it was also an answer to my prayer to get me out of the deficit I found my life was in financially. Can you see all these things tied together for the good of the mission at hand? That was a part of God's plan. It's so plain to me now, but it was not so when we first got to Iraq. You can see how God always knows what we need, when we need it, and how need it.

You and I can now see with 20/20 hindsight why the dedications meant so much to my heart. I truly believe God was preparing my heart for where we are now in our walk. All of the dots now make sense. Can you see now why the Sergeant David J. Salie memorial project and dedication ceremony moved my heart so much? It was just a couple of months before this time. With the examples of courage from Captain

Christopher Cash, CSM Faulkenberg, and SFC David J. Salie, God knew I would need a strong foundation on which to face this storm head-on. I remember thinking about the courage these men displayed, and I thought about the courage their families would need through these difficult times. As I walked through the valley of the shadow of death, my faith would prove to be sufficient, because there is nothing else. I would needed that grace given by God for the days that would follow. My wife needed a husband who was grounded in his faith, my kids needed a dad who was strong in his faith, and the people I would deal with needed to see the strength of God at work.

The Long Flight to Germany

Are you ready to take that seven-hour flight to Ramstein, Germany? At 0200 hours, we boarded a C-141. (It may have been a C-17, but I do not think so.) We would be traveling to Ramstein on an air ambulance flight. Like in the C-130, the passengers sat on web seating against the outer walls of the plane. These planes are noisy, yet as I sat in the web seat along the exterior wall of the aircraft, I was not sure that a silenced engine noise would have been beneficial for me at this time. There was no real desire for conversation at this point anyhow; I needed to walk this part of the lonesome valley on my own, knowing that my God is sufficient. My mind once again was tracking like a UFO. With the turns in direction, I found it hard to keep up with as it switched so fast. Sometimes not making any sense; and then at other times, there would be no thought at all, the lull in the thoughts came as a numbing relief to the incomprehensible direction my mind would take me. I was mindlessly floating away in never-neverland, not very aware of my surroundings became a time of welcomed relief from the pain within. My heart would seem to seize up when that gripping pain would surface. Then there were those times when the memories of Phillip would come to the forefront of my heart and rescue it from the pain that gripped it. They would be memories of Phillip with the family or his friends. Some would bring a smile that seemed to be at the time administered with the intent of a good measure of medicine for the soul now and then.

My mind would settle for a short time as we left Iraq behind, and I would concentrate on the connecting of dots of my life. With those thoughts, I could feel the song "Amazing Grace" deep within my soul. I could hear in my mind that old gospel song "Precious Memories," a favorite of my mother's. Wow, what a mighty God I serve to bring all these dots together at this time to accomplish a mission. "You have to walk that lonesome valley" would again follow those memories, and when I would allow my heart to be grateful, that time would end with "There will be peace in the valley." Those thoughts and songs came to mind because God gave us music for the ears to soothe the sorrows in our soul and to rejoice in the goodness of the Lord for those days He made for us. Remember our morning walks with "This is the day the Lord hath made; I will rejoice and be glad in it." Did that mean only part of the time when things were going good and rejoicing and being glad was easy to do? Ah, grateful for that dot connects, that part of the internal spiritual gyroscope to stay my course maintaining an even keel.

As we continue our flight my heart was reminded so often that I was not alone. God understood. He had been there, and my heart understands that He too understands the pain of losing a son who gave His life for others. So yes, God understands the depth of the pain in my heart and in the hearts of all. Though I cannot reach deep enough to the sorrow at hand, God is more than capable of doing that for me. It is in those times that I can feel the peace He gives my heart. I now know after nine years, only God can know and understand the deepest sorrow, the width of the loss, and the longing of my heart to lay my eyes on Phillip.

Are you ready for the final approach to Ramstein Air Base? Are you ready to wait with me for the next part of our walk to escort my marine home?

The Wait at Ramstein Air Force Base

When we land at Ramstein, we will have been twenty-eight and a half hours into this mission to escort my son home. I am truly grateful that you are still walking this with me. God has walked this valley with us; He is the source of my strength as we continue our walk in this valley. I do not believe my mind would have allowed sleep to come if I had wanted it to. These strains are without doubt tough on the body as it is on the emotions. Can you see how God knew all of this ahead of time?

I had never experienced this level of emotion before, even when I lost my mother at twelve years old. As I began to think about the loss of my mother, later my father, and then my three brothers along the way, God allowed my heart to understand the distinct difference between those losses and the loss of a child. He created us to experience those at different levels. It is right now, at the time of this writing, that I realize that this is why people say what they do without malice but, rather, out of a total lack of understanding and, most of the time, not considering the better part of prudence is keeping one's mouth shut. Only a kindred spirit can identify with what is going on in the heart. That kindred spirit also resides within the heart of God.

I ask myself, how could I have been more prepared for something like this? The only answer I know now is that I could not, except by the grace of God. I could have done nothing under the sun to make my heart ready for this. It is for that reason—a strong spiritual foundation is the only rock from which you can face into the storm. It is the only foundation from which you can walk that lonesome valley, but you can walk it on your own without being alone. It is the only foundation you have while you walk that valley that can bring you out the other end and never have to return to it.

Now we wait at Ramstein Air Base for five hours. Not a problem. My focus is on my mission. We will find our way to a passenger waiting area. After being on a flight as long as the one we just finished, sitting in a web seat, you will find any seat a welcome relief. I do not think I am going to be much good company at this point. You may want to pour yourself a cup of joe and just kind of tag along while I slip into another world. As I settled into my seat with my thoughts still on what seemed to be a mindless rampage at off and on times, I tried to close my eyes on the off chance that my heart would settle down and the thoughts might bump head-on with an off switch. Sitting there, I began to think about what a chunk of my heart had been all but literally ripped from my body.

My mind began to recall all the dots that before the morning of the phone call had no reason to connect. There were the dots that connected, making the projects we were on easier, and sometimes even possible. All these dots connected as a part of our job we had the joy of doing while on a mission we did not know yet. What we have walked through together to this point is impressive.

When I think about those who will pick this book up and walk through it with me, I realize this is a story with a God-given mission. This book has been intended from the time we left Houston to this point and has been a part of this mission. The fact that you are still with me on this walk serves as proof of this fact. Without God, this story could not be a story about a dad escorting his marine home. Without God, without this mission, I would only have a story about taking advantage of an opportunity to make more money than I had ever considered possible in my life. Without God, you would not be walking beside me from the start to now and through to the end. Forever 22, I realize, is the result of the love God has for Phillip, my family, his friends, and, yes, you. Because you have read this far and have walked with me, then you are where God wants you to be. It is not just a story about a dad escorting his son home. We will find a lot more dots to connect as the pages are turned and this mission proceeds.

However, we will find that God's purpose for our lives is more than just our comfort through this life. I truly believe He has a mission for each life he created. It is also my belief that it is our responsibility to humble our hearts, for it is only with a humble heart that we come to understanding of that purpose and mission. Once we find that purpose, then we can set out on the mission. It is our responsibility to reach as deep within ourselves to come up with the passion for that mission. God does not work alone in our lives but with us. You have seen that time after time in your walk with me up to this point.

As we wait for our time to pass for the flight to Dover, I would occasionally feel the urge . . .to wonder how others have handled this same situation. I know I am not walking through this valley as the first traveler. For the first time, many others are passing through it right now. I do believe that this walk is very personal for each individual, and that is why we have to make that walk on our own. I am beginning to understand that part of my purpose in writing this book is to help you not to have to walk through your valleys as many do alone. How you choose to walk that valley is a choice you have to make. You are the reason I am sharing my experiences. God intends for us to make a difference in each other's lives. That is why I invite you to walk with me through this story rather than simply inviting you to read it. I hope I have so far made that difference.

I have searched my heart extensively, and to this day, I am not able to tell anyone with any amount of certainty how to deal with such a storm outside my own set of circumstances. For this reason, you will find a purpose in this book for you, and a big part of that purpose is that you allow God to be yours. The whole point is not to get you to try in some way to feel or understand the pain of my sorrow. Only God can do that. The entire purpose to this point and beyond is to help you, the reader. As you walk this walk with me, understand the importance of building that solid foundation—a foundation built of faith that you can stand on to face the storm. My prayer as we travel through the rest of this journey is that your thoughts will begin to turn toward the condition of your own foundation. Upon examination, if it is not where you would like for it to be, then now is the time to do something about it. If you have not started, then I hope your walk with me will leave you with a sense of urgency to start building it. When the time comes, it will serve you well, as you have seen while walking with me to this point.

Getting back to the story, again, I simply do not remember the details at times. I am not sure of them at all, but the events on that timeline I recall very well. You and I have been sitting in the waiting lounge for at least a couple of hours. My body feels the toll this has taken; however, my heart and my mind would not allow sleep no matter how I felt physically.

We have been sitting by ourselves for some time now. Then a young mother with her two young children at her side walks into the waiting area and take a seat. Now we have some company; we strike up a conversation. She was a good conversationalist, wanting to know where I had traveled from and where I would be going. When I told her I had traveled from Iraq, I could see the change in her face. Maybe she was a bit confused. Then when I told her I would travel to Dover from Ramstein, that opened up more questions. I found her curiosity to be quite a relief. We talked about why I was in Germany, and we talked about Phillip. I had no problem talking about my memories of Phillip because he was such a great son and because the memories were so great and I was so blessed to be his dad. God knows when to cause our paths to cross with others. When her husband showed up, she sent him to get some food for her and the children. When he returned, she asked me if I had eaten. I answered no. It was the last thing on my mind. She explained that they had taken the liberty to pick up a hamburger for me. When their departure announcement came, they left. My thoughts started running absolutely all over the gambit of time.

My heart was able to be grateful for the conversation and the hamburger. God knows us. He knows what we need, where we need it, and when we need it. Is God not awesome?

God Provides a Time of Peace During the Storm

I had just settled in with my thoughts again, and I began to realize that time was not very relevant to much of anything at this point. My solitude within the waiting area was to end shortly when a young female airman, in the air force females are referred to as airmen, appeared in front of me and asked if I would like to go upstairs to the coffee room for a cup of coffee. I was more than glad for a change of scenery, and being an avid coffee drinker I was ready for a cup of joe, and it did not have to be fresh. I followed her up a set of steel stairs to the break area. She pointed out where I could find cups, cream, and sugar. I did not need anything but a cup and coffee.

Just being somewhere different in the same building for a change felt good. Just sitting in the same spot for very long was not my nature. I have always needed to be moving, even if it is in the wrong direction, as the old saying goes. This was not a lot different from the waiting time at Camp Anaconda. I had no idea about anything other than I would be flying to Dover Air Force Base in Delaware. Beyond knowing where we would be flying next. There was nothing more than just me and my pain that keep each other company. The pain would work its way to the surface without warning. My thoughts turned to my family at home, and I wondered how they were doing. I had no way of contacting them until I got at least to Dover and settled into a hotel.

I had managed to get a couple sips of the hot joe down when the young airman opened the door and planted herself in front of me. She was not sure of what she should say. Therefore, she just did what she figured to be right. "Mr. George, I don't know if I should ask you or not, but your son's body has just arrived. Would you like to spend some time with him?" My response was, without hesitation, yes. I

followed the airman down the stairs without a word. We came to a
stop in front of a door that had a security code lock. We stepped into
the huge refrigerated room. I would guess the temperature was a few
degrees above thirty-two. We stood there for a few seconds in total
silence, and she asked if I would like her to stay. I replied that it would
not be necessary. She turned quietly and exited the room. I would not
have minded her staying had she not asked. My time was silent, and
just between God and me. This was just a time for the grateful heart of
a father to know that his son's body was finally going to be on its way
home. I was in the room for about fifteen minutes, the temperature
was not a factor as I concentrated on the aluminum transport box, and
with a grateful heart, I thanked God for allowing me to do this, and I
knew that by His Grace did I make it this far. It was time to start the
next phase of the mission. As I wrote the last sentence, I realized that
at that point, my eyes were seeing the aluminum transport box in the
middle of the floor without the American flag covering it. Now it makes
more sense what happens on board the C5A. The dots would continue
to connect even nine years later.

When I exited the refrigerated room, the airman was waiting for
me, and I thanked her for allowing me to do this. She took me to the
departure area, I would be able to board shortly. She informed me they
were in the process of loading Phillip's body onto the plane. It would not
be much longer before the airman led me out a door and I recognized
the C5A. It was a monstrous sight. I had never been this close to one.
The C5A can be loaded by lowering ramps from the front and the back.
We approached the front ramp, and as we entered the cavernous cargo
space, my eyes immediately focused on the aluminum transport box. I
could see that it had already been secured to the cargo rails on the floor.
I was still at peace with myself and rested in God's grace. My soul was
at peace with the knowledge that Phillip's body no longer housed his
eternal soul. I thought of it as a sacred temple that had been a host to
his eternal soul.

The crew made their way from various parts of the plane and
formed two lines just in front of the lowered ramp. I was behind those
two lines with my backpack that held everything I was taking with me
on the trip home. I was OK with where I was—that is, as it should have
been for military protocol. The pilot descended from a set of winding
aluminum stairs from the upper deck. Once all of the crew was in place,

an air force chaplain came up the ramp. The chaplain did a small service with prayers offered in honor of Phillip's service and sacrifice. He also prayed for a safe trip to Dover.

When the chaplain finished, the pilot asked for the American flag, which was custom-made to fit the aluminum transport box. A young airman had to speak up and said, "Sir, we don't have one." The pilot's reaction could be read by anyone as being anything other than pleased.

When I heard this, I spoke up and said "Sir, I have a flag." He asked to see it. I had my backpack at my side. I unzipped it and pulled the Never Forget flag out of its box. The Never Forget flag was unfolded so the pilot could see it. The pilot quickly said, "Not a problem. After the Never Forget flag made its way to the front and present to the pilot it was then placed over Phillip's transport box. What happened next will be a vivid image in my memory forever. The pilot reached across his chest to his left shoulder, pulling the American flag from off his uniform and then placed the flag at the head of the transfer box just above the Never Forget flag.

On the "Angel Flight" Home

After the service concluded, I was shown the way to the upper deck by way of the spiral stairs to the passenger section; the C5A seated thirty-four. I had to research this bit of information, and in the course of my research, I found that the C5A was described as not very good for bus service. It was a long ways from the commercial flights I had gotten used to when flying in or out of Dubai. At this point, that did not matter. I was grateful to be on board with my son's body and ready for the flight home. I was still on a mission.

I lifted the arms up on three seats so I could stretch out and get some much-needed sleep. At fifty-eight years old, I was a long time from being a spring chicken. My body and my mind—especially my mind— were ready to shut down. I had been up and awake for about thirty-two hours by now. Another part of my mission had been accomplished: Phillip and I were headed to the United States. We were headed home on what would become known as the Angel Flight.

I have heard the song "Angel Flight (Tower Radio Remix)," and it has become very special to me. To have been on an Angel Flight, this song brought home the feeling of closing a chapter in a faraway land. The trip home for that warrior meant that his final sunset had come. His mission had been completed; the war would no longer be his to fight. The lyrics go "Come with me, brother / come fly with me / I am flying you home tonight," but what my heart heard was, "Come with me, son / come fly with me tonight, son / Dad will take you home tonight." Right now, as I relate this to you in written word, my eyes grow moist and my vision blurs as I watch the text of what is on my heart appear on the computer screen. I can feel the emotion in the tips of my fingers as they strike the keyboard keys. The hole in my heart is still there. It is as tender as the day of this flight, and the grace of God gives my heart a reprieve.

I just wanted to stretch out this six-foot, two-hundred-fifty-pound carcass. I have always been able to go to REM sleep stage as soon as my head is down. If there is any sort of preliminary stages, I skip all of them. Once my head is down, I am out. I had no sooner reached the very edge of REM sleep than the flight engineer tapped me on the shoulder. He should not have done that; I almost decked him. My kids learned a long time ago not to touch me when waking me up. I guess it is a throwback to Nam. He asked me if I would like to be up front for takeoff. Well, yes. Sleep could wait.

I spent about two hours up front for takeoff, strapped into a seat just behind the pilot, with a set of headphones on my head. The takeoff was an unbelievable experience—worth every missed minute of sleep I might have gotten. Once we were in the air, I talked to the pilot, copilot, and the engineer for about two hours. I learned that the copilot was about to get married soon, that was a good thing. I finally came to a point where I had to say, "Guys, I have to lay my head down." And that is what I did solid until we approached Dover Air Base. The engineer once again woke me up; only this time, he stayed away from me. He wanted to know if I wanted to be up front for the landing. Oh, absolutely. It was about 2200 or a little after when the wheels touched the runway. I had managed to get some solid hours of sleep; I did not know how much longer I could have stayed up, and was grateful not to have to find out.

It was amazing to watch the pilot steer that mammoth plane with the steering wheel off to the left side, no bigger than about six inches. We taxied to a stop, and by the time I made my way down the stairs, most of the crew was already in two lines. The chaplain was just coming on board when I reached the back spot of the crew. I was fine emotionally throughout the service. When the crew moved to the side, I knew that there would be a Marine detail coming to take Phillip's body to the morgue. My heart was strengthened by the fact that the soul of Phillip, the son that I had spent so much terrific time with was in heaven. There was no doubt in my heart at all about that fact.

My heart was also grateful for the fact that he was on American soil. I find it hard to explain how much that means to a family. A veteran would understand more than others. My eyes followed the length of the tarmac from the lowered ramp of the plane to a blue bus and a van parked behind it. I knew why it was there. I understood who would be on the other side and why. That knowledge did not bother me; my heart was still pretty much OK I had seen this enough times in Iraq. It was not until I saw the marine honor detail march between the bus and the van that my heart and mind kind of when into a stall mode. I think the reason this moment struck me so hard was that they were coming to take him; there was an element of being final I had not had to deal with until this point. I could literally feel my heart swelling my chest and knotting up. There was a sense of permanence to this action. I could not only see the detail clearly as they marched toward the plane, I could also feel the cadence of their shoe soles as they struck the tarmac in time with each other. I had no urge to follow the aluminum transport box. God has already given me peace on this issue.

Three Days at Dover

I am glad you are still with me. At this point, I would like you to know I would never wish you could understand or walk in my shoes through this part of my life. It is my desire, however, that what I have experienced by the grace of God will make a difference in how you see the power of God in your own life by His presence in my life through this storm. As you and I go through the next three days, you are going to see how God continues to be in the past, present, and future of those lives that belong to Him. Miracles are not limited to miraculous healings or sightings of images that remind us of Jesus. They exist in the everyday, ordinary lives of people simply walking through life the best they know how.

The fact that I was on that Angel Flight was a miracle in itself. As you travel with me from the air terminal to the hotel at Dover, you will see the angel of mercy at work. The air force chaplain, a full bird colonel, who did the service on the tarmac also drove me to the military hotel on base. On our way to the hotel, he swung by a USO building, where he pulled up to the curb to a woman waiting with a couple of bags in her hand. She handed the bag to me through the window of the sedan, explaining the she was waiting for us, and that the USO had been closed for some time now. She explained that one bag contained a hot meal and the other essential items. The USO handed the essentials bag to our warriors returning from Afghanistan and Iraq. We both thanked her, and the colonel drove us the short distance to the hotel.

The young female clerk greeted us from behind the registration desk. When I surveyed the lobby, I felt as though I had just stepped into a five-star hotel. That is exactly what it was. She asked the colonel how she could help him, and he told her what he needed. She told him that they had no vacancies at the time but that the junior officers' quarters had some.

I could feel the emotions almost radiate from the colonel's words as he asked her, "You mean to tell me that all of the rooms on the top floor are taken?"

She replied, "No, sir, but we cannot put him there."

The colonel said, "Young lady, do I need to make a phone call?"

The clerk replied, "No, sir." She understood what the outcome of that would be.

The colonel had handled the situation with authority and dignity. What he understood and the young clerk did not was that he had a father who had just lost his son in Afghanistan, had just completed a long trip home with his son's body, and he was not about to shuffle me to another building, especially this late at night. He thanked her after the paperwork was completed and then accompanied me up to my room. He told me that I would be at Dover for three days, and then it would be on to Houston. I thanked him, knowing I could never put into words how much my heart appreciated him.

Before he left, the colonel offered his advice for me to consider. And consider it I would. He suggested that because I would need to be at

Dover for at least two days, I should get a good night's sleep and then head home to the family the next morning. He thought that I could do more there than staying at Dover. He also made it clear that he understood that I had authorization to escort Phillip home. I thanked him and genuinely meant it.

A Busy Night

I took a few minutes to get familiar with the room. The quarters were unbelievable; the suite had the bedroom at one end of a formal living room, a dining room off the other end, and a kitchenette off the dining room. The shower just off the bedroom was huge. For a common country boy, this was impressive; this was the first time I had ever been in anything like this. Now I told you earlier that I'm an avid coffee drinker, so one of my first tasks was to make a fresh pot of joe. The next thing I did was eat the most welcome meal provided by the USO. It hit every spot that needed hitting. During my meal, I called home to let Penny and the rest of my family know that I was at Dover with Phillip, and that I was in the hotel room. When I talked to Sara, my daughter who was still at home, and Aaron, who was married and living in Austin, they both said without hesitation, "Dad, stay with Phillip." That response struck my heart so deeply. It showed the unselfish love they had for their brother. The phone call sealed my decision to stay to escort my son, the fallen marine, home

As soon as I settled into the hotel room, a gunny sergeant called me. He explained that he would get together with me in the morning, that his assignment was to be the marine liaison. I was familiar with the mission of the liaison from working with the military as a civilian in Iraq.

After finishing my meal, I took a shower. I had not had one in over forty-five hours. A hot shower after that many hours can probably wash hours of fatigue down the drain with the soap and water. I guess you might say I was beyond needing one. Shortly after my shower, I thought I was ready to turn in for the much-needed feel of a real bed and a good night's sleep. I had no sooner gotten into the bed than the phone rang. It was a gunny sergeant calling from Houston, a casualty assistance officer (CAO). It was about 2230 hours, and after he introduced himself and his mission, he said, "I hate to ask you this so late, but I need some paperwork signed so I can get it to the funeral home tonight. Would it be OK if I come by and get you to sign it?" I told him that it would be fine if I were in Houston.

He responded, "Well, where are you?"

I told him I was at Dover and he asked why I was at Dover. I explained that I escorted my son home from Germany. I did not wait for a solution to his need; I simply suggested that he fax the forms to the hotel and I would have the clerk fax them back to him. That was a good solution to the problem. Not a problem, right?

A few short minutes later, the clerk knocked on my door. As soon as I opened it, she handed me the papers. I signed them and took them downstairs so the clerk could fax them back to Houston. Once back upstairs and in the room now, I could lay my head down. I cannot remember if I had enough left in me to petition the Lord consciously or not. I doubt I did, but the neat thing about humbling your heart, and ultimately your life, to God is that he knows my heart and my needs even when I am at my wits' end.

We are truly creatures of habit, some more than other perhaps. I was up at 0500 and ready to face the day. I had no idea how that day was going to be or what I had to do, I knew I would find out soon enough. For this the reason we are cautioned by the scripture to take one day at a time. First things first, I had a fresh pot of "Joe" brewing as soon as I got out of bed. I looked forward to the first cup. I focused on the last few days and with a grateful heart knew God had been with me and would continue to be with me. I now had a good night's sleep and as He always does, when I need God's wisdom He is always faithful to provided it. You need to ask for it.

It was about 0830 hours, I suppose, when the gunny sergeant called to let me know he was in the lobby waiting for me. When I made it to the lobby, there was no mistaking the gunny. He rather stood out. He introduced himself and asked if I had eaten. I told him no, I had not, and that I was certainly ready to eat. We went to a restaurant on base, and the breakfast turned out to be good. We talked some small talk, and then he laid out how he was there to help me with whatever I needed. He told me the first thing we needed to do was move me to a room available in the officers' quarters. That did not bother me at all; my mission had more important elements to it than staying in a fancy hotel room. I was on a mission, and where I laid my head at night was not an issue for the short time I would be there.

The gunny was a man who knew his job and presented himself no less than one would expect a marine to. While at breakfast, he told me that if I was to be a part of the escort, I had to have a suit. This bit of information did not surprise me. I informed him that all I had with me would be in the backpack. He told me part of his job as liaison was to assist me in any way he could with whatever I needed. I told him that I needed everything to be properly dressed. That bit of info took us to a couple of men's stores after we checked in at the junior officers' quarters. Nothing they had would fit me; I have always been hard to fit. My arms are long, which reminded me of Phillip. At that time, I weighed 250 pounds. I have broad shoulders and could still bench-press two twenty-five for warm-up. Wish I could do that today. We ended up at J.C. Penny's. The gunny said he knew a woman who worked there and had helped him out before with similar needs. We found the woman, and I told her that I needed everything from suit, shirt, shoes, and a belt. I was quick to let her know that I was a T-shirt and blue jeans kind of guy, and that I would rely on her judgment. In no time, she had everything picked out, and all I had to do was pay.

This was the second day of my stay at Dover. When we finished, Gunny found a steakhouse, and it was an honor to buy him dinner. He had been a real help. I did not want to imagine having to do this chore on my own. Not that I could not have done it, but considering the circumstances, this was a godsend. We enjoyed our dinner, and Gunny briefed me on what would take place in the morning, what time, where, and then it would be time to leave. At this point, I only knew that we would fly to Houston with a marine escort.

That evening at the hotel, I called the family. I let them know that I had to go shopping to be properly dressed. Knowing that I had someone to assist me with it was probably a relief for them as they think I don't know how to coordinate colors. I went to bed early. I guess I was still catching up a bit from all that had taken place over the last six days. The load was heavy to carry from the morning I found out that Phillip had been killed in action to the morning that we were to leave Dover. God had given me the grace to be at peace with myself, allowing me time to focus clearly on the mission at hand. God's grace continues to be sufficient, which allows me to focus on the task I have in front of me.

The next morning, at 0500 hours, my eyeballs pop open. I am out of bed and headed for the coffeepot. You need to know that I can make it through the morning without my cup of joe in my hand, but I would rather not. As I sipped on my hot cup of joe, my heart was in the state of "This is a day the Lord hath made; I will rejoice in it and be glad." You might be wondering how I could take this to heart in light of the burden my heart had to deal with at the time. This is all part of preparing your foundation ahead of time. I understand this to mean that because God has made this day, I can rejoice and be glad in it. Not because the sorrow has been taken away from my heart or in any way diminished, but because God shares that burden of sorrow with me. I would not know anything more than today I am heading home to Houston, Texas. My son, my marine is going home.

At 0800 hours, the gunny showed up at the hotel lobby. We put my backpack in the backseat, and he drove us to the morgue. I think out of respect, he was mostly quiet. My mind was going in a thousand different directions and a distance too far away to measure. I would not have been a good conversationalist at this point. We arrived at a brick building. After parking, we walked to a waiting area. It was a nice antiseptic waiting room. The gunny stayed with me throughout the briefing. I found it very hard to concentrate on the moment

After a short time, an air force junior officer appeared and gave instructions to those waiting. If my memory serves me right, I was the only civilian. The others were in uniform: Army, Navy, Air Force, and Marine Corps, all in dress uniforms, and their purpose for being there was to escort a fallen warrior home. I remember I felt the burden of those escorts and the families who waited for them to arrive home from that last trip. I never felt out of place or ill at ease with the military, maybe because I was an eight-year Vietnam army veteran and this was where God wanted me to be. I got my discharge from the army as a staff sergeant; my draft date was November 1966; my one-year tour in Vietnam was 1967–1968. I reenlisted in December of 1969. I don't know why this popped into my head; maybe it tied my being at the morgue with the duty of the warriors in that room. I certainly identified with the mission each one of them was about to undertake.

Shortly after the briefing, I met the young marine who would be the marine escort for Phillip on his final trip home to Houston. The military escorts are very special because this is strictly a voluntary duty.

Just a few minutes later, we would be in a different room. When the time came to escort Phillip, we walked behind Phillip being carried by an honor guard detail in full dress uniform. Once we were out the door, the marines turned to the black hearse that was waiting under the portico. With all the dignity and respect of the military, Phillip was loaded into the back of the vehicle and locked into place. At the time of introduction to the marine escort, I found out we would travel by vehicle to Philadelphia, where we would then board a Delta flight to Atlanta, Georgia. Then we would transfer to another Delta flight to Houston. As we pulled away from the brick building, I saw that both sides of the driveway was lined with uniformed personnel holding a crisp salute as the hearse made its way past them. I could see the gunny standing on the sidewalk that followed the curve of the driveway from the morgue. He stood at attention, rendering a hand salute until the hearse had passed.

Trip to Philadelphia

I spent the short trip to Philadelphia mostly in silence, watching the countryside go by for seventy-one miles. I could not corral my mind as it flitted from Vietnam to Iraq and then end somewhere in between. I was not sure I felt I was anywhere; everything was too surreal at the time. No matter how hard I tried, my mind simply could never go beyond Phillip's present age of twenty-two. To this day, I try to imagine what might have been. I do not stay there too long because my mind cannot go beyond that point in his life.

The fact is that he will be forever twenty-two to me, and I am at peace, by God's grace, with that.

That point will also give credence to the eventual title of this book: *Forever 22*. I did not know at the time the significance of understanding this fact, but I do now, and it helps me in two ways. It helps me deal with the fact that Phillip will never be more than twenty-two years old. His legacy will start at that point. Understanding this also helps me not to waste time being at that point with the heavy heart that goes with it. Phillip would not want me to be where he is not. Phillip is with God, and God is with Phillip's soul in heaven, not in the body that housed his soul on earth. The question now is why would I want to be where

God and Phillip are not? I reason in my heart that if Phillip is with God and God is in my heart, then that is where Phillip is.

You will notice that the more I take you into this trip with me, the more dependent I will become on God to sustain me. I realized while staring out the window of the hearse that life is brief, even if we live far into old age. I would think about the things Phillip accomplished, the lives he made a difference in and the sacrifice he made for a nation. Then I thought about this multiplied by the numbers of the few who were willing to answer the call of duty and serve others in the protection of the freedom often taken without thought to its cost. My mind would wander for the seventy-one miles we would travel to Philadelphia.

The Flight Home

The marine escort and I made our way through the airport to the terminal from which we would fly out. The hearse backed up to a dock where Phillip would be offloaded from the hearse to a storage cooler after the casket was removed from the hearse. The marine physically checked the tag on the casket against the set of escort orders. He and I stood at attention as the casket was retrieved from the hearse and then we rendered a slow three-second salute as the coffin was taken out of the hearse. I understood the importance of this detail, as once while stationed in Berlin, I had the duty of escorting one of my men to Frankfurt. He was a live soul dishonorably discharged from the army, and there too, every detail of the mission had to agree with the orders of the document.

With body and casket officially turned over to Delta, the marine and I went to the Delta counter to check in. This was before the airport security system we see and experience today. After checking in, we went to a food court to get a hamburger. As we made our way to a table, it was so heartwarming to hear people thank the marine for his service. I feel that at this point, I need to apologize because I do not remember the marine's name. I wish I did, but I do not. I cannot thank him enough for volunteering for the honor of escorting a fallen hero home.

A Flight to Atlanta and Then to Houston

A Delta employee found us and led us to the tarmac where Phillip would be loaded onto a conveyor belt. Once again, the marine read and documented the ID tag against the number on his orders and made an entry on those orders as the information was verified. As the casket made its journey up the conveyor belt, the marine rendered a three-second salute, and I did the same, as Congress had passed a bill authorizing veterans the right to render a salute. With the casket secured in the cargo hold of the Delta flight, the marine and I would board the plane from the exterior stairway ahead of the rest of the passengers. My emotions were beginning to go numb at this point as my mind ran the gamut of random thoughts. I was taking my son home.

The flight to Atlanta departed on time, and we were due to land in Houston at 1900 hours that evening. The flight, like the hearse trip, was spent in silence. Most of the time, I stared out the window with no rhyme or reason to the thought process my mind was going through. Knowing that my son was in the cargo section was tough to get my mind around. So to speak, Phillip was in the presence of the Lord. He was my son, and I was his dad, period. The evil of Afghanistan could never take that from us.

What happens next I have heard many times from news reports covering a fallen warrior making that final trip home. As our flight approached the Atlanta airport, the pilot spoke over the PA system. "Ladies and gentlemen, may I have your attention. We have the honor of having two fallen heroes and their escorts on board with us. We have a soldier and a marine. The marine is accompanied by his father. As we make our final approach and taxi to the terminal, please stay seated as the escorts exit the aircraft." I will never forget the silence of the passengers to show their respect. We deplaned using the exterior stairs, and once again, the three-second salute was rendered as the casket came down the conveyor belt to rest in front of the marine escort and me. The marine checked the information on the ID tag against his paperwork and documented the information.

Delta took charge from that point, and the marine escort and I went into the terminal to check in for our flight to Houston. We were to have a layover of only a couple of hours. It was raining when we arrived in Atlanta, and the severe weather made its way to the Atlanta area while we waited for our next flight. Our connecting flight was delayed due to a storm system at its point of origin. I was used to delays, and besides, there was not a lot we could do nothing to change that fact.

I engaged in a conversation with a young girl setting across from me. She turned out to be a delightful chatterbox. She was a marine going home to Indiana on leave for the first time to see her mom and dad. I told her about Phillip and how I came to be a dad escorting his son home. She was busy writing a letter as we chatted. I figured it was to some friend either back at the base or a friend at home whom she may not be able to see in the short leave she had. It turned out that because of the storm system at the origin of her connecting flight, she had been there for a number of hours. I asked her if she had eaten, and she said that a couple of men had bought her some slices of pizza a few hours prior. She said she did not have any money because she had put everything in her sea bag, including her money and calling card. It was apparent that she was not accustomed to traveling because her sea bag was in the cargo area, and there was no way for her to get to it. I gave her a twenty and told her to go get herself something to eat, which she promptly did.

While the young recruit was gone, I managed to strike up a conversation with a man and his wife. It turned out he was a retired two-star general. We talked about Phillip and other military topics until the time their flight was called for boarding. Meanwhile, the young marine returned. She was worried about not calling her folks. She needed to let them know that she was OK. This is how God is where we need him, when we need Him, and how we need Him. I remembered the calling card I had gotten for the USO at Dover, and I did not need it. It had a hundred minutes of call time on it. I handed it to her and told her to go call her parents. She did and was so relieved when she returned.

Shortly after that, her flight was called to board, she stood up to leave, but first, she handed me the letter she had been writing. I thanked her and wished her the best. Mother Nature caused the flight delay, but God's Divine Providence caused the paths of the young marine and the retired general and his wife to cross our paths. His own will glorify God. As flight after flight was either cancelled or delayed further into the night and we were coming up on the last window of opportunity that would get us out of Atlanta that night, I thought, *Not a problem.* I knew that God was still in charge of the winds and the storm, and that the delay served His purpose. The mission he had put me on would not be deterred by any reason other than his own. Sure enough, the call came to board for Houston, the last flight of the night, some five hours late. That did not matter. God was in control of this mission. This is where a grateful heart and a solid foundation can help you overcome any setback and maintain a sense of sanity when a situation goes south in a hand basket. The flight to Houston was short, and the plane was almost empty. None of that mattered, and the time was irrelevant to the mission's end.

The plane taxied to a stop, and the procedure of offloading Phillip was repeated with familiarity. As the marine and I made our way to the baggage area and he picked up his luggage, I headed to the stairs leading up to the upper level. From the top of the stairs, I could see Sara rushing down the steps with tears streaming from her checks. Aaron and Diana were there, followed by my son and my daughter-in-law; Penny, my wife; and Phillip's Aunt Susan. There were hugs and tears. How do you find the words to describe the pain you see in your son's heart knowing that he will not be greeting his brother again? How do you find the words to measure a sister's sense of loss for a brother that she looked up to as a source of strength and for direction in life? As it will be repeatedly shown, there are no words.

The marines had a detail there, and the gunny sergeant came over and introduced himself and let us know that if we needed anything, we should let him know, and he would be contacting us in the morning.

At the end of the day, I know when I turn the lights out that with God, all will be right with my soul. It would certainly be the case with this day too as we made our way home from the airport. As you can imagine from our walk through this, there are still some rough days ahead. You will also know while walking with me through those days that all will be right with my soul.

CHAPTER 7

Laying My Rest My Marine

As we walk farther into this story, you will see things will not get easier. Escorting my son home is without doubt the hardest thing I have ever had to do in my life, but it was also the most honorable thing I have ever done. As I think about how to approach this chapter, I think I have concluded that to spend a lot of time here is not what Phillip would have wanted. This part of our walk has everything to do with laying Phillip's mortal temple to rest and honoring and paying respect to that tradition for the sake of family, friends, and comrades.

Getting from Dover to Houston is out of the picture now; that part of the mission has been completed. As we walk through these days, I still need to be mission oriented. There are many things buzzing around in my heart and mind for me not to be focused on a main task at this point. An example of that is I do not remember the trip from Hobby Airport to our apartment. I think either my mind just shut off for that trip home from the airport, especially considering the events of the day.

As you and I are now used to saying, all is well with my soul. That is the way it was from Dover to the end of the flight in Atlanta. This portion of our trip is undoubtedly blessed with fair skies and favorable winds, as the ship's captain had prayed for. We reach Atlanta in time, only to find changing weather conditions that are not conducive to flying. The closer we approached our scheduled departure time, the worse the weather became. Flights from around the affect area started showing up as cancellations on the inbound board. Then as the bad weather made its way to the Atlanta area, outbound flights were being cancelled as well.

Call it what you may, but I never felt a need in my heart to become concerned about making it home with Phillip. We are on God's mission, and our responsibility lies in focusing on our part of the mission, and that was not worrying about the weather. Like the storm on the Sea of Galilee, the control of the weather is all in the purview of God's hands. Our mission is to get ourselves with Phillip to Houston, not allow a weather delay to become an issue.

As you walked beside me, can you imagine doing this? As a Vietnam veteran, I have never had a higher honor. Our WWII, Korean War, and Vietnam War veterans certainly understand how tough this duty would be, as a lot of them have experienced it. All of them can certainly understand the honor involved. Then most of the younger generation has at least seen the images of the flag-draped coffins as our heroes return home with honor.

There were times when I came close to thinking the physical and spiritual laws that contend no two things can occupy the same space at the same time were wrong at last. As you and I move forward on this walk together, we will find out if that is proven to be true.

I cannot recall anything that happened from the time I got up on this morning to that evening when I was standing at the funeral home. There was a viewing for Phillip on August 24, 2005, at the Rosewood Funeral Home in Pasadena, Texas. That evening is still a blur to me. No matter whom I talk to or how much I try to recall the details of that evening, I simply do not recall much. I can remember there were many people there. I remember that Barry, who worked for me in Iraq, showed up with his girlfriend. Bill Sanders, my buddy from the generator shop in Iraq, could not make it home, but I definitely remember his wife and his son introducing themselves, that was a special blessing. Barry and Joyce Prater I remember; their son was a marine with Phillip, and Phillip had visited them with Chase one time.

From this point, everything goes fuzzy. I was just kind of there in body, and to this day, I have no idea where my mind got off. It certainly was not there with me. During such a time that the heart is dealing with such intense pain, I think God protects us from physical and mental overload by shutting down certain functions, kind of like the overload protection of equipment. I know that many people showed their support and love for Phillip and my family, and for that I am forever grateful.

Phillip's funeral was on August 25, 2005. The morning started out in much the same state as the day before, only with a shorter waiting time. The funeral service was at Grace Community Church, and we were there around 0900 hours. This church had a Christian school at its previous location; Phillip attended the school the last two years of his high school days and graduated one of eight in his class. Suddenly this question crossed my mind: how does one go into detail about a funeral for someone so close? I think what my heart tells me is that you spend as little time in that spot as is necessary. Because what comes to my mind is that is the way Phillip would want it. I think to spend a lot of time in this spot and in this is time is only detrimental to our own ability to move forward with our pain.

I find myself revisiting a notion from earlier; that notion is that I have no doubt that God was present at the funeral, and then therefore, Phillip had to have been there in spirit as well. I also know that God did not stay in that spot and in that time; that would somehow suggest that God is present with a temple that no longer has a soul. This simply cannot be; hence, why would I ever want to be where God is not? This kind of notion that we should spend an inordinate amount of time and energy here is no different from staying in the valley of the shadow of death. Again, God and your loved one are no longer there. Phillip is in heaven, as is God; and yet at the same time, they are present in my spirit because my spirit is alive and belongs to God, and my body, which is the temple to my soul, is where you will find them. God taught my heart this earlier and is emphasizing it now. There is a reason God has taught my soul these concepts, and they are for my own benefit and for the benefit of those who struggle with creating shrines made of images and inscriptions that seem to take the place of their loved ones. The plot of ground my son is buried in is hallowed ground, for sure, but only his mortal body that served as the temple for his soul is there. He, being his spirit now, is in heaven with God. That is part of the reason this book was written. I ask you as we continue to walk, is that not a powerful thing to know and understand as this understanding allows us to move forward with the pain and the hole in our hearts to what God has for us? I cannot emphasize enough that our loved one is not in the places we can go and touch. I would never suggest to you that you get over it because I know I cannot go there.

This is about the fourth time I have gone back and made significant changes to my writing, and that is OK. When the spirit in me is satisfied, then I will click on the Send button to the publisher. If I do that out of a natural haste to declare a project or mission complete, then guess what, it will not fly, and that dog will not hunt.

I remember waiting for the line to go down as people filed by to pay their last respects. When the line was gone, I remember standing in front of the casket alone. It was just a natural thing, and the right thing, for this Vietnam veteran dad to render a final salute to his son, who died a proud marine doing what he knew was his call to do in life. The thought came to my mind, *His final sunset has come, his mission completed.* I remember thinking, *In honor we stand* and *in prayer we remember.* I am proud to call him my son. I am proud that he served his country well. The final salute of a father to a son was the image printed in the *Houston Chronicle.*

Channel 13's Elma Barrera approached me outside the church as we were heading to the car and asked if I minded talking. Elma had interviewed me when I came home on my first R&R. Our church had made a special stained glass for me to take back to Iraq. She asked me at that time what I thought of our presence in Iraq, and I obliged with what I held to be the truth as to how I saw our efforts over there. I thought we needed to be there. Do not ask me or, for that matter, anyone else for an opinion if you do not want the truth as I see it. I have never felt the urge or the need to be politically correct. Now, less than a year later, she is asking me if I could have talked my son out of joining the Marine Corps, would I? She knew my position on the war on terror, and especially our being in Iraq.

Without hesitation, I told her I would not have tried to talk him out of joining the military. I wish I had told her what I thought about the problem I have with the premise of letting someone else pull the load. What makes my son any more valuable to me than someone else's son or daughter to them? Are there certain families whose sons and daughters are less valuable and therefore more expendable for the good of those who think somehow that theirs are more valuable and not expendable? I don't believe Elma meant to imply that or anything other than she was being a reporter. She may have been hoping that I had changed my thoughts and would rail against the war, and possibly against the military or the president, but that's the way I am going to see it anyhow.

We will make the trip to the Houston National Cemetery. It was a long drive with a long procession of vehicles traveling with us. Can you imagine a day like this? Everything seemed to bring the sense of finality to it. The day was a typical hot August day. As we sat at the hemicycle for the service, the sun's relentless waves of heat bore down on us. I think the combination of the long trip and the weight of a heart with a huge hole in it just kind of shut me down a bit. Again, I will say that sometimes that is a good thing as it acts as a buffer against total overload and then collapse.

This was a typical August day in Houston, Texas. The temperature was a hundred degrees or more, and the humidity was heavy. The sun's glare bounced off the concrete beneath our chairs as well as off the walls of the hemicycle to our right. The sun seemed to pinpoint the top of most uncovered heads, and sweat would roll down places we did not know we had. Time remained an irrelevant factor in my mind. I suppose it was a good thing that my mind was somewhere else. Perhaps it was off with Phillip somewhere. My heart was at peace, something that only the grace of God could give. As "Amazing Grace" played on the bagpipes, the sound of Taps played by the bugler and the twenty-one-gun salute fired the last volley, Phillip's final sunset had ended. His body was ready for eternal rest, and his soul to live forever. He would truly be forever twenty-two on this eighteenth day of August 2005. He lived his life well, served his country, God, and family; his mission was completed. His soul would live on in eternity with the desire for those who his life touched would finish their missions against their final sunsets, with the example he had set for others to follow. He had made a difference. Their lives were enriched because of who he was. His legacy will live on as long as we remember who and what he became. From this realization, we can see the dots connect in a way that will guide us to the next part of our mission.

From this point, it became my duty and responsibility, as well as the nation's, to honor and remember Phillip. Honoring and remembering is a part of the responsibility of a grateful nation. If we do this, then their legacy to this nation and its people is a never-ending gift.

I was certain Phillip was looking down from heaven. I could see him so clearly with those long arms crossed across his chest, his face sporting that smirky little grin he was known for and uttering a soft-spoken "Oh, good grief, Dad." When that image pops into my heart, I would know that all is well with my soul and that my son lives on.

As we were leaving the cemetery, I could feel the spirit of God closing this chapter of life in my heart. I did not believe for one minute that the pain of that early morning in Iraq would not return. I do mean, however, that I only had to bury my son one time, not every day. I do not have to bury him each time I am at his gravesite.

I do not go to the cemetery as often as many people do. I believe the plot of ground Phillip's body rests in is hallowed ground, but Phillip is not there. He is with the Lord. It is good for my soul to visit when the spirit moves me to do so; My heart is in a state of sincere prayer as I write that all of this makes sense and that I will help move those in this spot to a point that will get them beyond where they are.

Collecting Frayed Ends

Well, you and I have been through some truly good times from the time of that newscast early on in May of 2004. We have walked many miles in Iraq and clocked many hours and been blessed in so many ways. We have made it to the mountaintop where my life took U-turn. We have seen how God allows our lives to make a difference in others'.

We also sailed together through some high and rough seas as the storm brought its devastation to my life from the time I made that phone call home from the big sandbox. This is the ugly part of our time to walk together. I can only hope that in your walk with me, you can see how my God has always been there for me. He was there when my heart took a horrendous blow that ripped a part of it right out of me. He was there when we walked that lonesome valley, though I had to walk it on my own. We walked it together and made it through to the other end by the grace of God.

Now you are about to walk with me as he continues to be the solid foundation my life stands on as we move forward. Walk with me when the answers to when I lay my head down do not fail me. You were with me in those early morning hours, sharing a cup of joe and pondering life, which is necessary for moving forward. The frayed ends are gathered and mended as far as it is possible with choices that will move my family and me forward. Honoring Phillip's life in a way that he would not have to say "Oh, good grief, Dad." Walk with me as God continues to answer my prayers as "when I lay my head down" remains the biggest weapon in my arsenal against those things that would steal my joy and try to derail me from my mission.

We are about two weeks into my emergency leave. It is decision time. The time is at hand for me to decide if I am going to be returning to Iraq to work or not. This is not a decision I can make independent of the family. I was prepared to deal with whatever decision the family made. Blessed I would be by whatever they decided on the question I had to put to them. So I talked to them individually for the most independent answer possible from them. They all said the same thing: "You have to return, because that is what Phillip would want. They understood the mind-set of their brother and respected what they knew he would want. He most certainly would not be a happy camper if he thought in the least bit that he was the reason for any of us not moving forward that scenario would have been so foreign to him. God has taught my heart a principle here. Phillip set out on his mission aiming to fulfill it to the best of his ability, and he did just that. He would not understand at all any of us giving up because he had completed his mission ahead of us. Therefore, the mission of Forever 22 begins to make its purpose known around its edges. The Forever 22 mission started at home. Could there be a better place for a mission to start? We are always making it our aim to finish the mission, for we too are working against a final sunset that we cannot know. As I think about purpose, the words "making a difference" stand out. This is really what our lives are to be about, no matter who we are or whatever our place is in life, we are to make a difference in the lives of those around us. If you will remember, this was a part of our reason for being where we were and when we were to make a difference.

Contact with the KBR travel office in the Houston office resulted in airline tickets mailed to me for my scheduled departure back to Camp Warhorse. The plane tickets were in my mailbox within days. I was pleased with the decision the family made. I was glad I was headed back to Iraq. I felt my mission in Iraq was not yet complete. God has a way of bringing hearts into agreement when the need is for the mission. I agreed with the family's thought that I needed to finish my mission. They did not want me to have to deal with asking later, what if I had not? What if I had gone later on down the road and it was too late? Can you see what a unique and good family God has provided for me? As a couple of days would go by, I just felt the need for thirty more days at home. There was something in that feeling that I just could not put my finger on and to the time of this writing, I still do not know. When God moves the heart on something like this, you need to pay attention and not worry about the details because He is right in the middle of the details. If I could get a thirty-day extension, would I feel in my heart what God wanted me to do?

During these times when you are paying attention to God, you may not always understand it; however, you and I know that understanding does not always determine whether we proceed as God would have us to go. OK, we are ready to be obedient to what God has instructed our hearts to do. What we need to do now is get in touch with Houston HR and let them know the desire to spend an extra thirty days without having to go through the hiring process again. I would go back as scheduled because it was clear I needed to go back. You will see this is one time I did not procrastinate, I have been good at that all my life, but not this time. I began to make calls to the Houston HR number. After a number of reasonable attempts, I could not get an answer. I was running out of time.

I have always thought the best answers to a problem was to think outside the box and go outside the box. Where we were inside the box was not going to get us to where we needed to be in just a couple of days. You and I learned from the first fifteen months in Iraq that there is great power in the wisdom of God and how He would handle a situation. I made an honest attempt to get the Houston office to answer, but to no avail. That night, "when I laid my head down," I simply needed God's wisdom. I would be running up against the impossible in the next few weeks.

The next morning, the first thing to take care of was to put on a fresh pot of joe to brew. Then we sat down at the table with a fresh cup poured and began to ponder our next move. After a number of sips and pondering, the result of the pondering came down to the use of a phone book. As my fingers went down the list of names found under the KBR bold letters, they stopped on a name: *Steve Arnold*. He was a VP living in Virginia. If he answered his phone, I felt I would get results. What I did not know was if he would answer the phone. But that was not a problem; God had given me the answer to our prayer. He did not answer, in fact. Not a problem, right? I left a message for him to call me in regard to the dilemma I found myself in after not being able to contact anyone in the Houston office.

The next day, we did get a call from Steve Arnold's office. It was his secretary letting us know that she got the message and that Mr. Arnold was in New Orleans at the time due to the flood caused by Hurricane Katrina. She assured me that he would call as soon as he got back to their Virginia office. Sure enough, I got a call from Steve Arnold the following day. I love it when a plan comes together. A Team. George Peppard ails, Hannibal Smith. I explained my situation, and he gave a number to call in Houston. It was the HR supervisor's number, and there was a side note to call him back if I needed to. I really did not think I would need to do that. I called the number and explained that because I could not get the Houston HR number to answer, I conferred with Steve Arnold. I think we can make a good guess here. Steve Arnold's name was all that I needed to say. After that, I just needed to let him know what I needed. The HR supervisor knew that I could not have called him on that number if I had not talked to Steve Arnold as I said I did. This was all I needed for the wheels to start spinning. I explained what I would like to do. I am only reckoning here. It amazes me when the lower echelon of workers think they can do things like not answer the phone. I have a very distinct feeling that this HR person only answered calls from friends. This bordered on being criminal. I had worked with KBR long enough to understand the mind-set of some of the lower-level workers. I was set; all I needed now would be to call the travel department for new airline tickets. As we continue to walk together, I hope you can start telling yourself, "Not a problem." It really works, and it makes life a lot easier too.

With this out of the way, could have that additional thirty days with my family. My heart was relieved, and to this day, I am not sure why I did what I did. I just knew I needed to do it. I think it was more for my need than the family. That is part of walking in faith: you do not always have to understand everything ahead of time, or even at the time. It may be that I was the one who needed the time; maybe I needed the extra early mornings at home with my cups of joe and my ponderings of the things in my heart. I am grateful for the answer to "When I lay my head down."

You and I will be on our way back to Iraq in thirty days. We have a mission to complete. I could feel that when I returned, things would be different. Not different because of what we have just been through, but different because the climate of war was changing, the winds of the nature of our troops being in Iraq were shifting. Their mission would change from hunting the bad guys to advising and building the Iraqi army. There is no doubt losing Phillip has added another dimension to the mission we would be on. I don't believe the original mission changed because God knew this all along. Now we will see the mission with more clarity and purpose. We will meet the challenges of the mission with a more intense purpose and passion. This is where God wanted us to be at this point. You and I both have learned that with God, all things are possible. Sometimes we can know things on the surface, but then deep down, the question is, do we really know them?

In Honor We Stand, and in Prayer We Remember

Remember the chapter where we learn about the dots connecting. Understand that dots connect for us all. We just have to be where God wants us to be; otherwise, life is purely circumstantial and coincidental. That is not the realm my God works from to guide me through this life. The dots of my life will connect for me the rest of my life, because sometime ago, I decided to do it God's way. My way failed big time. One such connection I realized right as I was writing "In Honor We Stand." I wrote this piece while stuck in Dubai.

This piece is the result of God correcting an attitude I had copped. I was in Dubai, ready to return to work at Camp Warhorse. All air travel bound for the Baghdad International Airport were being suspended. The first two days of delay in Dubai, not a problem. I was fine with that, and the extra time really felt good. What a shame, right? It was after two days that I began to have a problem with. I began to grumble in my soul. I will never forget this. I was sitting on the edge of the bed when my heart was just really in a gripe mood. This was so far out of character for me; all I knew was that I wanted to get back to work, and sitting here in Dubai was not going to allow me to do that. God got my attention quick. It was as though I could not move. Then I heard deep in my soul, *Why don't you shut up?* There was no mistake about the message or the messenger. I did not need more convincing to know the chastisement of God was upon me. You do not want to go to that woodshed on a regular basis. When the hand was lifted, amazingly, so was my attitude. I got busy and wrote the following:

In Honor We Stand

As a young soldier, some thirty-three years ago, I stood,
In a faraway land.
Now I stand in honor of a younger group of soldiers,
In a faraway land.
I salute those who give of themselves for our freedom,
In a faraway land.
I stand in humility and honor, such a small price on my
part, to those who gave the ultimate.
In a faraway land.
I stand owing a debt I cannot pay
For the Stars and Stripes
Symbolizes freedom;
The soldier guarantees it.
In a faraway land.
I am not a poet or artist
But I was a soldier and
I stand in honor now.
In a faraway land.

God inspired my heart to write this on my return to Iraq in 2004. I went home in October that same year. We had our family Thanksgiving a month early. I was home from Iraq, and my next R&R would be five months down the road. Phillip was home on leave, and we had a great Thanksgiving and had so much to be grateful for at the time. Little did we know that that would be our last Thanksgiving with Phillip. You can call it anything from happenstance to luck. I prefer to believe God knew what we needed as a family and when we needed it, and he provided it.

I had no idea when with my grumbling heart in Dubai that one day what God gave my heart would end up in a book and a tribute to not only my son but also to other fallen warriors, to those who served and to those who were wounded. I had no idea that it would become a tribute of honor to the Vietnam veteran. God knew, though.

CHAPTER 8

Camp Warhorse to Camp Speicher

Sometime in early February 2006, KBR moved me from Camp Warhorse to Camp Speicher in Tikrit. It was all within God's ability to know what I needed according to His purpose of when, where, and how. God knew that my work was winding up at Camp Warhorse, just as I believed in my heart. He knew I would not be content with the changes that would come to the camp and the work that we would be required to do—or maybe a better fit would be *not* to do. The challenges would be gone, as our jobs would switch from construction and maintenance to simply routine maintenance alone. Please do not misunderstand me. There is nothing wrong with being in maintenance, but if that is not your bailiwick, then it is no good for you. As we walk deeper into the mission God has us on—I say us because I feel that in the end the mission is not exclusively mine—we are going to understand more about purpose and making a difference. With the changes coming to Camp Warhorse, I think by the time we end our mission at Camp Warhorse, we will also understand that we have to be who we are.

For a long time, KBR had used many of my photos for company use, and for slide presentations for meetings either within or with the army, and I was happy with that. In fact, it was a blessing. Once I bought my first Nikon semi-pro digital camera, a Nikon D70, I was in camera hog heaven. I had been shooting with a small point-and-shoot Kodak. I was able to get a lot of Kodak moments with that little camera, but what surprised me was its cost. I bought it from the PX. I had to shell out three hundred dollars for it. I would shoot with it for about six months, and I was pleased with the digital results; but every time I would shoot and thought about the size of it, and having to shoot with the rear monitor instead of an eye viewer, I would think, *I need a real camera in my hands.* That is when I made the decision to buy my first TTL Nikon. I still shoot with the D70 today. My passion for photography came back with the full force of my heart. I fell in love with photography as I had when I was a twenty-year-old kid in Vietnam, which was where this simple farm boy bought his first camera. When I think of those days, I think of Phillip. At twenty, our lives had many similarities. I did not realize this until just now. I bought my first camera, a Fujica range finder 35m, from the PX in Vietnam as well.

On our walks through the first months of this journey, we saw how God used lessons and experiences from way back in the past to connect with the needs we find ourselves in now. I think you and I need to sit down with a fresh cup of joe and really ponder what we are about to be taught. What is the old saying? "All roads lead to Rome." That is it? Well, we are on a road where all roads from the past lead to today's larger highway. With a fresh cup of joe, we can start pondering where we are and where we are going. It is easy to recognize the roads of the past. I suppose seeing some of them pop up is not a bad thing, just a surprise that they connect today. Like the road that connects the first camera bought in Vietnam and now connecting some thirty-eight years later, this dot from the past will have a huge impact on our mission and the direction it will take. That dot from Vietnam will also make a difference in the lives of people around me—how awesome is that? All of these dots led to Forever 22, which you will see as we walk on in this story.

My passion for photography had to be placed on a holding pattern. The time simply came to a point in life where if my family was growing, the money and time for my hobby simply had to take a backseat. There was not but one clear-cut choice here. Love for my family was far more important than my love for photography. As the years passed, I would continue to read as much as I could about photography. The passion was still there, and I knew in my heart that someday I would be able to take it up again. God has blessed me with being able to see a project, a situation, or a thing completed. Therefore, when I was able to afford my first digital camera from the PX in Iraq, it was like a dream come true. My age at this point may have tampered with my outward show of excitement, after I was thirty-eight years older. I do remember when I sat down at my desk upon my return from the PX that I was like a kid in a nickel candy store. The overwhelming joy I felt in my heart could not be in the least dampened by anything as I unwrapped my new digital camera. I knew I would someday pick up a camera again and renew my passion for photography.

Remember, in the chapter about the stained glass—we saw how God connected the dots out of my need in high school to take the industrial arts class. This is another one of those times. While a young soldier in Vietnam, I bought the first camera of my life. I would develop a love of photography. I taught myself as a hobbyist, and although I needed to put it on hold when I left Germany with an additional daughter to our family, I never lost my desire for it. I reckon at this point I needed to encourage you to be grateful for the good things you learn. As we have seen, God can reach way back and connect those dots to today.

As we travel through Camp Speicher on our way back to Camp Warhorse from a trip to Hawaii for a memorial service for the marines, the two-thirds lost in Afghanistan, a door will swing wide open for us that will affect the rest of the time we spend in Iraq. I needed to be in the area for some reason; maybe it was just to visit Stephanie. The door for the dot from Vietnam would connect when the temporary project manager walked into the room. When he saw the Nikon around my neck, the connection happened. We started a conversation about cameras and photography. We ended up in his office and talked for a long time about photography. He had just bought a new Nikon. He saw the Nikon around my neck that started all of this.

Before we left Camp Speicher to return to Warhorse, he said, "You know, we really need a photographer/historian." He asked if I would be interested in the job. Are you kidding? Of course I would. With my job at Camp Warhorse changing drastically, this is one of those unbelievable doors that God opened when it was needed and where it was needed. We will return to Camp Warhorse with new hope in our hearts. We would not notice the changes right away, as they were small in nature, but the cumulative impact was large. I think what made the biggest difference for me was the nature of the influx of new people and some of the policy changes that made no sense whatsoever. We realized that Camp Warhorse had lost its individualism; part of its character that made it a joy to work there had been snipped away. People no longer work for the common good but are rather self-serving. After seeing these numbers of subtle changes, it was evident that the camp was going to change forever, never to be what it once was. While the proverbial handwriting on the wall was very faint, we needed to prepare for it.

Staying focused on the mission will oftentimes gives us a clue as to what is coming down the pike, as it is often referred to, when the end is obvious but not official. Staying focused on the mission had one other advantage—it helped keep us above the fray. This is a term I used a lot when giving advice to someone who sought advice. You never want to allow yourself to mire down in the trenches where there is only the muck of despair and strife. Staying above the fray, so to speak, permits you to spend your energies wisely on freethinking and have space to breathe.

Stephanie, our lead operations specialist, had been transferred to Camp Speicher while I was on emergency R&R. That was a surprise. We would have someone in the area to talk to now. I was excited, and I let my boss, Ralph, know that I'd been offered a job, and I would like to take it. I knew God had opened another door before we made it back to Warhorse.

I did not bother Stephanie with excessive e-mails to ask her about the job because I knew in my heart that God had opened the door. What happens to us sometimes is we begin to think God has had ample time to make this or that happen. We either doubt God or get very grumbly as we begin to think in terms of our own period we put on what is truly in God's control. Or out of our own impatience, we give ourselves over to negative thoughts, and we end up doubting it was ever of God to start with. We slough it off to just a wish of our own making. That is what happened to me after waiting a whole three months—yes, a whole three months. Now wasn't that just awesome of me and my test of faith?

The moment I gave up on trying to figure it out and resign to the fact that this was of God's doing and the timing of it would be His timing. When I accepted the fact that I would be going to Camp Speicher as a photographer/historian according to God's timing, I became content in God where I was. I got a radio call from Ralph to come see him. I honestly had no idea what it could be other than routine stuff. What we see here is being content with where we were in God. When I got to his office, he simply told me to pack my stuff, as I was going to Speicher. Within a couple of days, I was at Camp Speicher as the photographer/historian. What we have at hand now is a brand-new job with no official slot. The plan was to create a slot from the excess of slots the operations office had. That was not a problem, right? I was on a mission that transcended the title of a job slot. I was excited about my new job makes, no mistake about that. As we focused on the mission given to us from the beginning, our priorities would stem from there and in that direction. It did not matter to me what that position was called; I just wanted to do my new job.

This was a joy to my heart. By now I had brought my photography skills up to speed somewhat anyhow. I had my new upper-level amateur photographer Nikon D70 that I enjoyed using to no end. I was happier than a tick on a longhaired dog. In fact, when the Fifty-fourth Dust Off unit found out I had just gotten my new camera, they took me up to about three hundred feet, and I was able to lean out the gunner's window and shoot Warhorse and parts of BaQuaba. Of course, I was strapped in. I love the results of the Nikon over the little digital I bought in the PX. I was grateful for the little Kodak, however, because it gave me back the passion for shooting and the desire for a real camera in my hand.

Settling in at Camp Speicher

Once we arrived at Camp Speicher and had settled into a hooch, the project manager explained what he had in mind for the new job. I liked what he envisioned for the new position. It sounded good, and I felt an eagerness to get started. We would have to at first play the job by ear since it was the first of its kind for this operation. We would have no problem with that after spending fifteen months at Camp Warhorse meeting all the challenges it presented. We would have a lot to learn and we would be welcome. That was okay. There was challenge brought to the job, and that was where we would do our best. We would take on the new challenges with a grateful heart. With the move to Camp Speicher, we realized that we have to be where God wants us to be; we have to be what God created us to be and how he wants us to be. This is where we will find the most fulfillment in life. We have learned that anything short of being on the page we are supposed to be simply will not work. I know that last sentence, while it may be grammatically correct, may have to be read a couple of times.

It is somewhat strange how things come together, and then I think about it and discover it is only God still connecting the dots. Throughout the first part of this book, I struggled a bit with the content connecting with the title of the book. From writing the last paragraph God connected the dots I needed connected to settle that issue from this point on. I really think writing from this style gives me the flexibility I need to slip from having you walk beside me through most of the story, and then being able to go alone in those times where it seems only I can be living through an. I find it neat, and I am comfortable with it. My hope is that you as the reader can feel that you are a part of what is going on, putting your heart into the story at the same time. As we walked through getting to Camp Speicher and the satisfaction we felt knowing we were once again going to be able to feel the joy in doing our job and take on our mission with increased fervor, I was reminded of Phillip.

I know and understand at this point my purpose for life and in life has changed and will continue to change as mission and vision become clearer. Which brings me to the point of being who God created us to be. I am beginning to understand that there will be a connection between this thought and Forever 22.

We will see again how God was always ahead of us and at that point stopped surprising me. I still had no idea what all of this was to lead to; all I had to know was this was where I was supposed to be. We will come to understand that mission and vision are two different things and do not always travel as companions; they do at some point according to God's timing cross and connect. I realized now that I probably would not have recognized it or understood it had it been given. I did know now that all the things that happened to this point was God's way of getting my heart ready for the moment I was living and experiencing at the moment. We have seen that with each next moment, God has been there and it is ready for us to occupy. It was God's way of getting my life to where I am right now. Writing this book never entered my mind until after I finished with Iraq. The dots simply did not connect at that time. I knew I was returning to Iraq to finish the mission, from that time forward Phillip would become be a part the mission. I would take one day at a time because it would be the day the Lord would have made for me; I would rejoice and be glad in it.

With that in my heart, I was determined to do my best. I cannot fail to complete my mission no matter where it led me. I knew without doubt that I needed to continue teaching the glass class after settling in at Camp Speicher. We have seen that the classes are more than just a glass class. It was a way of letting folks experience God in a different way. I knew the task would have to be approached differently than the way I approached it at Warhorse. Since this was our area's operational headquarters, I needed to pay attention to protocol. People's egos were a little bit more in play here than at the more laid-back operations of the smaller Camp Warhorse. Not that ego was not at play there; they just tended to cut down a couple of notches a little faster.

One definite bright spot about being at Camp Speicher was the fact that when leaving for Ra&R or returning, that would be the only stop from Camp Liberty in Baghdad. I have no real complaints about having to go through Camp Speicher while at Camp Warhorse; however, not that I do not have to do that I am not going to miss the procedure of the past.

God Teaches My Heart

Moving to Speicher taught my heart a lot about people, and I realize now that learning is usually associated with most missions. We will spend almost exactly one event year at Camp Speicher, for a total of thirty-three months in Iraq. I learned a lot at Speicher, my heart felt the joy of doing my job, and I have always been a people person. That is the way it is when you do things God's way.

When we decide to give God control, you have to allow Him to be in control all the time. It cannot be that you take control from him when you think things are going great and you do not really need Him at the time. We have learned that kind of thinking will only send you back to square one. Sometimes when we do this, it takes us a while to figure out that God did not move away from us, but we moved from God. There is no power sharing with God. We do not get to choose who is in charge on an as-needed basis. If you allow God to be in control, then you have to trust Him. He will always be where He needs to be, when He needs to be there, and how He needs to be there.

God had crossed my path with those of Major Green and Captain Porter. We will make a trip to their office with Stephanie, and she will introduce us to them. She told them ahead of time that I was a Vietnam veteran and was a father who had lost his son in Afghanistan. Stephanie also knew from our time at Warhorse that I was a Christian, and so were Major Green and Captain Porter. Stephanie had known both men long enough and knew that they were Christians. She also knew I needed their friendship and fellowship.

The friendship quickly developed between Major Green and Captain Porter, and they would invite me to go to chapel service with them, and that was a true blessing. We would stop at the Green Bean coffee shop on the way to the chapel. The Green Bean was a special place for the warriors; it was the desert version of Star Bucks without the liberal hate toward our military. I realize now, as I write this manuscript that God was preparing my heart and preparing the way for where He wanted me to be.

You and I have seen that sometimes it is hard to connect all the dots and things do not seem to make any sense. So at that point, you simply say, "OK, Lord, I trust you." That is exactly what He wants to hear. I knew more now than ever that whatever I did at Camp Speicher, it would take me a step closer to mission accomplished. We are learning that you cannot focus on the end of the mission; you have to focus on the day you have been as of right now. Not tomorrow or the next day because they may not be yours to have, which reminds me of how grateful I am for the todays that I had with Phillip. I am grateful for the days I have each time with my family, because tomorrow is not promised to me; only the breath I draw right now gives the life for the next. We are on just another point to get us where we need to be.

We are in tall cotton as we walk this part of our journey; we will have one of four offices in our building. Our office is the first one you see when you enter the building, so all foot traffic to the other offices has to come though ours. We do not have a door to close. We will take it without hesitation or prejudice in our hearts. The building has its own bathroom and a kitchenette—that is five stars over where we came from. I don't know about you, but I liked our digs where we came from. However, I am not going to complain about what we have here. We will not be spending that much time here if I have anything to do with the way we get to operate anyhow.

One definite bright spot about being at Camp Speicher was we would no longer have to travel to Camp Speicher and spend most of the time three days before leaving on our scheduled R&R or, upon returning, have it be the only stop from Camp Liberty in Baghdad. I have no real complaints about having to go through Camp Speicher while at Camp Warhorse; however, now that I do not have to do that, I am not going to miss the procedure of the past.

CHAPTER 9

Photographer/Historian

I have never had a nickname in my life until I moved from Camp Warhorse to Camp Speicher. When we first got to Camp Speicher, the first thing we had to do was set up in the office assigned to us. We would be in a building adjacent to our area of operations. Most people called it area operations; all C-sites were then controlled from there. There was also a bit of a class warfare that went on between the people who worked in area and those who took direction from and reported to them. For that reason, we would be very happy being in the building we were assigned. It is kind of like in politics, where there are times you want to distance yourself and your operation from the central head.

Our office was one of five in the building. We would share it with three military offices and one other KBR section—the laundry section. Terry Johnson was the head of that section; he was a retired army master sergeant. We would hit it off and become good friends. There will be a dot to connect a little later as we walk through this story.

When the front door opened, you stepped into the office of the photographer/historian. For that reason, we had the largest office. That would turn out not to be a negative thing for us. All the traffic to the other offices had to go through ours, meaning that gave us a high volume of contacts. That is, once we had made it recognizable as a photographer's office.

First, we had to settle in before we could do anything. The desk of the photographer/historian consisted of a carpentry-shop-created square plywood box with a multilayer shelf that sat anchored on the front side. Roger Miller's "King of the Road" comes to mind. Do not ask me to make a logical connection here, and this is definitely not a God thing. It is all on me. When we finished with the setting-up process, we had two laptops, one monitor, one printer, and a phone that actually worked. Some of the camera gear was strategically located on the desk. This was for eye appeal and for impression for our mini press release to the folks back home. Phillip would have had fun with this situation. The digital record was made of the first Camp Speicher photographer/historian workstation. Using a 10mm fisheye attached to my camera, I could capture all the high-tech setup in one frame.

Next, e-mails went out to the family. An e-mail to Aaron was most certainly going to bring a quick, witty response. He promptly replied as expected, and it simply read, "Dad, you look like a high-tech hillbilly. I told that to a couple of friends. Guess what, it stuck I reckon. I had a nickname after all these years. For most people, I was the cameraman. They could not remember my name but the camera around my neck told them who I was. If someone needed to find me, the camera man was who he or she should ask for in operations. It was a lot of fun. We were now ready for our job as the new photographer/historian of the C-sites. We were also ready to carry on with our mission at the same time. We were beginning to get a good feel for the theme of the mission as far as we knew it, making a difference in honor of Phillip and the other fallen warriors and their comrades. That is a broad mission; however, that was as narrow as we could get for now.

Before we could get our job designation recognized as a legitimate slot, our chief backer transferred. In this entire time, God was right in the middle of it, making sure that doors we could not possibly open, and some of them we would never have thought of. When God wants you to be somewhere to do what He wants you to do, we have learned no man can stop that. You call it what you will, and we will call it the providence of God because we are there.

God Has the Best Security System

There is no higher level of security than the system we find at the hands of God. He is the master of His domain. A breach by anyone or anything at any time for any reason would be impossible. God set His security system up to protect his mission we were on at this point in Iraq.

Stephanie introduced us to Major Green and Captain Porter; their offices were adjacent to our building. Major Green was army. He worked for the DCMA office, and Captain Porter worked with Major Green. She told them ahead of time that I was a Vietnam veteran and a father who lost a son in Afghanistan. Stephanie also knew from our time working at Camp Warhorse that I was a Christian. Now, is it going to surprise you that so were Major Green and Captain Porter? Stephanie knew both men long enough and knew that they were Christians. She also knew I needed their friendship and fellowship. How is that for connecting the dots ahead of the need? While we were in Major Green's office, Stephanie asked if the major could prepare a letter stating that I was the KBR photographer/historian, not a problem. Been a while since we have heard that used.

The friendship with Major Green and Captain Porter quickly developed. There was a standing invitation to go to chapel service with them on Sunday mornings, and that was a true blessing. We would stop at the Green Bean coffee shop on the way to the chapel. That was always special, even though I still had my zero dark thirty cup of joe and my time for pondering. The Green Bean was a special place for the warriors; it was the desert version of Starbucks. I realize now, as I write this manuscript, that God was preparing my heart and the way for where He wanted us to be.

Making Our Own Assignments

Now it is time for us to get to work as the C-sites photographer. The problem is, we had no formal issue of direction; everything was left with the temporary project manager. So at the end of the first few days, we would just get a feel for the day-to-day operations. At the end of each day, I would lay my head down and expect God's wisdom the next morning with that fresh cup of joe and my time of pondering. After a few days, we would begin creating our own projects. They were projects that were productive; we could feel good about that aspect, given the fact that we had to make our own assignments happen. We were on a learning curve—that was a certainty. This attitude will go hand in hand with trusting in God's wisdom as we lay our heads down each night. Can you feel that in your heart as we walk through the story?

Most people in the operations office had no idea what I was supposed to be doing. I was used to thinking outside the box and dealing with the not-so-normal. This was not a problem. There were a few times someone from the operations office would try to get me to conform to be an operations specialist; they would soon give up on that. I was not an operations specialist and had no desire to be. Then someone else would try, especially when they needed a body to stick on the night watch. That did not go anywhere either. Sometimes you just have to have the chutzpah to stand your ground, so to speak. We did this without ruffling too many feathers. I would very diplomatically remind them that I was a carpenter who also happened to be a photographer. I do not believe there were any more attempts after the initial failed ones. This rather conjures up images and thoughts of a failed coup d'état. Sounds good anyhow. I simply knew in my heart what God wanted us to be doing.

We were to be about making a difference, and we could not do that submitting to being just a warm body to satisfy a night position because no one in the operations office wanted to do it. They chose the wrong hillbilly to try tapping for that. When we went through times like this, my thoughts would turn to Phillip. I tried very hard to teach my kids to think for themselves, to be who God created them to be. Hence, we have a connection here to Forever 22 and its mission. Sometimes we have to stand up to external and internal forces that would cause us to fail in accomplishing our mission. This is one of the reasons I have come to cherish my early morning routine with my cup of joe and my time of ponder what God has planned for me.

I found that the camp manager's attitude toward his job and the people he was responsible for was quite different from the attitude and treatment of employees by the project manager. We really enjoyed the self-assignment of photographing the camp weekly safety meetings. The photos we would take were handed over to the camp manager, who really appreciated them. He would go through them and pick out what he wanted, print them, and post them on a bulletin board in the hallway. When the crafts people came through, they would be surprised to see their photos there.

This posting of photos became very popular with the workers. I would often think of Phillip when doing projects like this, because it made a difference. It was making a difference that made Phillip who he was. We could have just waited for instructions and drawn a paycheck. Being selected to do the job of photographer/historian because someone trusted we could do it made a difference in our desire to do that job. Not taking the initiative certainly would not move forward the mission we had before us. God's wisdom is that we do the best job possible because He is with us every step we take on the path that He lights ahead of each step. I oftentimes think of the confidence I see from Phillip's life and the lives of others, and they give encouragement, inspiration, and hope to my heart.

That is why Aaron is a police officer and my girls are nurses. Their desire is to make a difference, and that ultimately comes through. That is where God wants to find us in life, being who he created us to be, and, through that, make a difference. I would find a lot of photo work to do for the camp manager, and we were just fine with that.

Connecting to Forever 22

You might be wondering what this has to do with Forever 22. Well, you are not by yourself at times. I did not see the connection back then either for many of the things that would connect and I would recognize only much later. That is just the way life is at times. You do not stop moving forward because you cannot see the use in it at the time. All I knew was God put us on a mission, and we were going to complete that mission. We had no idea at that time that God was teaching the heart and honing what he had already given us. God was teaching the heart about the importance of networking, a skill we would need when we got back home and have to take on a new phase of our mission. This just reminds us that God is always ahead of us, lighting our pathway. *Networking* was a term I understood by, of which I had exactly zilch experience in at all. He was confirming what I already knew and loved doing—that is, making a difference in someone else's life and then to be blessed by it to boot.

Focus on the Good

In our time spent at Camp Speicher, we will make many friends, which makes each day "a day the Lord hath made and we will rejoice and be glad in it." I have to take the time to ask you if you are friends with that early morning routine and a hot cup of joe. We wake up each morning expecting to rejoice in our day. Rejoicing for the day because God made it for us will make each day special and allow our time spent in it to be memorable. As I read my devotionals these days, I find that they speak volumes to that very issue. My heart will never forget how God prepared it for the mission to continue once our time in Iraq ended. We will continue to learn while at Camp Speicher. The heart will learn new lessons and concepts as the days pass. Many of these lessons learned will then be placed on a back burner, so to speak—in the heart. Where they will lie dormant, to later be brought forward for implementation at the right time for what we now know and refer to as connecting the dots. We are seeing that connecting dots to things either we do not understand now or we may not even see is becoming a major part of our mission working itself out. I am convinced at this point that the relationships we build, and how we build them, are central to our mission of making a difference. They are also a part of the central reason for this book. That is, to you the reader, for your encouragement during those impossible times. To inspire you to, if you will, "when you lay your head down" and to show you an example of what worked for me through that walk into the valley of the shadow of death. As the story has been lived again in my heart, I am not alone, because I have you, the reader, walking with me and my God.

If you do not have an early morning devotional time, I strongly encourage you to have one. I wish now I had started this a long time ago. The good news is that God is always ready to bless you from where you are. Now is the time for you to do that.

If you are still walking this walk with me, then at least, as a reader, you are getting up early in your thoughts as you go through the chapters with me. My prayer is still that some of it will rub off on you. You do not have to be the avid drinker of the joe I am to enjoy those early morning hours with just you and your God. It is such a pleasure for us to get out before my work hours start at 0700 hours and drive around base at sunrise. There are some amazing sunrises for the shutter release and lens to capture, creating an immense sense of joy in the heart as we thank God at the same time for the day ahead of us. It is during these early morning times that my heart would feel so blessed with the memories of Phillip. As we stand alone with the only one who could understand what lay at the bottom of the heart only He could reach and let us know He understood the heart completely. I think everyone would benefit from adjusting their morning routines to include a special time for just themselves and God. Can we really have a better way to start our day than with the only person who is capable of reaching far beyond our own very short reach?

I cannot begin to imagine doing things any different to honor who Phillip was—a young marine and a son. I cannot imagine the pain I would cause his spirit if I choose to stay in that dark valley or if I try drown my sorrows in a bottle. I cannot imagine doing that to him. Now I am getting the connection of my time at Camp Speicher to the story of Forever 22. I can feel the hurting hearts of others in this spot of their lives, and I want so badly to reach out to them and let them know that I understand their hearts. That I know they do not have to stay in that valley, that they can walk a lighted path and honor their warrior. They can walk forward with their pain and know that there is hope.

God was teaching my heart about people and relationships with people. This is what Phillip's legacy would be built around. That is who he was—a marine who cares for those he was responsible for, a young man who cared about people and put them ahead of himself. I have a charge in my life to complete a mission that I cannot do with any less fire in my belly than will bring forth a passion that will carry me to complete this mission against the final sunset of my life. I now see this a part of Phillip's legacy.

Repeatedly I would hear this one point from friends of Phillip's and people who only met him in passing. All of them would say he had made a difference in their lives in some way. We will find out as we move forward how this characteristic will become a vital part of Phillip's legacy. The results of his sacrifice, which preserve his legacy, rest squarely on my shoulders and the shoulders of a nation who enjoy their freedom. Our lives are designed so that all things work together. There is nothing under the sun or moon that happens without some degree of cause and effect. Are you ready to answer your call of duty, completing that mission against your final sunset? Are you still in that valley wandering around, looking for something that left that valley sometime ago? My hope is that you can take from my "when I lay my head down" and when you wake up, the wisdom you seek will set you free to walk out of that valley knowing that you are no longer walking it alone. I will walk it with you through the pages of this book in honor of my son and so many other sons and daughters. This is truly a part of their legacies to you.

CHAPTER 10

On the Road in Search of a Niche

We will not have been home long before the opportunity to be on the road would be available as a means to search for that niche in life God has for us to find. There were a number of events for this accounting of our search to find the niche. We will load up and walk through these trips as they stick out the most in my memory. We will run the road together from Houston to DC a number of times. Each trip will take a week or more to get there and the same on the return side. This time on the road will give us plenty of instances of laying our head down at night, and the early morning hours we have become used to by now.

April Trip to DC

When I was a young soldier, there was an older master sergeant I had come to respect for his seasoned wisdom. He would often say, "Nothing ventured, nothing gained." I knew the motor home needed some work done to it, so I had Penny ask a friend take the motor home in for some repairs that was covered under the extended warranty. One of those items was the engine A/C unit. It had stopped working the last time I drove it. At that time, I had no idea where I would be going in it or when. I just felt it would be a good idea to get it ready now, and I would be able to pick it up from repairs when I got home.

Welcome back on this walk with me through the rest of the story. I found out from Families United, a group Penny and I belonged to as Gold Star parents (parents of a fallen hero) that there was a group leaving California and would be caravanning across America. They would stop to rally support for our troops at designated stops. When they would get to DC, they would join a number of patriotic groups to counter an antiwar protest sponsored by MoveOn.Org, the bus tour group would link up with a group of patriots in support of our troops. I looked at their itinerary, and they were due to come through Dallas, in April. That would be a perfect spot to join the caravan for the rest of the trip to DC, the rig would be ready to before then, and that would work fine. Now I have a plan from which to work. The words of the master sergeant came back to settle in my heart prompting me to make plans to link up with them in Dallas

Getting us from Houston to DC for that event using the motor home would prove to be an interesting and challenging time. I knew I wanted to be on the road, and this event provided me the opportunity to do just that. During my morning cups of joe and pondering, I would start laying out my plan of action in my mind.

It was a good thing the plan of action to use the motor home was in my mind. The day I needed to leave, the rig was not yet ready, but I was promised it would be ready in a couple of days. That time came and went. They had to do some unexpected work and order parts. Now I was at a point that if I was going to go, I needed to be linking up with the group. I thought, OK, I could catch up with them as they made a swing to the south from Arkansas. It wasn't ready for that possibility either, so now I needed to go with or without the rig. I had a couple of days. Then, if I was going to catch up to the caravan before they made it to DC, I would need to go in the car. You guessed it: the motor home still was not ready. I hopped in the car and drove straight through to Atlanta, Georgia, nonstop, with the exception of a half-hour power nap in New Orleans. I pulled to the curb in front of the Omni Hotel in Atlanta, Georgia, just minutes after the caravan had departed. Merilee Carlson, chairperson of Families United, had stayed behind to ride with me to the next stop. Marilee said she would wait for me, and we could go on to catch up with the caravan at the next stop. When I pulled up to the corner, Marilee was standing there waiting for me. We put her luggage into the back. She got behind the wheel, and I occupied the passenger's seat. As Merilee pulled away from the curb, I immediately set my seat to maximum recline, and I crashed as we headed toward South Carolina to link up with the caravan.

When you know God is in control, you do not sweat the details. That does not mean that you do not have to pay attention. It means that by God's grace, you can get to where you need to go at times when it might seem everything comes your way to derail you. Not a problem, right? With God's grace, you will get to where you need to be in peace. I had gotten the sleep I needed by the time we made it to South Carolina. We were right behind them; we even had a visual on them at one point. When we arrived in town, we had a scheduled stop, but we could not find them. We decided to go on and catch up with them a next stop. We would learn they had problems of their own in finding where they needed to be, they were in the wrong city. As it is, most of the time, things do work out. We were able to catch up with them in North Carolina for the next scheduled event there.

It was quite a relief to get to the hotel in DC. I was in a room and ready to call an end to the traveling portion of the day. Then down to the restaurant for a meal and some meet-and-greet. When we finished, the bed was the most welcome sight at this point, because we would need to be up early, eat breakfast, and then load a bus for the park, where everything was set up and there were flags everywhere.

I was up at 0430 hours and made a pot of hotel joe. As I sat in the room, my mind pondered one familiar question: *What am I going to do next, and how?* I knew I was still on a mission, and part of that mission had to do with Phillip's legacy. That fact established itself when we returned to Iraq with the blessings of the family. We also know from our experiences getting to Iraq from the start to the point of leaving Iraq that we would not be going back. As I empty the last sip of joe from my cup just before leaving the room, God allows my heart to be at ease knowing that all is well with my soul.

Mid-April, and it was still cold in DC. In fact, there was snow on the ground. The antiwar folks were supposed to have a huge group. We could only hope to be noticed for our point of view. At the end of the day, our group outnumbered them, probably three to one. The newspeople, of course, were there. They covered the antiwar group, but not the patriots. It is rather ironic when some thought is given to the fact that it is the patriots who are the people willing to pay the price for the freedom of those who are willing to openly display their ignorance and lack of respect for them. I am at a loss for any idea of how they think they came about being free individuals. The patriot serves to preserve the freedom for the nation's people, not based on whether they agree or disagree with our points of view. That, my friend, is why men and women have died for the principle of freedom. Therefore, if a person or group of people choose to show ignorance and ingratitude as opposed to gratefulness and appreciation, then that is also a part of freedom.

I have found that these people do not have a clue as to what it has taken to fight for and die for the right affording them the very privilege to have their very ungrateful-hearted protest. If it were a show of disagreement of policy or action taken, I would have not one iota of problem with the effort. That is why veterans are veterans; that is why any of us serve. It is for that cause we fight and die. It is the ignorance and stupidity of the actions and words that come from these groups that raise the ire of those who serve and those who believe in the goodness of America. Not that anyone dares to disagree with us. I have always believed an opinion that differs from that of my own is due respect if it is a heartfelt belief with some moniker of consideration. However, with that right comes the responsibility to respect my opinion at the same time. I thought of Phillip often during the course of the day. I thought about his brother and sisters and the cross they had to bear with the loss of their brother. My thoughts would then turn to the protesters, those who were of my kids' age group. I thought of how misguided they were. Most of them were so clueless concerning the truth. Then there were those who had gray hair, what used to be the symbol of maturity and wisdom. Toss that idea out the window as a truth when considering this particular group of old geezers from the sixties as being wise. These folks I have absolutely no respect for. They had not learned from their youth in the sixties. They were just as arrogant today and mean-spirited with the spit of their youth. They would bear a heavy burden for the misguidance of the younger folks. They were old hippies still without a clue. Having said that, I realize that part of the connection for me here is understanding that we have to be active in order to make a difference, Phillip was engaged in what he believed in; hence, he made a difference.

We spent the day with temperatures just above freezing. Intermittent snow had started falling in the later hours of the afternoon, I did not mind that. You might think at this point that I might be a wee bit off the rocker. However, when considering that we just spent so much time in the extreme heat and dry, and then you might think, maybe I may not be off my rocker.

That evening in the hotel lobby, Merilee would introduce me to two of the Patriot Guard Riders from Houston. I met Jerry Turner and Joe Ace. That introduction would be a dot that would connect down the road. That introduction will be a start to a terrific friendship with Jerry and Joe and with a group of people who were patriots that I would come to love and respect. We can see as God did during our walk through the time in Iraq bringing people's lives onto a path that would cross my own at the appointed time. Jerry Turner and Joe Ace were both Vietnam veterans. We became instant friends. They invited me to join the Patriot Guard when I returned to Houston. Like so many times in life, the offer went by with no thought given beyond the last words of the invitation. It was no different than the night Penny said "Maybe that is what you ought to do."

I truly believe that had I not made that trip, I would have never given a thought to join the Southeast Texas Patriot Guard Riders. We now know the rest of the story, as the late great Paul Harvey would say. I would join the Patriot Guard Riders when I returned. A motorcycle was not a requirement for membership. That fact, not owning a motorcycle, is still a part of my being a member today. Even though I took a motorcycle riding class, there is just this small warning in the back of my thoughts whenever I think about a bike that says *No, this is not the path for you to take.* We have to pay attention to those warnings; they are for our benefit.

A number of mornings after the return from DC, with undocumented numbers of cups of joe and hours of pondering, I think a conclusion is ready at this point. We need to understand if the trip to DC made a difference.

Finding My Niche

Now as you walk with me through this part of our journey together, we will be spending a lot of time and effort trying to find my niche, as some would say. I knew it would not be an easy task, but I also knew I had to start somewhere with the intention to move forward. We have come to understand and appreciate this concept when it comes to listening to the spirit in you. We have come to know beyond a doubt that you need to move on after your prayers have been answered. You cannot find much of anything just sitting like a bump on a log. We have learned the valuable lesson of those early morning hours with a cup of fresh joe and God to ponder the day with. This pondering of the day is very real. It's the instrument used to open the door to so many answers while we seek answers in the direction and success of the day while in Iraq. Never discard a method that is working; in others words, do not try to fix something that is not broken.

Becoming a part of Families United was a blessing that would help down the road in deciding which direction to take. Sometimes we just need to be involved in order to know what and where we do not want to be a long way down the road to finding that niche. What we will find as we move forward is that we keep the one thing we do know about our mission always at the forefront of our thoughts. Being a part of this group helped me with just being involved in something. I was moving.

I had not been involved in much of anything before leaving for Iraq. I had stopped being involved in church. As I look back now, that was in part because I felt that I had nothing to give. I was just sort of floating through life. Now I have this huge hole in my heart to contend with, it would seem I would be entitled to certain emotions that evolved out of that loss. To the contrary, the distance you and I have walked thus far in this story, we know for sure that we are not entitled to sit and do nothing, especially if you claim to believe God is God. We have seen God provide His Grace and Mercy during that walk through the lonesome valley.

"As I lay my head down" is the last thing on my heart each night at the end of the day. The mornings start with a fresh pot of joe. We will start our day with what became routine. We can call it traditional, if that fits, pondering for the day. We saw it work so many times, so it would be so counterproductive not to rely on it now. On this morning, as we sip on our cups of joe, at the end of the pondering time, we have at least one thing. We have a theme that attached itself to our hearts, from the time we returned to Iraq after Phillip gave his life in Afghanistan. That theme was making a difference. That became a part of the mission for the rest of our time in Iraq.

With our mission unchanged, and the call of "make a difference" in our hearts, we at least have a sense of mission. What is needed now is a vehicle for that mission. In Iraq, it was the job. I do not have a job right now. After a few more nights of laying my head down, followed by early morning pots of hot joe and a number of hours of pondering, the day came when we would have our answer. The vehicle for the mission's forward path will be in the things we would involve ourselves with.

Time of Remembrance, 2007

We find ourselves in this part of our walk together, being a part of Families United. We will join them for a Time of Remembrance program that will take us to DC. For this trip, we will find that the motor home is out of the shop and ready to roll. Penny and I would head back to DC for our second Time of Remembrance ceremony. Only this time, I will not be returning to Iraq.

We will leave on this trip from Houston with Penny flying to DC later. I would meander through Kentucky, just the motor home and me. I am very much at home with this type of travel. I love being on the road, on the move and with my cameras. The one thing that would be on my heart, especially during those early zero dark thirty hours, was the question I had for myself during the time I was sipping on the cup of joe in my hand and pondered in my heart, *Am I making a difference?* The question was always there, and it was hard to see how all the dots would connect. I knew first that there would be dots to connect because we saw how the dots connect from the time of the application for a job with KBR and the dots that followed that through the following thirty-three months, all of which connected to bring us to the point God wanted us to be.

God opens the doors, and we need to step through them. It is OK to take the time and effort to make sure it is a door God indeed opened. But that opportunity my go away if you do not trust God enough to know that he is with you and has your back if you make a mistake in interpretation. I think what we have to see here is as the old saying goes: "Do something even if you are wrong" applies to those many times when we are faced with choices. To sum it up, wisdom tells me that to do nothing is no better than doing something and it is the wrong something. When we take a closer look, we will find that there are consequences to both paths taken.

My last trip to DC was in April, for the Move America Forward effort. This would be my first voyage in the motor home since returning from Iraq. When you are seeking God's mission for your life, you will find it among the things you are already doing most of the time. In this case, we will find the vehicle to a mission we are already on. God meets us where we are, and from that point, we need to allow Him to lead. It does not always mean a change in what you are doing; sometimes it is an addition to what you are doing. Each trip will supply us with more than a bushel of learning reaped from each trip. The sum of the parts still adds up to the whole. As we start this walk, we have come to know to trust the adding up of the parts, the dots God will connect for the sum of the whole. We do not know what the vehicle will be that allows us to continue on the mission, but we do know the answer is there. It may be in part or completely in this trip when it is over. We set out with the one thing we do know about the mission: we are set to make a difference.

Penny and I would make another trip to DC during the middle of May for our second year of Time of Remembrance. I will leave ahead of Penny in the motor home and take my time getting there. I had my cameras of course, so you know I would be busy shooting whatever photo ops that would pop up. On my way through Tennessee, I would stop in Paris, Tennessee, to see Stephanie and Jeffery Archie. Remember Stephanie from Camp Warhorse and Camp Speicher operations? This visit will bless my heart, and I will never forget until the end of my days. Stephanie had become a momma, and absolutely loved it. Jeffery was one proud dad, and that made my heart fell blessed. This is the way life is supposed to be. As I'm feeling this blessing, I can also feel a compelling gratefulness in my heart. I can also feel the connecting of dots to Forever 22. Stephanie and Jeffery made a difference while they worked in Iraq, and they are living their lives in order to make a difference now.

As the visit with Stephanie went on, we talked about the eighteenth of August and the impact it had on her and others. Our lives are supposed to have an impact on others for the good. God created us for this interaction with each other. Likewise, I will never forget Stephanie and her part in getting me ready administratively, and her efforts to work with Major Matthews and Major Daniels to get me out of Iraq through the army so I could escort my son home. Stephanie made a difference, and Phillip made a difference. Neither Stephanie nor Phillip knew that at the time. God did though and connected the dots as only He can do. I would have dinner with Stephanie and Jeff that evening and then be on to my next unscheduled stop somewhere in Kentucky.

I would make my way to DC from Paris, Tennessee, going through Kentucky, taking my time going to Russell Springs and then across the Blue Ridge Mountains, crossing at Morgantown, West Virginia. I loved the Blue Ridge area. The trip brought back many memories of crossing the mountains when I was in the army going from Fort Ritchie to Illinois. There was just something about being in that part of the country that puts my soul at ease. After a good night's sleep, we will start the day off with the routine cup of early morning joe and with a time of pondering during the trip to DC. We would leave Russell Springs early and would make it to DC, pulling the car behind the motor home, right at 1700 hours and rush hour traffic. Not a problem, right? The motor home was bigger than most of the traffic. I found that putting the turn signal on and then turning the front wheels in the direction I wanted to go before moving forward worked to get the opening I needed. This was not something God taught my heart, but rather, the study of human nature did. We would find a KOA campground located in Millersville, Maryland, where we found ourselves leaving right after getting the motor home parked and the car off the tow dolly. I needed to be at Regan International Airport to pick up Penny.

Driving to DC is worse than Houston. I would get not exactly lost because I kinda knew where I was and knew I did not want to be there and at the same time kinda knew where I needed to be. I just needed to figure out how to get there. I made it, and Penny did not have a long wait after getting her luggage. I was grateful for the fact that I did not have to make a trip to the airport on our return going home.

The next day would be the Time of Remembrance event at Monument Mall. There would be three-thousand-plus families of the nation's fallen warriors. The event was great and a terrific tribute to the families who will continue to pay the price of freedom. Lunch was atop the FDIC building cafeteria. I never did find out who hosted this for the families, but it is appreciated with a grateful heart.

Our stay in DC did not have an expiration date on it. When we made our way back to the KOA camp, after talking to the folks who operated the camp, we decided to stay through the Memorial Day weekend. Our stay at the KOA camp was terrific, and the folks who ran the place were awesome. When we shared with them about losing Phillip, he then became very special to them. This would become a part of my learning curve. Making a difference took on more meaning during this stay at the campsite. The reaction to Phillip's sacrifice meant so much to us as parents. I learned that telling Phillip's story first is not about me. It is all about our warriors making a difference. Making a difference is becoming a steadfast partner of the mission as we find ourselves moving it forward as we walk on through this story.

At this moment, as I wrote this last sentence to this point in time, I realized, when I tell the story about losing Phillip that God has taught my heart this moment that from now on when I share the story of losing Phillip, I am sharing with them the fact of what he has sacrificed in order to make a difference, along with others who have sacrificed for the nation with all the other fallen warriors, our wounded and those who have served and those who are serving now. It most certainly is about the price my family has had to pay and will continue to pay. He made a difference, which brings pride to my heart as I think about the often-used line "All gave some and some gave all."

We will walk through the rest of this story about making a difference become a recurring theme of Forever 22, giving credence to the phrase "never forget," because in order for the legacy of these brave men and women warriors of freedom—freedom in this land that is American exceptionalism because of exceptional Americans—there has to be a remembrance of the price they have paid for us. This call for recognition of this fact is never to be an in-your-face moment but, rather, to rally those who understand the cost of their freedom. For those who have not, they have an absence of understanding of what their freedom cost someone else willing to stand for them. They end with the missed opportunity of having a blessed heart knowing someone cared enough to stand for them against an enemy of their freedom. What difference do the selfish really make in life?

Those who make a difference do not choose the American who will benefit from their acts of courage and unselfish giving. They give to all Americans and America. As we walk on through this story, at this point,

I have thought about the call to recognize why you live in the land of the free because of the brave. I love that phrase, and it goes to the heart of why I do what I do today. The survival of our warriors' legacies depend on the voice of those who understand and appreciate them give to it day in and day out. We are finding at least a starting thread to continuing on our mission here at home. When we think about life, we realize just how much life goes and comes back full circle. God created us with a purpose. As our lives move forward, we live it one day at a time making choices that decide the path we take. At the end of life's journey, we find ourselves having made a full circle, with all the dots of our lives being connected to the end once again facing God's purpose. Understanding that the legacy of your life depends on how well you are remembered for the difference you made in life before your final sunset. At that point, can you look back and say all is well with your soul? How will you end the life you were created to live. Will you have made a difference?

I did not realize at the time of the event that this time would connect not only to Forever 22 without realizing it until just now. It will also connect the dots of Never Forget as a part of Forever 22. This trip to DC would be a point of continence of Phillip's legacy of making a difference. It will be a point of answering a call to mission to keep the connection to the legacies of all of our warriors' sacrifices in making a difference. As they are laid to rest, there is a promise that they will not be forgotten. This is a solemn promise given by our government on behalf of a grateful nation as the family is presented with the Stars and Stripes that cover their coffin during the ceremony of laying that hero to rest. I would not see this connection as clearly until I started writing this book.

Rolling Thunder, Memorial Day 2007

As I pointed out earlier, we had no plans to stay in DC after the Time of Remembrance ceremony, but when we got back to the KOA Park, we were told about the one-hundred-plus Rolling Thunder members who would start coming to the camp for the weekend that has come to be known as the Run for the Wall. With the usual practice of "when I lay my head down," when the early hours of the next morning came with the smell of the fresh brew it was time for the morning routine. Sitting outside the motor home with a fresh cup of joe and pondering the trip back home to Houston, everything was well with my soul. At the end of several cups of joe and a conversation with Penny when she got up, we decided to stay through Memorial Day. With no idea of what we would do, we did know that a lot would be going on during a major holiday in DC. We had no real plans that would require being back home. We took a nature walk on trails through the woods adjacent to the camp. These well-traveled trails presented many photo ops to a photographer. We saw some of the most incredible blossoming trees, bushes, and wildflowers. Of course, this was right up my alley, and of course, I had my Nikon with me. You can see these photos in a gallery if you go to.

Most of the Rolling Thunder group started arriving throughout the day on Friday for the Run for the Wall. The park personnel told us how much the park looked forward to them showing up each year. They had been doing this for the last twenty-five years. What a tradition to get to witness.

Apparently, the caretakers of the camp told them about us being a Gold Star family. The next day, they invited to us to be a part of their Blessing of the Bikes ceremony. They made a point to honor Phillip and his sacrifice. Most of these folks were veterans, and those who were not were patriots. As we walk through this, our minds can go back to our walk together in Iraq and know this is part of making a difference. Honor and Remembrance cannot bring a loved one back, but it can ensure that their legacy moves forward on its mission.

This was the Rolling Thunder's annual Run for the Wall. Riders from all over the country would converge in DC to bring awareness to our POW/MIAs issue and to make sure we do not leave anyone behind in the future. When Penny and I arrived at the parking lot of the Pentagon, it was an unbelievable sight. All I could see from the top of the hill that led down to the massive parking lot was a sea of motorcycles. Seventy-five thousand motorcycles was the official count. The sight made the heart feel a joy that so many were willing honor the fallen heroes and remember. This sight would stick with me as I began to search for a clear vision of my purpose and my mission. The Patriot Guard Riders had a special section in the ride from the Pentagon parking lot to the Memorial Mall. They would have Gold Star mothers on the backs of their motorcycles for the ride to the mall. The lead vehicle for this group was a WWII Jeep followed by a Vietnam era

2½-ton truck. Standing in the back of this thing brought back many memories for me as I climbed up onto the bed. I had two Nikons—one with a wide angle lens and the other with a telephoto lens. Penny was on the back of a motorcycle of a Patriot Guard Rider. From our starting point, both sides of the street was lined with people waving flags, giving a thumbs-up, and a resounding support of clapping. The sight and sounds made it hard to focus at times, as my heart would flip from the pain of losing Phillip to the huge swelling as my pride in our nation swept across it. This was the scene all the way to Monument Mall. We passed the marine who stood at attention for the entire procession. What a sight. I realized as I finished the paragraph that the intent here was to make a difference.

A special memory was the night before the ride from the Pentagon, we were invited to a meet-and-greet type of affair at the hotel where the founder of Rolling Thunder, Artie Muller, was staying. Penny and I had a chance to meet him. Can you conjure up what it is like to walk in a sea of leather and chrome? Check the photo gallery out on my website for Forever 22 at www.designedphotos.com.

A Visit to the Oval Office

Our Families United group received an invitation to a White House breakfast for Monday, May 28. It would be during this event that Penny and I would have the honor with about four other families to meet President Bush in the Oval Office. What a follow-up to the Rolling Thunder event.

As we walked into a room off the dining room, Keith Hensley introduced us to General Peter Pace and his wife, Dana Perino, who at that time looked like a little kid. We met the sergeant major of the army and General Scott, who I had met before in Iraq, and so many more people. I was most impressed with General Pace. As a rule, the position of a person does not impress me. It's the content of that person's heart that catches my attention.

When we had finished our breakfast, we were escorted to a waiting room outside the Oval Office. Keith had become a friend to the Families United group and had many dinners with them during our visits to DC. There was a short briefing on how the visit would proceed. Can you imagine the chaos without this level of organization? After a short time, we walked through the door to the Oval Office. It's hard to describe the feeling I had as a veteran and the father of a fallen warrior. President Bush was already in the room when I entered. I needed to check my cameras in with security before entering the Oval Office. That put me behind the president. The rest of the group was in front of him. Being the last to enter the Oval Office, I ended up behind him. I got to see something the others did not. A fly had been flying in front of him. He swatted at it a number of times and then got it. He opened his hands, and it dropped to the floor. Then he kicked it with his loafer and kicked it under the back of the couch.

The president talked to our families from his heart. Remember that God has taught my heart to listen to the hearts of the people to whom I am listening. I did just that when listening carefully to President Bush, coming away with knowing what he said and felt was from his heart. You do not have to always agree with some in order to accept what comes sincerely from their hearts. He spent about forty-five minutes with us; that time included everyone having a chance to ask questions we might have for him, and then time for the White House photographer to take photos of each family with the president. When the meeting had concluded, President Bush turned to walk out one exit, and we exited an opposite door. President Bush stopped to turn toward us and asked, "Anyone want to ride with me to Arlington?" Well, what do you think? We walked downstairs and out the front of the White House to where the president's limo was waiting, Penny and I rode in the Secret Service SUV that was right behind the president. We had a great chat with the guys on the trip to Arlington. When we got to Arlington and got out of the SUV, we could hear some people wondering who these other people were.

I have some awesome shots of the president during the ceremony at Arlington. What a trip to put into the bank of memories. I have many photos and ask myself, *What in the world am I going to do with them?* Well, they will become connected to, as other dots, that I had no idea about have been connected to this book and the mission of Forever 22. Making a difference is the reason.

We crossed the Blue Ridge Mountains and were at the bottom just as the sun was rising. I looked in my extra-large side-mounted mirrors and saw the sun rising to make its debut of the new day. The sun rising over the mountains made my heart extra grateful as I thought about what I was witnessing. Now that I have seen this sunrise in the mirror, there was no way as a photographer that I could let that photo op pass. I found a safe place to pull over and stepped out of the motor home and started shooting. As I shot frame after frame, my heart felt the presence God. He will do this if we just take the time to allow it to happen. Stopping often for photo ops become standard operating procedure.

We headed back to Houston the following day, by way of Ohio, to see my sister. This was followed by a trip to Lake Cumberland for a couple of days, where we camped at the state park. My heart felt blessed and was full of joy. At this point, I still had no idea what God had in mind for me, except that He knew the message "Make a difference" was coming through loud and clear. The challenge now is, *What do we do with it.*

On our way home, we will have one more time that is special. As we made our way back home to Houston, we stopped in Paris, Tennessee, to see Stephanie and Jeffery. Penny had the opportunity to meet Stephanie and hear her explain how Phillip made a difference in her life and how she would never forget it.

Invitation to Korean War POW Reunion

Somehow the Bakers got my name and contact information from Marilee of Families United. My first meeting with the Bakers was through an invitation to the KWVA, the Korean War Veterans Association. I attended the meeting, which was held somewhere in the Dallas area. Mr. Baker was a three-year POW of the Korean War and an instant friendship started between us on that day.

We will receive and invitation as guests in Charleston, West Virginia, to celebrate a reunion of Korean War ex-POWs and their families. What an honor this was, and another opportunity for a motor home trip.

Penny and I left Houston and made our way to Arkansas, where we spent a couple of days with Phillip's buddy's parents. We would leave Little Rock to drive to East Memphis, Arkansas; and then we will turn north to Illinois. We would be in Illinois to pick my second oldest daughter; she would be coming back to Texas with us. With stops in Ohio to visit with my sister then onto Charleston, West Virginia, if you ask a fella from West Virginia where he is from, he will undoubtedly answer with a hearty "West by God Virginia." Go figure out that one right.

There were about three hundred Korean War veterans there, and the trip and event were an absolute blessing. Listening to and watching these amazing men and women who served during a time when their service to the nation referred to them as the forgotten war veterans. This was an incredible experience. This has a connection to Forever 22. My mission would be centered on the effort to keep our heroes remembered and honored, to keeping their legacies alive. There was still no clear vision as of this time. I understand I had more to learn before I could see the vision as a clear part of the mission. I think the point here is that while we are opening our hearts to God's mission, we should be grateful for the fact that we know we have a mission and that it will be a part of our life.

I have come to learn that God doesn't want us walking around in misery with "Well, I have to do God's work." No, God wants us to experience life to the fullest while dealing with all the ups and downs of life. Here is the connection to Forever 22 and a message for you if you are reading this book. God didn't call me to sacrifice my life beside Phillip. I would have had it been possible; however, it was not, I would have been more than willing to do just that, as I am sure you would probably be ready to do for your own kid. It was not God's intent nor was it Phillip's intent for this possibility to be the case. For that reason, I can move forward with life with a mission because of Phillip's sacrifice and his willingness to make a difference in the lives of those he touched. Another set of those dots God will connect where the connection needed to be later on in this story

While I did not have a vision of what I was supposed to do; I do know that if I just stood still, I would never find out. We have seen throughout this walk that there are times when God wants us to be still and know that He is God. He wants us to live our life out trusting Him. If I take a wrong turn or chase a wild goose, at some point, it will become clear, and I can make a correction to my direction and always walk away learning something and be blessed by it.

As I finished recounting this event, I realized that in whatever we do, we should consider the difference it may make in someone else's life, good or bad. Do whatever you are doing; do it with the intention in your heart to make a difference in someone else's life. Sharing Phillip's story is a tribute to the brave men and women of our military. When I share his story, the intention in my heart is not for recognition for myself in any way. The story becomes about who he was and what he became, resulting in what he did for a nation, hoping that it makes a difference in someone else's life. I cannot share his story without knowing that whatever God has in store for me, making a difference will always have to be a part of that mission. This is keeping their legacies alive for those who have given their lives to a nation.

CHAPTER 11

Glass Class at Camp Speicher

With a renewed passion in our hearts, we are ready to do whatever it takes to do the job we love doing and continue the mission God has given us. With that amount of passion for the job and the mission, we cannot fail to do the best job and to complete our mission no matter where it leads us. I knew without a doubt that we needed to continue teaching the glass class after settling in at Camp Speicher. We have seen that the classes are more than just a glass class. It was a way of letting folks experience God in a different way. I knew the task would have to be approached differently than the way I approached it at Warhorse. Since this was our area's operational headquarters, I needed to pay attention to protocol. People's egos were a little a bit more in play here than at the more laid-back operations of the smaller Camp Warhorse. It is not that egos were not at play at Camp Warhorse; it was just easier and quicker to take them down a couple of notches.

April Kicked Off the First Glass Class

Are you ready to start up a new glass class at Camp Speicher? Starting this class was different from starting the class a Warhorse. We found ourselves with no place that we were in control of outside the office; we had to look around for a suitable place. As we have been doing for a very long time now, "when I laid my head down" was no different at Camp Speicher than it was anywhere else. In fact, we probably needed it more now than ever because our mission was becoming clearer. Then add to that the fact that the people were different and the attitude of the operations was different.

I became friends with MWR workers in my role as photographer. They liked what we were doing for the safety meetings. He wanted us to spend some time at the MWR shooting different events. Of course, this was right up our alley, and we were glad to do it. This was why we were there as photographer/historian.

You can always know when you are slightly behind the proverbial eight ball when there is that nagging feeling in your heart every time you seem to turn and it did not seem to matter which direction. I needed God's wisdom on this matter, for sure. I simply did not have a clue. At the end of the night, literally, before the lights in my hooch went out, I thought, *OK, Lord, I give up.*

The next morning, I was a little bit earlier getting up. I did not spend the time in my hooch these days for my early morning routine. My computer and everything else I needed were in the office. I walked to the office with the glass class on my mind. After I unlocked the door, the first thing I did, as usual, was to make that fresh pot of brew after the lights were turned on. By the time I checked my e-mails, the brew was ready. With a fresh cup of joe at my side, I would prop my feet up on my desk and settle in for my morning pondering session. Nobody but me, God, and a pot of joe. By the time the others started coming in, I still did not have an answer. What I did have was a peace in my heart from knowing that the answer would be in hand today before the lights were out. That was all the assurance I needed. It had never failed before, and my heart was satisfied.

My friend Terry came in, turned the lights on in his office, and checked his e-mails; and then we were ready to hop in his vehicle to go to breakfast. How much better could it get for being in a war zone? We should have had it so good. I was beginning to think more and more of Phillip these days, as our mission and reason for being in Iraq became clearer. We were to make a difference in all things, big or small. We were to do whatever we could and when we could to give someone a little bit of a brighter day.

After breakfast, we left the office to meet up with the MWR guy, Bill. I had some photos on a disc for him, and we could be certain he would have something new for us to shoot. He took the disc and placed it on his desk. Then led us out to the game room, in the corner, where there were some mats on the floor. He explained that he would like the sumo wrestling photographed. He explained to me the way it would come about and showed us the thick foam suit that the contenders would put on and then pretend they were sumo wrestlers. Now this ought to be fun, right? On our way back to his office, I mentioned needing a place to teach stained glass classes. He jumped on the idea and suggested we teach at the MWR. It would be a natural. After a few quick queries, he showed us to the library, suggested we could use it twice a week to teach the class. This was perfect as it had individual stations built in and tables. The only thing we would need now was a place to store everything. That was not a problem either. There was a huge room at the end of the building, most likely used for that anyhow.

By the time we left the MWR, we knew God had answered another prayer. There was never any doubt that the answer would come by the end of the day. We went about the morning searching for photo ops. The building of the new mess halls were always on the agenda of morning and afternoon shoots.

Once back to the office, we needed to work on a flyer for the upcoming glass class. I would need to let operations know what I was going to do. Not a problem: Stephanie was still in charge, and she knew how well the glass class worked out at Camp Warhorse. She handed the project manager a copy of the proposed class, and he liked it.

We designed a flyer, printed it, and distributed it with the MWR being our biggest promoter of the upcoming classes. Once again, as we have seen before, God opened doors and the hearts of the people we needed in our corner. When the lights went out on that day at the office and the door was locked, I would turn to take my usual look back and then continue to my hooch, knowing all was well with my soul. I was ready to lay my head down for whatever God would have for me the next day. I know this might sound a bit farfetched, unless you walk beside me or in my shoes how do you know it does not work?

The one thing I did not have to figure out this time was how to do a 33x44" drawing. The grid system was a tried and proven method by now. The Camp Speicher glass class was different in many ways from the class at Camp Warhorse. What would not be different would be the blessing that came out of this class, and my soul would be blessed again.

This project came about from the same need for wisdom to find a unique teaching project, as did the kneeling soldier project. The projects I understood in my heart had to be special for the time and place we found ourselves. I was up against a deadline again for an idea for the teaching project. Not a problem, right? All I had to do was lay my head down and ask for God's wisdom with a humble heart and in an earnest seeking mode.

During my morning cup of joe, someone had sent me at the right time, as if that is unusual at this point, an e-mail with the picture and bio of the now-famous three firefighters. Would you not know, after about the third cup of joe and reading the article about the New York City Firefighters, raising the flag over the Twin Towers rubble? This e-mail of the firefighters went hand in hand with another e-mail I got a couple of days after I arrived home with Phillip from Dover. The e-mail I received at home was from the New York City Fire Department. It simply read something like this: "Mr. George we understand your pain. We are the Ladder Company who lost the most men in 9/11."

The community-teaching project decided by the time I finished the cup of joe I was sipping. We are used to things working this way. My heart was overwhelmed with gratefulness. A depiction of the three firefighters raising the flag over the Twin Towers rubble of 9/11. What an honorable choice. I do not believe for one second that would have been the case had it not be for God's wisdom. The sips of joe may have had a wee bit to do with it. This project came about by the connection of two e-mails. Once again, we see the dots connecting, Phillip's legacy, making a difference, and being on track with the mission in Iraq. Walking with me this long, you are probably not surprised by what God does by now and are thinking, *OK, what is next.* I wish I could find the e-mail, but I cannot.

The three-firefighters glass will be a part of Forever 22. I know that now, but I did not know it back then. I suppose I need to keep that point clear every so often.

During the introduction of the first class, I was able to give them a thumbnail sketch of how the class started and ended at Camp Warhorse. More importantly, I was able to let them know that God had His hands on this mission as well as Camp Warhorse. Then I was able to tie in the connection between the teaching project, the story of Phillip, and the e-mail I received from the New York Fire Department. This connection is another example of God knowing what we need, when we need it, and how we need it. These connections started before I ever thought of the title of this book. The two thoughts bumped into each other, and a teaching project was the result. Did they really just happen to bump into each other, or did God cross their paths? I suppose no matter how much evidence there is, those who prefer to, believe in themselves and their luck. I think by now, you and I know better than this.

The first class started the second week in April. There were more warriors signed up for the class than we had at Camp Warhorse, mostly likely because of the much larger size of Camp Speicher. Once you see the makeup of the class, you will see army, navy, and air force. We had one Dyna-Corp worker, three Iraqi American Christians, and three or four KBR people. This was an example of God crossing people's paths. In the class were three Airborne Rangers from the 101st. I truly believe each person was there by design.

The three 101st soldiers chose a depiction of the band of brothers. The project was five feet long by about two feet tall. One of the men found a place where, once we had gotten to know each other, he could share his concerns about his little girl who was having some health issues. We would pray with him before we would start the class. He would share with us about the worry he had concerning his baby girl back home. You can see from one thing how the classes were the vehicle for so much more than cutting glass. Can you imagine being a soldier? These men were outside the wire more than they spent inside in safety, with worries about their child back home. God had a reason for the young warrior coming to the class, and that was the real purpose for him being there. There was a civilian in the class who had lost his daughter some thirteen years ago, when she was only seven. Then I had my experiences not only of losing Phillip but also as a Vietnam veteran. We had a navy chief petty officer who was dealing with his concerns for his daughter back home. Captain Porter was also a man who believed in prayer. Therefore, the three Iraqi American women believed in prayer. They would pray with us as well as the other soldiers who were there. How unique was this? Was this coincidental, or was it by God's design that these people who had a strong faith came together? Cutting glass was not their only purpose for being in the class. How about you? We have walked many miles together. We have been through a lot together.

The three American Iraqis were a blessing to have. They were unique individuals, with unique stories to share as Arab Christians. The youngest stood out in particular. She was seventeen when she and her family moved to the United States. Her project was a map of Iraqi states with a Christian church in the center of Iraq. It gave you the feeling that her desire was for Iraq to be a Christian nation. The church with a steeple became the focus of her project. She was such a pleasure to work with. When we started, she was so sure she could not do the project. When she finished, that doubt banished from her. Never again to be revisited. She was so proud, and we were proud of her. The class, like Camp Warhorse, developed its own personality according to the needs of the class. Like Camp Warhorse, it was a place where the warriors could feel the release of tension experienced from everyday military pressures. When we stop to think about a stained glass class in the middle of the dessert, and in a war zone to boot, that becomes at least unusual.

The first class started in April, as announced by the MWR, and by mid-August, the project was completed. Captain Jake Porter worked on the project, and when he told his father in Carbondale, Illinois, what we were doing and what we planned to do with the glass, his father asked if he could make the frame for us. The beautiful oak frame arrived from Carbondale. Captain Porter and I put it together. We had everything spread out in the middle of my office floor. We assembled it, and it was ready to go into the crate made for it from the carpentry shop at Camp Speicher. I often consider the question of how we could have been more blessed than we are right now. People stopped by either the class or the office to check on the progress of the project. Most of them would leave offering to help in any way they could. A carpenter from the carpentry shop offered to build a shipping crate for it, and he did.

We crated the glass, and it was ready to take to the DHL office. They have a small office at the airfield. How is that for having your needs met? We will ship from DHL at Camp Speicher to New Jersey, where it will arrive at Captain Porter's mother-in-law's house. Things work this way when God is involved. People get involved helping others. People are blessed in so many ways. Now that the glass is on its way to New Jersey, it is time for us to hop on a plane in a few days to be on our way to Houston. When I paid for the shipping, I did a lot of praying that it would get there in one piece.

Stained Glass from Iraq to New York

I think God would have me take the time to talk just a little bit about what continues to make my time in Iraq so different than most. It is not because I am anyone special; it is, however, a result of allowing God to be active in my day-to-day walk while in Iraq. When it came time for R&R, like anyone else, I welcomed it with open arms. I was always ready for it and blessed by the chance to be at home with my family. That aspect of my life has taken on a completely new perspective that reaches all corners and crevices of my life and my family's life. My outlook on how I operate day to day from this point forward starts with an increased passion for the mission I know I have in life. As I continue to write, I still wonder how what I have written to this point ties in and focuses on this being about escorting my son home. Then my heart gets a reminder: this has to be about God first. A story about Phillip could not exist without how He has connected all the dots for this to be a story. At this point, my heart is at ease once again, and you and I will continue our walk through this story

Folks, this is how God works in our lives. The flight from Camp Speicher to Baghdad, where a night or two will most certainly be spent at Camp Liberty. We are for sure to spend it with an anxious desire to not stay any longer than necessary. When we were at Camp Warhorse, this was kind of a mixed blessing. It was nice to have the big food court to choose meals from and a huge PX to shop from mostly on return trips. Then we would be on our way to Dubai. For most trips out of the country, one night here was a great relief before taking off for the ten-hour flight home. It was during that flight that with nothing to do but be alone with God and my thoughts, I began to realize that Phillip's legacy had started a long time ago. This is the point of my recognizing that and understanding that I am his voice for that legacy to continue.

My heart needs a lot of teaching in the coming days, and I welcome that. The question becomes, *Am I willing to humble my heart enough to hear the directions God is giving me?* This part of Phillip's legacy has already started with the stained glass mission from Iraq to New York. It is in remembrance of Phillip that the two e-mails crossed paths to inspire the choice of the teaching project. The flight home was hours of pondering this or that, resulting in some light being put on things I needed to understand to move forward. Phillip's life would flash before me in my mind as though I was seeing it on a big screen. The memories were such a blessing against those times when the pain would seem to rage against the very core of my heart.

Houston to New York

We make it to Houston. We will only spend a couple of days here, getting ready for the trip to New York. At the end of that couple of days, my wife, daughter, and I loaded up the motor home and headed for New Jersey, then on to New York, with a stop in Little Rock, Arkansas, for a visit with one of Phillip's buddies' and his parents. We had our car on a tow dolly hitched to the back of the motor home. We were ready to head for New York City.

Before leaving Iraq, I spent time exchanging e-mails with the public affairs woman of the fire department in New York City. This would allow them the time to get the wheels turning for the presentation of the glass to the fire chief. Doing this sort of thing was a first for me. This called for some real thinking outside the box. When I laid my head down, the next morning, pay close attention to the wisdom God provided. When we left Camp Speicher, we had names, phone numbers, and addresses. What more could we want or ask for? You got it—we are on a mission.

We made it to Hope, Arkansas, and developed a problem with the motor home. We just happened to stop at a truck stop to eat; but when we were ready to leave, it would not start. I pulled the engine cover and could determine I was not getting gas pumped to the engine. There was no way I could get to the fuel pump without tools and jacks. The truck stop had a repair shop but did not work on gasoline engines. They were strictly a diesel repair shop, but they did manage to get me the phone number of a couple of brothers who could do it. These guys were supposed to be mechanics. I guess that statement may have given you a hint to the dilemma that would come.

These guys showed up in a pickup truck, and sure enough, they had jacks and tools. They determined quickly that no fuel was being pumped to the carburetor. Yep, no doubt about it. I reckon the fuel pump had given up the ghost. I felt sorry for these guys; they worked hard for about six hours to get the fuel tank dropped. This was a one-hundred-gallon steel tank. With the old pump out, they went to town to buy a new one. I felt better about them when they did not ask for money up front to pay for the new one. I do not know if it did anything to boost my confidence in them, but it spoke volumes about their integrity.

With a new fuel pump in hand, they began the process of installing it and getting the tank back in place. They had two kids with them; and being kids, they became restless after a couple of hours. I reckon they had not figured on the job taking them longer than that. Once the new fuel pump was in and they actually checked to make sure it would pump, and it did when power was applied directly, they put the tank back in place. You know these guys had to have been praying as they crawled from under the chassis of this 33½ foot monster; it had just eaten their lunches as it goes. They turned the ignition on, but nothing. The engine turned over, but no fuel. Now these bubbas were at the end of their expertise, and they had a failed mission to boot. I really did appreciate their effort. They worked hard, and they worked earnestly. I asked what I owed them, and they asked if three hundred was too much. Well, the fuel pump was right at a hundred, and they had paid for that so I was more than glad to pay them three hundred. It was worth it to know that someone would put forth such honest effort. When these two brothers exhausted their mechanical expertise, I still had the problem I started with. This small episode on our way to New York is about allowing God be seen in all things.

"What are you going to do now" was her question, and my answer was "Not a problem." Now Penny does not have the same relationship I have with "Not a problem." I called our friend who lived thirty miles away in Little Rock, the parents of one of Phillip's marine buddies. I would call our roadside assistance number for a heavy tow truck to get the rig to our friend's house. Barry would come to where we were spending the night with them and get a mobile technician out the next morning. We got a good night's sleep, and the mobile repairman came out the next morning. He started with checking fuses under the dash panel, especially knowing the bubbas had installed a new pump. In a short time, he found the blown fuse, replaced it and the engine fire right up. He told me that he wished he could find the source of the short but could not at that point. I understood that reasoning from the eight years in army electronics. It was another three hundred, and well worth it. With a very grateful heart, I gladly paid the man, and we were on our way again.

My thoughts at this point bring back so many memories of Phillip and me working together. For the most part of my life, from a lad to today, I have learned to think outside the box. I taught this concept to Phillip as we worked and spent time together. I believe in what is capable of allowing us to do. I feel it is a part of my mission in life to encourage others to think outside the box they find themselves in at times.

Well, I needed to think outside the box while dealing with a motor home in the lower forty of a truck stop in Hope, Arkansas. Not a problem, right? You have been with me long enough now to feel in your heart that it really is not a problem. We have roadside assistance with our vehicle insurance policy; towing, then, is not a problem. Where do we have it towed is the next item that needs to be solved. We are just thirty-three miles from our friends in Little Rock. The answer to the problem is to call them for help in finding a local mobile technician. We can then have the rig towed to their place. While we locate and get the rig worked on, we can visit with our friends. Not a problem. The call goes in to our friends. All is well with them, and the last thing to do is call for help from a tow company. At this point, I am reminded of when George Peppard's character in the TV series *The A Team*, when he would conclude a mission with "I love it when a plan comes together."

Faith in My Daughter or Nutty Dad

What happened next the next day about thirty miles east of Little Rock, we still talk about it today. Sometimes you just have to take a chance on those around you and in your life. What I do next may be a real test of faith, you might say. It may simply be the confidence of a dad in his daughter. At that thirty-mile mark east of Little Rock, I pulled the rig over. I got up from the driver's seat. Penny thought something else was wrong; she would also think I was out of my mind. I looked at Sarah and asked her if she wanted to drive. She looked at me and said "Sure" with the confidence of a seventeen-year-old. I just knew in my heart that she could do this. She had a two-lane highway and a straight shot all the way to Nashville, Tennessee. Not a problem right?

It was not. After she adjusted herself to the steering characteristics of the rig that left her barefoot, she was comfortably resting on the dash as she drove to Nashville, Tennessee, and north. Sara drove to just north of Nashville and was so excited when she made her first left turn to head north on I-65 toward Bowling Green, Kentucky. I can still see the excitement and being proud of what she had just accomplished. "Dad, did you see that? I made my first left turn?"

After she made that turn and found a safe place to pull over, she was ready to exit the driver's seat. Now there will be a connection made of this new challenge driving this big rig to Forever 22. As I write about this account, I realized how much she was like her brother. If saying yes to the opportunity of taking the wheel meant that she was confident enough to know she could do it, then that is what I needed to do for her at that time. We have to believe in our kids; we have to trust them sometimes with things that may seem out of their league, so to speak; and we have to risk letting them take the chance. I saw in Sara a quality that helped make him the Phillip he became, and what he became was one hell of a marine. I do not know any better way to say it.

We made it to my brother's business, where we were able to park the motor home, take the car off the tow dolly, and spend the night with him and his wife. God was definitely with us and ahead of us on this mission—and what a mission it was. While at my brothers in Bowling Green, Kentucky, I noticed that my brakes were a little soft, so I decided to have them fixed. At the same time, I decided to have the oil changed in the on-board generator. It ended up I needed a sensor for it. Not a problem. It could be ordered from Nashville and be there the next day. We were still in good shape as far as time to get to New York on time. God was certainly watching over us and blessing us along the way.

We needed to get Sara back to Houston so she could be there for a test that she did not want to miss. We drove her to Nashville, Tennessee, to catch a flight back to Houston, where we would stay for a couple of days. Again, this would be so like much like Phillip, making sure that she took care of what she needed to. The next day, we picked up Aaron and his wife, Diana, from the Louisville airport. From there, we continued on our trip toward Lexington. That was a trip with an awesome view through that giant windshield. So far, by the grace of God I was not behind schedule; I had to adjust the time I spent with my brother in order to get back on schedule. All of this brought back so many memories of Phillip and the way we would handle issues that would come up on a job we were doing.

Mechanic Problems: Not a Problem

Aaron and Diana flew in from Austin, Texas. Penny and I picked them up from the airport. We were about thirty miles or less outside the west side of Lexington when I pulled over and asked Aaron if he wanted to drive. He said sure, and off we went again. Aaron drove an armored truck in Austin for a while, so there was no doubt that he could drive the rig. The break for me was a good thing. Aaron had only been behind the wheel maybe ten minutes, more likely less, when the engine stopped. It is during times like this that you can really appreciate the fact that God made you the way you are. Not a problem, right? I told Aaron to pull over when he could safely do so. He was moving at about six when the engine stopped. I knew we had enough momentum to get us to a safe place to pull over. I asked him to turn the emergency flasher on. It did not take long to find a safe place to pull off the road. We looked around outside. It was pitch black, and we could not see much of anything even with a flashlight. We were not looking for the problem, but to make sure we were off the road far enough, and we were. Without a doubt, I knew the fuse had blown again, and I knew at this point that I was going to have to get the short found and repaired.

Roadside service called again for a tow truck. The roadside assistance found a tow truck, but it would not be able to make it until morning. That left us with the question of what to do next. The rest of the family simply was not too fond of the thought of spending the night in the motor home, stranded on the side of the freeway, even though the power plant worked perfectly. I did not cherish the idea of them being there and being very uncomfortable. Not a problem, right? God had given me the ability to think outside the box a long time ago. At this point in my life, my heart knew two concepts—the first being "when I lay my head down" and the second being "not a problem." I needed not a problem for this immediate issue.

Aaron and I unloaded the car from the tow dolly. Now it was ready for them to drive the twenty-two miles into Lexington, Kentucky, where they would spend the night. We would be able to get the motor home towed once again to a shop. You have walked with me since May of 2004 with this story, you have seen the many times God has had our backs. This time is no different. I would spend the night in the motor home, and Aaron would drive the rest of the family to a hotel in Lexington, Kentucky. Not a problem again. Once they were on their way, I called the roadside assistance people again to arrange for a tow to the repair shop. The assistance people informed me they had a company to tow, but they would not be able to get to it until 0700 hours the next morning. This tow was not a problem. What else was I going to do? I went to bed in the motor home that night and did what I had come to make a routine part of my day. When I laid my head down, I asked for God's wisdom. The tow truck showed up as scheduled, and once the rigs wheels were off the ground, the driver asked if I had someplace I wanted to take it. I did not have the foggiest of ideas, but he did. He said he knew a fellow right next to the Lexington Airport. I agreed. I knew God was in charge and that this technician would be someone I could trust.

I spent that night in Lexington with my family, and the next day, we stopped by the repair shop. The mechanic said it would take a while to run down the short. I understood that from experience of chasing shorts down in equipment when I was in the army. He asked where we were going, and when I told him New Jersey and then on to New York, he had a great idea. He said, "You don't want to drive that motor home into New York City anyhow." He suggested I leave the rig with him and drive on to New York, as it was not that far. We would be gone long enough for him to find the problem. That sounded like a plan to me. I loved George Peppard when he was Hannibal Smith of the A Team, and I love it when a plan comes together.

We Came to a Fork in the Road and Took It

The next day, we went back to the Lexington Airport to pick up Sara. Aaron had rented a car so he, his wife Diana, and Sara could drive to West Virginia to visit with Diana's brother and wife. With all the time we've had share to this point, you know that our walk is in God's hand. That would be the last time Diana would see her sister-in-law. She would pass on from medical complications; so seeing her when she did, has to be chalked up to a God thing—that was a true blessing. They would catch up with us in New York City. All was working according to plan, and I can look back now and know that all was well with my soul. Not a problem.

There are times when I wonder what Phillip would think. Without doubt, we enjoyed the trip so far, even though there were mechanical problems. As I ponder the question of what Phillip would think, there is no doubt as to the conclusion of that question. He would be extremely pleased of his family, for being strong enough to honor him with being able to understand the price he paid for our freedom to enjoy life. Which brings me to a point I hope does not pass over my readers: our men and women, from the beginning of this exceptional nation, die for us to have a life and live that life in the freedom they paid for. The price of freedom did not include or intend that our life wither on the vine of the choice of staying in the shadow of the valley of death. I sincerely pray that God will move the hearts of those who find themselves stranded in that valley; they will not find their loved one there. Eternity will pass, and they will still be searching that valley alone with their sorrow. I cannot in good conscience sugarcoat this fact.

The kids head to West Virginia, and Penny and I headed to Captain Porter's mother-in-law's house in New Jersey. Penny and I made it there around 1900 hours. Captain Porter's wife, Jill, and her family greeted us when we walked into the house. This was so awesome; they made us feel so welcome. The glass was out on a table, and they were just about finished with cleaning it up for the trip to New York. God continued to connect the dots. The next morning, we got up and loaded the glass into the back of the car, a Pontiac Vibe, which was perfect for accommodating the glass to lie flat in the back.

It is time for us to get on the turnpike to New York City. We were definitely blessed. We said our good-byes with a grateful heart. It had been years since I had driven a turnpike. Not a problem right? We are on a mission. It is amazing what does not bother you when you are on a mission given you, and you do it with all the passion you can gather from deep within your heart. I think Penny believed we would never make it, until we came to the Holland Tunnel, or at least I think it was. Not a problem. It was a tunnel, and it was going into New York City; the rest would be elementary. The New York City Fire Department had already arranged for our hotel. Again, some of the details like that are fuzzy. After being temporarily lost, we found the hotel. Drove the car down the ramp in the parking garage. When we got out of the car with the luggage, ready to make the trip up the ramp with us, I looked back at the parked car, and I knew I did not want to move it until it was time to head back to Kentucky. The stained glass would be fine in the car until Aaron and I would pick it up the next day for the presentation.

What is not fuzzy is the care we received from the Fire Department of New York City. I am reminded again as I write this part of the story that a part of Phillip's legacy started from a ladder company of New York City. The e-mail from the New York Fire Department to Iraq, and now in New York, to present a stained glass window depicting the three firemen raising the American flag over the Twin Towers rubble of 9/11. This is what legacy is all about, through our remembrance of how our heroes made a difference in our lives, by the things we do in honor of their sacrifices. We owe them so much. I heard a prayer offered on behalf of our fallen: "If they could speak, I believe they would say to you, 'You are our voices now. Never forget.'" As I write these words, my heart understands that not forgetting is a living testimony passed on from generation to generation as a mission that has to endure if we are to remain a free nation.

Can you picture an image in your mind of me and my son carrying the stained glass window from the parking garage to a waiting vehicle a couple of blocks down the street to take us to fire department headquarters? I had no idea other than the fire department's public affairs woman would meet us in front of the hotel Aaron and Diana are staying the night in. When we reached the rest of the family, we saw a New York Police van parked at the curb in front of them. As Aaron and I reached the rest of the family, the two police officers stepped out of the van. They walked up to me and Aaron and asked if I was Mr. George. I answered, "Yes, but I didn't do it." I was only trying to being funny. I think I really did say that; however, my kids would probably tell me my memory is just getting old. They explained that they were there to take the glass and us to the fire department headquarters. They strapped the glass in the backseat of the van. Then we all got in and started the trip to the fire department headquarters. What none of us expected was that before the officer behind the wheel pulled the van into traffic, the emergency lights had been turned on and the siren wailed as he pulled the van from the curb into New York City traffic.

How awesome was that? With lights and siren, we made it to the fire department headquarters in no time. Not a problem, right?

Now that our police escort ended in front of the fire department headquarters, we were next taken up an elevator and into a huge conference room, with Aaron and me carrying the stained glass. A young lady entered the room and introduced herself as the chief's assistant. She told us that the chief was running late. He had a busy schedule with the 9/11 anniversary. She took the time to offer us something to drink and brought in a plate of snacks. She stood in front of the massive windows looking out over the city; then she pointed out where the Twin Towers once stood and told us how she was standing in this very spot on that horrific morning. Can you imagine carrying that image with you for the rest of your life? Especially knowing now the cost of life taken that day. This brings to my mind the thought that evil takes lives and good gives life. This thought will be with me for as long as my mission in life goes.

We waited for the fire chief for about an hour, and that was OK because it was 9/11 and his schedule was understandably busy. It was an honor simply to be here to honor those taken by the evil perpetrated on a city and its innocent citizens, and it was an honor that our warriors were a part of this mission. At 1400 hours, the chief appeared in the conference room with a photographer. The small ceremony was short, but the mission was completed, and big blessings do come in small packages. After all, this mission is not about me. It is all about those who gave and served a city and a nation.

After the ceremony concluded, we experienced a terrific treat when we escorted by a fire department van to the Empire State Building. We were whisked to the top on the VIP express, avoiding the wait in the long line of the regular elevators that opened onto the observation deck. With two Nikons around my neck, I could hear Phillip's "Oh, good grief, Dad." As we sped our way to the top, I could feel my anticipation as a photographer building. If you have never seen the sunset over the Hudson River, it is a sight that your eyes will bless your soul with. Once again, God was in control. We spent four days in New York as guests of the fire department. They would send a van by each morning to pick us up and be with us for the entire day.

CHAPTER 12

Tragedy in the Early Morning

I will never forget that particular morning. Nothing was different as I unlocked the front door to the office. As you know by now, I drink a lot of joe, so I had a pot on a stand behind me at the desk. We were just about ready for that first cup when the phone rang. Now that was out of the ordinary. It was a call from operations. They needed me to go to the far mess hall with my camera. There had been a fire, and they needed photos of the damage. It sounded urgent. Besides, getting to the scene of something of this nature imperative to getting the best photo details possible before the scene would become less preserved as time passed and foot traffic through the area increased. We would grab the camera bag with the extra lenses in it. Leaving a fresh pot of joe was not something I did unless the matter at hand was really pressing, and this one was.

We had a real photo investigation to do. Driving to the scene, all kinds questions would come to my mind. All I had at this time was which mess hall it was and nothing more. I knew this was one of the earlier constructed mess halls, they were huge canvas tents designed for temporary use on a FOB (forward operating base).

When shooting something that could involve a large area and great heights, it was a real advantage to have a number of lenses, depending on what you were focusing on. I did not even have a chance to make a fresh pot of joe. I got a call from the front office. I needed to get one of our mess halls as soon as possible with my camera. There had been a fire, and they wanted photos of the damage. We got into the vehicle and headed toward the mess hall. We had keys to a vehicle solely for our use for getting around Camp Speicher.

En route, my mind tried to build a set of guidelines from which I would work. That way, I would not have to slow down to think about these things once on the fire scene. This was our first assignment of this urgency. We could feel like a real photographer/investigative type. Well, maybe that is a little overreaching, but we did feel it was the most legitimate of the assignments we have had to date. As we parked in the parking area some couple hundred feet from the mess hall, we could see evidence of the damage the fire had caused as we walked toward the canvass structure. One of the first things we would notice was Camp Speicher's fire trucks. From what we could see immediately, the fire had been out for some time. This was evident by the number of people milling about the scene. Half of them probably had no need to be there as they could not add any expertise to the situation at hand. Self-importance has always been a point of curiosity for me. We had no problem entering the scene proper. Most of the people there knew me and were used to the cameras. That made my mission on all levels much easier. This was a blessing with KBR and the military. An officer stopped me one time. I showed him the letter I had from Major Green, and that satisfied him. Actually, it felt good to know he was alert.

As we stepped around the piles of broken slabs of concrete, the smell of smoke was heavy in the air and the foam from extinguishing the fire was everywhere I looked. Someone had overfilled a huge washing machine with suds of detergent. There were small pockets of smoke swirling from various areas as some items still smoldered. As we neared, the space between a charred fuel truck and a generator, we saw a lump on the ground covered with a fire blanket. No one had to tell us that a body was under the blanket. At least one worker had lost his life in this incident.

From that point, it was not hard to piece together some rudimentary facts. One thing a photographer has in his favor is we tend to see things in a photo frame, and we tend to see things others do not. Seeing the covered body of one of the fueling truck works tugged at my heartstrings. I would think of his family back home receiving that notice of death. Because I knew that person would have family somewhere. The weight of receiving the notification of the death of a loved one could weigh heavy on my heart. The memory of that phone call home, only to find out that Phillip died in Afghanistan, was still very fresh in my mind. I was on an assignment with a real mission, so we will press on. We paused to take a couple of photos of items that may or may not be of interest to the investigation later on. In this day of digital images, it was better to trash more than you kept than not have one that might make a difference in finding the cause. I was fine with doing my job as photographer, until I saw a couple of the firefighters come out from behind one of the parked fire trucks. Then there was that overwhelming pain from the depths of my heart that only God could reach.

All I could do was stand still and know that God is God and that this unreachable place in my heart that caused such pain belonged to His Providence. That pain would grip my heart at times without warning, as it did now. You see, Phillip wanted to be a firefighter when he got out of the Marine Corps. He was about a year from that time when he gave his life in Afghanistan. There is no doubt he would have made a good firefighter. Now we see one more dot to connect to Forever 22. I knew most of the Speicher firefighters; I would shoot their training session from time to time. You'll catch some of those photos on the website.

I had the safety department lead come up to me; I knew him from being out photographing the construction projects. I told him that my office had sent me to do a digital record of the incident. He showed me around and explained what had happened, as they knew it to that point. I realized that I was fortunate to get the information I was being given. It would help us narrow our focus and look for certain things. Apparently, the fire started with the scheduled refueling of an external fuel tank. The fire spread quickly when the explosion occurred. The canvass walls of the mess hall, once splattered with flaming diesel, quickly went up in flames. They are used throughout our military bases in Iraq and are the best alternative in a war zone to a hard structure being available. They were quick and temporary; temporary could stretch into years if required.

My heart went out to the two men who worked the fuel truck. The one under the blanket was the American expat, and the Indian helper was in a cash unit and would die later of the injuries he sustained. We would stay focused on the mission at hand, and I learned quickly that I could overcome my emotions that wanted to surface when I focused on the mission by the grace of God. He strengthens me in all things. As I walked about taking photos, I felt confident in what I was doing. Do you remember how we have seen how God uses experiences from our past to help us accomplish a part of the present? Well, I did not think about it until I started writing this book.

When I was in the army, I managed to take a number of courses in law enforcement from Hagerstown Junior College. The classes were held on the base at Fort Ritchie, Maryland. One of those courses dealt with the forensics of an investigation and the importance of the chain of evidence. That training kicked in, as did my work in electronics for eight years in the army, allowing me to understand the importance of grounding, which was a much pounded-on issue for KBR in safety meetings and in those jobs that required the grounding of equipment. With those dots connecting for me as a photographer, I think I was able do a much better job. With what I knew as an electronics technician, we would find ourselves paying particular attention to the rear side of the fuel truck for evidence of whether the grounding line had been attached. Especially since there was no evidence that there may have been some problem with following the refueling procedures. We made our way to the side of the truck, where we found the grounding wire still connected to the fueling tank's grounding point. After being satisfied we had enough photos, we thanked everyone for their corporation and started making our way back to our vehicle.

On the way to our vehicle, we came upon the large pile of chunks of concrete we had passed on the way in. I wanted to park my bottom there for a few minutes and go over that last hour or so. I did not want to leave any bases uncovered. We shared a huge chunk of concrete with a female soldier. She was a staff sergeant and was the chaplain's assistant. It was easy to see that she was upset. As we talked, I shared with her that the pain of death touches the heart in ways that probably nothing else can, and I think especially so since she worked in the chaplain service. This too was a part of God teaching my heart. God was teaching my heart the importance of listening to the hearts of others rather than just hearing the words they were speaking. This was a gift that God had blessed Phillip with during his short twenty-two years. This too brings us to a latter connection with Forever 22.

When we returned to the office, we downloaded the photos and burned copies to a disc for area operations. In fact, it was not long before we got a call from operations tell us that CID, the army's criminal investigation department, wanted copies. That brought back memories of my army days at Fort Ritchie when I would repair the CID radios. When the uniforms showed up, we had a great conversation, especially when I told them about repairing the first cell phone that belonged to the CID. Life was good when the dots connected. This would be by far the most serious of our assignments.

KBR held a memorial service for the expat. A friend of his asked if I could make a memorial photo for the service. It was my honor to do so. I used the sunset and tower as the backdrop.

CHAPTER 13

Mission to Iraq Comes to an End

The time spent in the KBR orientation center established the fact that this would not be a lifetime job. That fact was very often a side note to whatever information handed out at the time. The very nature of war would dictate the time of all things that evolved around it. Once we were on the ground in Iraq and realized that we were on a mission God had put us on and the need for a job paying good wages became the vehicle for the mission. With both the job and the mission we had to do to the best of our abilities, God would hold us responsible.

I remember someone telling me when we first arrived at Camp Warhorse that when the day came to pack up and go home arrived, we would know it. We can say at this point, "You know what, I think he was right." The new year had just gotten started; with each night I would lay my head down, I needed God's wisdom as much as ever for what was troubling my heart. The mornings following those nights would not produce an answer as quickly as we had seen in the past. As I sat at my desk during those early morning hours sipping that cup of joe and pondering the thing that weighed on my heart, I knew without a doubt that the answer would be there when it was time.

My thoughts would turn to Phillip. Making a difference, like a thread in the eye of a needle would find itself stitching the dots together. How he had become such a huge part of my being in Iraq, from the beginning when I had no idea that there would ever be a connection to what I did there to his life. Now the mission was the guiding factor that governed my life. The mission did not take us off the rails when it was time to consider the job we were there to do. In fact, it went hand in hand with the mission, as a vehicle it. We have talked about this before—how God works with us where we are.

I really had no idea what would be in store for me when I got home. God had not given me an insight to the vision He had something for me, and I knew He would. I just had to get home and lay my head down and count on His wisdom. I did know that Phillip's legacy was a part of whatever mission I would be on.

One morning, while I was having my morning cup of joe and my pondering time, I realized a small piece of the answer to my prayer. The work at Camp Speicher had come to that point we found ourselves at when we departed Camp Warhorse. The construction projects were ending with the ones already started, and now they were well on their way to completion within days. As you walked with me at Camp Warhorse, this is a phase that the contract KBR has with the Department of Defense that changes the dynamics of the work considerably. The workforce is reduced in all areas of operation, some more than others. This was just the nature of the beast, and what that produces in the nature of people trying to hang on to their jobs for so many reasons, chief among them being that they had adjusted their lifestyle to their income in Iraq, knowing fully well in their minds they would never make anywhere near that at home.

I could hear Phillip's response to this problem: "Oh, good grief, that was stupid." Phillip was very frugal with the money he earned. Therein lay a part of the problem some of these folks faced; they did not really earn the money deposited in their accounts each month. Life has a natural way of extracting from the greedy and those who take without giving back when they have the means to do so. We have seen how blessed we have been in our walk through the time at Camp Warhorse and at Camp Speicher. When your eyes and heart are set on trying to make a difference in whatever way, you can according to your own abilities, and God can magnify those efforts.

After our morning routine, we would still go to the mess hall for breakfast, still the most important meal of the day for this farm boy, even though I had not been on a farm since I got out of high school. Phillip used to say, "Dad, your taste buds are shot from eating too much squirrel growing up." We would usually leave the mess hall on our daily tour to shoot the projects going on that we knew about. We normally managed to stay away from the office as much and as long as possible.

The afternoons would be the time that we would stop by the different crafts to shoot whatever candid photo ops might pop up. That time of the day we used to build relationships was also that time in the day when people needed some cheering up. With the advantage of truly believing "this is a day the Lord hath made; I will rejoice and be glad in it," my spirits soared high most of the time. This made a real difference many times in the rest of the day for people. This no doubt was a part of our mission as we went about our job.

I still was able to get out and around the base at sunrise and sunset with my camera. These were my very special times to see the handiwork of God, his paintbrush on the canvas of the world I lived in. During these times, I had God's assurance that all was well with my soul. You will be able to see some of these photos on my website.

As the days would march on through the new year, and as the end of January was approaching, we can feel in our hearts that our mission in Iraq will come to an end soon. At this point, it is not up to us; God will let us know when it is time to pack it up and go home. There are those times in life when you can hold on to something a little bit longer than you should. Only to find out that there is no real benefit to anyone in the end. In fact, you may even miss the train to where you should be going either altogether or at least be where you should be on the late side of time. You and I will keep our hearts in tune with our mission, and when that time comes, we will board that big bird for a last homeward-bound flight with a grateful heart. That is another neat thing about doing it God's way—you can come to a fork in the road and take it without remorse.

As we closed out January and February started, I could see the end of our time coming. I could feel this in my spirit, and this part of my overall mission was coming to that point. There was no doubt the mission was not ending. The mission we were on was one that would be my mission for a lifetime, a mission I will finish against my final sunset as Phillip finished his. I decided one night while sipping a cup of joe in my hooch in late February 2007 to call it an end and go home. It was time to continue my mission at home. Can you identify with a point in your life like this, when you know it is time to move on? Hanging on to a thing out of fear is not living life to its fullest according to the abundance of life given us. It certainly is not where God would have us. It also makes us miserable company.

Time at Camp Speicher Comes to an End

As a photographer, you are always looking for those photo ops. They were becoming harder to find. The operations office changed dramatically after Stephanie left. A person as woeful, incapable, and overbearing as an individual replaced her. It did not take her very long to learn not to like me. I certainly did not like here either. That is unusual for me; this is one of those times. I understood the situation I found myself in; I still was not in a job position as a photographer/historian. Technically, I was an operations specialist.

You and I know better than that. After a few rounds with her, I found the answer I was looking for one morning while sipping my morning cup of joe. It was time to go home, and the number one reason was that I could no longer effectively do my job and be productive at it. That was important to me, as it was an issue with integrity and not just keeping a paycheck. The second thing was that as the vehicle for the mission changed dramatically, the mission stalled at this point as well, like a powerless boat lurching about in rough seas.

After my early morning routine, I went to HR to start the process. Once the paperwork was started, it was the point of no return. In this case, if this was what was in my heart, as a reasonable look at the answer to my prayer, then why would I want to change it? Remember, when you and I first started this walk together, we were at the starting point of a new direction. And because my heart had decided I had done it my way long enough.

We will not spend a lot of time here because it would be so counterproductive. We are on our way home; it has been an incredible thirty-three months. God has blessed my soul tremendously. It is time to take the connected dots and the continuing connecting dots on the mission from home now.

As we turn the lights out on our time in Iraq, we can look back and say, "All is well with my soul."

CHAPTER 14

Home from Iraq and on the Road

On this cold February day at Camp Speicher, I would for the last time sit at my desk and sip on my last cup of joe made in my hooch, and I would have my last pondering session of the "when I lay my head down" after a good night's sleep. As I sat and sipped the brew in my cup and ponder the depths of my heart, I wondered at the decision I had made. My heart and my spirit were set in agreement; that fact made facing the results of the decision a lot easier. I was making the right decision. My mission in Iraq had ended. Without a mission, there would only be a paycheck to stay for, and that was not the reason God brought me to Iraq in the beginning.

I would leave the coffeemaker in the hooch for the next resident. It was a 220V make; I could not make it work back home, and it would not be worth the shipping fees anyhow, regardless of the months of joy it may have brewed. I locked the hooch door for the last time. I took the time to stand on the sidewalk and take a final look back. When I turned toward the operations office, I knew all was well with my soul.

As we approach the office to get that final ride to the hill, as the camp area was commonly referred to, and a lot of the time by those less than privileged workers of the area. There was a feeling of peace that settled over me and saturated my entire body. Before I entered the office, I stood there for a bit to let it either pass or sink in. I shivered from it. I knew it was not from the cold morning air because I wore T-shirts throughout the winters in Iraq and seldom put on a jacket. This brought back some fond memories of Phillip, because he was the same way. It could not have been anything other than the grace of God at that time. When it passed, I walked into the office, and most of the workers were at the mess hall for breakfast. We would sign the travel log and wait for someone to take us to the hill. I remember when we were at Camp Warhorse, and I think it may have been Ralph, who told me that when it came time to go home, you would wake up one morning and decide that it is time. That is pretty much what happened about four days ago.

The flight from Camp Speicher on February 27 to Baghdad would be sometime around 1300 hours. We arrived at the travel operations to check in or out; whatever you want to call it, we did it. I knew most everyone in all of the offices, though the levels of friendship varied. Friendships for me never developed on what someone did for me or could do for me. A friendship formed based on mutual understanding and respect for each other. It has been forty-four months since we landed at Baghdad International Airport—are you ready to walk with me on this journey home? We are beyond the point of return, and I still feel in my heart that this is right. This would be the last time we will visit this question. We shipped seven large packages home, and still we have left many things behind.

The waffle maker I left behind—how do you take a tradition away if there is someone to carry on with it? That is very much unlikely, as the mind-set of most folks was such that if it did not benefit them, then they did not do it. I could not imagine living my life that way. Our departure meant the end of the photos for the safety meetings because no one else wanted to step up to the plate. That is OK, because we are all different, and that was a part of my mission, not anyone else's.

We would finish the checking-in process through security and other offices. Now we just had to wait. We would catch a base bus from the bus stop at the travel center to go to the mess hall for the last time at Camp Speicher. If you are reading this and thinking I am missing it, you would be mistaken. What I am feeling is coming from a very grateful heart for the time I am allowed to spend here on God's mission. What needs to be understood about this point in time is that when God says it is time to move on, then it is time to move on, and we must rejoice in it. As we leave the last new mess hall to open on the base, many memories come up. Then once again, in retrospection, we made a difference—that was our mission, and we did it while doing our job to the best of our abilities. "This is a day the Lord hath made; I will rejoice and be glad in it." That mind-set made its presence known and echoed in my heart as we stepped onto the bus to return to the travel center. That is not what it was officially called, but we will have to do these some eight years later. I will not let anyone or anything steal my joy.

At 1300 hours, the names are called off a fly roster, and we boarded the bus for the trip to the airfield. Everything today would be the last time in this place. There was no doubt in the heart that we were still on a mission; it would just be in a different location.

One difference I would have to get used to when we get home is not having a job that will take some getting used to. Because I really did not know a lot ahead of time about the mission, I had not given a lot of thought to it. I did know that God would let us know. One last look back and for the last time, and all was well with my soul.

We boarded the airplane. There was no seating order; you just found a seat and took it. The flight to Baghdad was less than an hour, if my memory serves me right. As we sat there, the engines finally came to life, and the plane started moving forward in the runway. We had been in this spot many times since first arriving in Iraq, but so much had changed. Flights out of Speicher to Baghdad had been flying about two years now. The days of helicopter rides to get us from Speicher to Baghdad were no gone.

It is strange what one can think of when taking off, while in the air, and during landing. Sometimes the thoughts are so frivolous they are not worth remembering. The flight from Camp Speicher to Baghdad just rather happened. One minute we were still on the ground at Camp Speicher, and then it seemed all of a sudden, we were on the ground in Baghdad.

On this trip, after checking in with operations, I did not go to the food court or the PX. I did not want to have to struggle with extra things to carry and keep up with going home. I think what I wanted more than anything was some quiet time. Are you kidding me? That is one commodity not available. I had it figured out, though, from the many trips I'd taken before. I would get some sleep from about 2000 hours to 0100 the next morning, and then I would get up with my laptop and go to the area set aside for reading or using my laptop. There was no access to the Internet, unless you had a KBR computer, which I had to give back when I checked out at Camp Speicher. That was

OK; I had many photos, and I needed to edit a lot. I was just learning Photoshop CS2; that software had cost me six hundred dollars. I never thought I would see the day I would be able to afford something like that. Never thought I would see the day I would have a job like the one I just left. Now you tell me there is no God who is not ready to join you right where you are.

My thoughts would turn to Phillip and the rest of the family. There really was no time when I would think about Phillip without the rest of the family. I had always been grateful for this, and I was, as my fingers stroked the keys of the keyboard. My heart overfilled with joy when I thought about my family and how I had been blessed beyond comparison. I had time during this early morning of relative quiet to sip on a cup of joe that had been in the maker way too long. It was a joe, and we have learned to be grateful for all things. I was able to think back on the projects we did—the glass classes and the memorials. I thought about how what we did and why we did it made a difference in the lives of those people. What a blessing to take home with us. We have discovered that making a difference is to be a part of our mission. What a blessing to realize that while getting to do a job that we loved and the joy to get up to each day and know that we were also on a mission given us by God. It truly has been one awesome experience, and I am so glad the you walked through it with me and will continue to walk with me as we discover so much more about ourselves and the mission we would continue once home. Believe it or not, most of the time, traveling through Camp Liberty, I keep to myself with my thoughts. For one thing, I could never be a part of the constant whining about the most superficial things.

Roll call is at 0330 this morning, and that meant that if your name happened to be on it, you would be flying. Guess what, we are on the fly-out-today list. One night at Camp Liberty is a cakewalk. It is when you have to spend two or more days stuck here that the nerves really have to be put in check.

When I stepped off that plane on US soil at Bush Intercontinental Airport, I knew I had no plans of leaving it in ten days, memories from Vietnam to California came to mind. What a feeling. I think one of the first things my heart was grateful for was the absence of sand on the ground and in the air. Then my eyes were blessed with so much green, even at the end of February. It truly was good to be back home.

Transitioning Was Not as Easy as I Thought It Would Be

I was used to sixteen- to eighteen-hour days in Iraq seven days a week. The first few weeks home were hard; I had a hard time finding something to do for eight hours, so transitioning was, let's say, a task in patience. I knew I had the time to work on this. My morning routine was only in part the same. I got up at zero dark thirty, made fresh pot of joe, and, while sipping the brew, I would ponder on the day. Only I did not have a clear direction to ponder. That point in my return had since faded from my memory; I know I had not done a lot of anything for a while.

For each morning I would wake up in the apartment, I simply would not feel right. I felt better when I was in the hooch than in this apartment. I have never liked apartments. When you have such a dislike and you have a choice of not having to be there, then guess what, you will correct the situation at some point. I would leave the apartment each morning, make the drive, maybe eighteen miles to the house, and spend the day there.

I had started on remodeling the house while I was in Iraq. That did not work out so well. Penny and Sara moved into an apartment. It simply was not in Penny to oversee the remodeling. I called it off after trying to manage it from Iraq and the times I was home on R&R. I suppose that was a lesson learned. If your wife is not interested in or doesn't have the experience to take on such a project, then do not expect her to do it.

I had to replace my power tools; they had been stolen, all of them. I had no idea who did this; all I know is they wiped me out. I have less use for a thief than any other type of person. I put a list together and made a trip to Home Depot. As I shopped to replace my tools, I thought of Phillip. We spent a lot of time in Home Depot buying material or tools for a job. I remember, when he drove to get us there he would always, without fail, park as far away from the entrance as he could get. I would ask him why he insisted on doing that, and he simply replied with that Phillip grin and soft-spoken voice: "It's good for those old knees of yours." Then as we were walking toward the store, he would hand me the keys to the van. "Why are you handing me the keys, son?" I would ask. "Because they don't belong to me," he would reply in all seriousness.

With the tools replaced, one of my first tasks was to finish my cave, or office, my room in the garage; that had been started by someone else. I needed somewhere other than that apartment to have my joe and pondering time. Every man needs a cave; in fact, we all, man or woman, need a place we can get away without having to leave the property for that personal time. My cave had the interior wall on the garage side kind of framed, so that is where I started. It ended up measuring 8' x 17'. I wish I had taken a little more and made it a couple of feet wider. I have been using it for about seven years now, and it has served me well. I have put a lot of time out here. It is my cave, as I call it, and so does everyone else. A friend will call out, "Are you in your cave? I will stop by." I suppose in a way, it sort of made me feel that I needed to be somewhere.

Anytime a person transitions from a situation that covers months on end and beyond, you are prone to experiencing a resistance to those changes in habits and lifestyle that need to be made at the time. By no means would I attempt to compare being a civilian in Iraq to the level of PTSD our warriors experience. I know there is no comparison between the two based on the time I spent in Nam. However, what I am saying is that you do not have to be in a war zone for this to be a culprit in keeping you from readjusting back into the normal life you had before. Retirees experience this upon leaving a job that they had been doing years. This brings home the point of having a solid foundation of faith. From that foundation, you can know that you can face the challenges that change presents head on.

To my advantage, I have learned many lessons well in the thirty-three months spent in Iraq. I have learned to wait for God's direction for the plan, and when it is given, I get up and start with one foot in front of the other. At this point, we can actually be so excited when understanding this is living "this is a day the Lord hath made; I will rejoice and be glad in it" to its fullest meaning and purpose.

The first few weeks were hard because I had no idea what I was going to do or where my mission would take me. I did know I would not go back to doing what I was doing before Iraq. That idea was completely out of the question—not a possibility I could think about, one of the most significant reasons being the fact that my body was worn out. I could not keep up with the demand of the job to do that kind of work anymore. I can just hear Phillip saying, "Oh, good grief, Dad."

I was confident that God had sent me on a mission that took me to Iraq and now back home to continue this same mission. I have not forgotten you are still with me. I guess I just needed to get some of those personal things out of the way. In Iraq, the many lessons my heart learned were a result of the many experiences I had, which are too many to be counted. Rediscovering my love for photography, for one, I think at times that God just tossed this in as a blessing. I had entertained the idea of making a living from photography, and it had to be one of the most appreciated benefits of being there. I have taken thousands of photos and need to organize them at some point so they can be shared. I had thought about the possibility of making photography an income source; I knew I could make money at it. I simply did not get the green light to make that work. I had most of the equipment I needed, and I did some shooting but there simply was not that feeling that this would be my niche. My passion for photography was still there, but not as an income source. It was going to take early mornings, fresh pots of joe, and a lot of pondering going on in the cave to get me on track. I had several advantages at this point; I did not have to have a job for the income. I had the most potent tool at my disposal. I had "when I lay my head down," which followed me everywhere these days. I would not leave home without it, so to speak.

I managed to get the new set of kitchen cabinets from the middle of the living room floor to hanging on the walls and the base cabinets installed. Next was the countertop. I installed tile on it. I really enjoyed doing the work, but there was something missing. I simply could not put my finger on it. I would think of Phillip a lot while trying to work on the house, but the memories were encouraging, especially when I heard the "Oh, good grief, Dad" in my heart.

Each morning, I would wake up with my cup of joe and time of pondering, I got nowhere. I did not get frustrated because I knew God had an answer.

CHAPTER 15

PERSERVERENCE FINDS PURPOSE

Finding purpose in life can be an elusive quality even when life is as close to normal as it can be. Trying to find purpose after a tragedy a strikes, and you find yourself with a loss that cannot be comprehended in any sense seems to be a futile effort much less becoming a mission. Finding that purpose takes on an even more elusive dimension as perseverance is called for beyond any that we may have in us . It is for that reason that reaching beyond one's self reaching out for God can that be found. It is when we stretch out our hands to God that we find while we cannot reach Him, He is more than capable of reaching and touching us. For my family and me there was definitely a sense of indescribable and incomprehensible part of our lives torn from the fabric of our family. Life tends to stop making sense for a time until that point of realizing the foundation we stood on during the storm is still there. We can still reach out to God and know that He can hear our hearts, then reach down to grab hold of us with his sufficiency's.

I have seen my family handle the loss of Phillip from the time the notification was given by the Marine Corp, through the blurred days that led to the time of laying him to rest as a Marine, a comrade, a son, a brother, a grandson, a nephew and a friend. I watched the days that turned into months, then eventually into years now. In the beginning our reaction was most likely not different from that I have seen of other families who lost their warrior before and since then.

What I have seen as a difference is in the solid foundation that was there for the family to stand on, supporting each other during and after the storm that came to our household. They knew deep within their hearts what they believed and stood on that belief then and to this day. I have since that tragic day seen so many families literally fall apart with the absence of a solid foundation to stand on. The causes range from depression so deep that the individual cannot cope, many times the individual will turn to alcohol to try burring the pain, only to find themselves with an additional pain added to what they already are experiencing. I have seen a multitude of other harmful actions come from the losses suffered.

Having seen a number of families react to their loss, I count my family blessed to have chosen a strong belief in God and that He is real and most definitely operates in our personal lives. I have also come to understand that families who also have that strong faith come to find purpose for continuing a strong love for the life they have because of the life their loved one gave.

I cannot prove in any way other than let others see Him through His working in my life. No words can match what the actions of one's life can speak. This is why I become so adamant about knowing what you believe, why you believe and believe it with passion so that in that hour of need you cannot be persuaded to abandon your faith. During my storm and to this day my foundation stands intact.

Phillip gave his life, I think it is important that we keep in mind men and women like Phillip gave their lives on our behalf. Friends who were grandparents told me that grandson had decided to decide to sign up for the army delayed entry program. Given what was happening in Afghanistan and Iraq at the time their reaction was not in favor of the choice he had made. Shortly after the young man made his choice, they had to attend a funeral of one of his young friends who had been killed in action. Standing beside the coffin at the viewing, their grandson turned to them and especially to the grandmother and asked, "Why is it okay for him to be there instead of me", the message struck home.

They were people of faith and had that strong foundation on which to live their lives. I often think of them and this time in their lives. I also think of the young grandson and his answer to the call of duty, just as Phillip and all the others throughout our history have answered the call of duty.

I have found that understanding the need for individuals to answer the call of duty helps me to find purpose in the sacrifices made. There are so many stories to be told of our young heroes, the phrase so often used; "all gave some and some gave all" applies to anyone who has ever served.

I think at this point in my writing I would hope that you fully understand that it was my faith in believing without doubt that God was my God and He was with me always. The two themes that I see in writing this book are connecting the dots of our lives and making a difference in life.

I have concluded that in order to find purpose for the rest of my life with the loss of my son, the words of King David of Old come to mind clearly; "but as for me and my household we will serve the Lord". In this scripture, I see choice; this is what we must all do when faced with the storms and circumstances of life. It was my choice and the choice of my family to believe that God had our backs so to speak. The continuance of this story is based on a faith that provides me and so many others with a foundation on which to stand and find purpose in live to its end.

Well, it is time for us to walk the toward the end of this story. As I continue to find purpose in my mission.

CHAPTER 16

Continuing the Quest for My Niche

In October 2007, we will find ourselves involved with a group that built custom homes with special features for our severely wounded. This mission would last for five years. This was a true blessing, and we will feel we are a part of something that will make a difference. With the need to know that what we are doing makes a difference, there is only one way, as we have learned throughout this walk together, to test the waters of any effort is to at least stick a foot in it. This organization and its mission seemed to fit what we were looking for to involve ourselves and carry out our mission at the same time. We will find out that it would be a way for us to get more directly involved. There are a lot of worthy causes, and as time goes on, there are a good many to stay clear of being in any way being a participant. The best remedy for this issue is "laying your head down.". Wake up the next morning early enough for a cup of joe and pondering time before committing yourself. You have to find where God wants you to fit in. If what you are doing does not fit the mission God set you on, then you may enjoy what you are doing, but there will be that sense of being off track until you find it.

I had one guiding light at the path of my feet that would light my way. I always kept in mind that a big part of my mission was to honor not just my son but also all of our sons and daughters who gave all, those who served, and those currently serving. This gave the search for making a difference a very special place in my heart.

Late October of 2007, Penny asked if I could go to a Gold Star Mothers meeting with her to take some photos of the meeting. Not a problem. I have not used that phrase in a while, and it feels good. We find everyone sitting at a conference table eating. Afterward, the group's president called the meeting to order. The meeting was conducted according to the Rules of Roberts, from the start of the meeting to its adjournment. There was a guest introduced as Carla Patton, who worked for the Energy Corporation of America (ECA). She was there by invitation for her expertise in fundraising. She would offer guidance and suggestions to the group, to help the Gold Star Mothers with ideas as to how to run successful fundraisers. When Carla talked about how she was organizing a sporting clays tournament as a January event that would benefit an organization building specially adapted homes for our wounded warriors, she had my full attention. The concept and its benefactors absolutely grabbed my interest. Carla gave me her contact information. This was possibly an organization that we could be a part of and make a difference.

I started working with Carla on the project. I found that I was able to get them a Huey helicopter that would take folks on rides from the event site. I was at a Texas Honor Ride event when I talked to the pilot of a Huey helicopter; they had flown it in for a static display. At the same event, there was a WWII 6th Cav reenactment group. I was given their contact info, and when I talked to the president of the group, his answer to the invitation to be at our event was yes. It turned out that the Huey had a young volunteer working with it, who was Phillip's best friend in high school. What a dot God connected there.

The event turned out to be a huge success, in spite of the fact that it rained for about three weeks solid prior to the event. The location had already been used as a sporting clays tournament site on part of a ranch located on the Brazos River, in Fulshear, Texas. It was a perfect environment for our event. At the end of the event, we could feel that we had made a difference according to the mandates of our mission. We would work on this event with Carla and an unbelievable team of volunteers for about two and half months prior to the event. We found a real connection with the event that blessed our hearts as a result. Enjoying the folks we had the pleasure of working with and get to know was a plus. Carla stressed to the max, and I would tell her that everything was going to be OK, but for people to rely solely on their own abilities and wisdom; this was not a comfort because they did trust only in their own abilities and wisdom.

On the opening day, she had given in to the idea that her company would not want to do another one. Before the end of the day, people were asking her about the next year's event. Telling her how much they enjoyed and agreed with the cause supported by the tournament. This goes to part of my point in writing this book: faith in God allows us to reach far beyond what we are capable of doing ourselves. His wisdom is far beyond any that we may possess. I truly believe God wanted this event to be successful. The tournament and its volunteers made a huge difference in the lives of some of our wounded warriors.

We will have four more years of tremendously successful tournaments. Many hearts blessed, as people were able to make a difference in the lives of some of those who had given so much to this nation. To those who say "Well, I did not serve," my question to them is, would they have if they had heard the call? And the answer is always yes. I believe that answer. I believe that answer because I hear the heart that the answer is coming from. I will try to get them to understand that the warrior needs the patriot. They are the reason a veteran becomes a veteran; they are the reason we have men and women serving now, and they are the reason we have heroes who have given the ultimate.

We had the tournament at the ranch location for three years, and then the American Shooting Center offered to host the event. There was a trade-off in doing this. We lost a lot of the atmosphere offered by the ranch's surrounding woods and the winding Brazos River. On the other hand, we gained a meeting place for planning in the months ahead of the event and the big gain was the better and bigger availability of the parking.

As we worked through the tournaments, it was hard to see the connection to Forever 22 until I started writing this book. As you and I continue to walk through this story, connections are easier to see now than when they were actually happening. We have no problem realizing everything we do connects in some way to everything down the road. I have learned that we praise the Lord and move on because it all will connect whether we see the connection then or not. I would not miss one year of the five tournaments.

The second year was a special blessing—for my family and the Patriot Guard Riders. I met General Wells during a Memorial Day event at the Houston National Cemetery. God will always have the people you need in front of you when they are needed. General Wells was needed; he gave me his contact card and said if he could ever do anything for us to just let him know. I gave him a call one day to ask him if he could attend the sporting clays event. He said he would be glad to. Then I asked him if he would be interested in retiring the Never Forget flag that covered Phillip from Germany to Dover. His reply was a resounding yes. The flag at that time had been with the Patriot Guard Riders on many of their missions for our KIAs who came back home from Iraq and Afghanistan. It was on missions the Patriot Guard Riders did in tribute to WWII, the Korean War, and the Vietnam War. It was also there for fallen law enforcement, firefighters, and EMS personnel lost in a helicopter crash. The flag had the honor of standing tall for so many missions. The Never Forget flag has flown in the Huey from the sporting clays venue in Fulshear to Ellington Field. Will Bowers did this in honor of Phillip, his best friend. Will had it flown in a Vietnam F-4 from Ellington to Randolph Air Base in San Antonio, then flown in an Apache at Ellington Field during the Houston Wings over Houston Air Show and at that air show. The ReMax skydiving team jumped the flag. Major Dan Rooney has flown it in an F-16 over Oklahoma. The most recent mission of the flag is that it went to Afghanistan with the aid of General Wells. The flag has a lot of history.

The Thursday night of our volunteer appreciation night, General Wells ran into a problem he could not shake loose in time to be able to make it through the traffic and then be able to make his appointment he had later on. When Carla told me that General Wells could not make it. I said to her, "Not a problem." How about if I can get Will to get him out to the site and take him back to Ellington by way of the Huey? Carla was the type who would not argue with you especially if she did not think an idea would work. I called Will, and he started working on it, he found another chopper to bring the general to the site, the Huey was not available. Again, it is a matter of thinking beyond yourself to make the seemingly impossible happen.

General Wells was a huge hit with the folks. He retired Phillip's flag from the Patriot Guard Riders, and that was a godsend because five of Phillip's marine comrades were there for the tournament. You and I have gotten to know the habit I have of saying "All is well with my soul."

The fall of the second year, I happened to be at the Hempstead, Texas, Watermelon Festival with the Patriot Guard Riders. Before the second year of the tournament, I happened to be at the Watermelon Festival in Hempstead, Texas with the Patriot Guard Riders. I was on the street shooting away when a godsend photo op appeared before my camera lens. What I saw was a group of cowgirls riding paint horses. What really caught my attention were the patriotic red, white, and blue western wear they had on. There was that huge tug on my heart.

Later, when I downloaded the photos and came across the photos of the Lone Star Cowgirls, the banner on their lead parade truck was very readable. There was no doubt that they would be a great addition to our event. I went to the website listed, got the contact information, and gave them a call. From that point on, they were in. These gals were so awesome leading the wounded warriors in with the Patriot Guards Riders following that second year of the sporting clays tournament. Those red, white, and blue outfits were right at home. God knows beyond any shadow of a doubt what works and what does not work. This was the result of keeping a mission on the front burner and being aware of an opportunity as God presented it.

The Southeast Patriot Guard Riders

You have seen the name *Patriot Guard Riders* quite a bit in the last few paragraphs because they have become such an important part of my life. Like so much of what has transpired over the last four years, that is where we are in this walk together. Writing this book has brought a huge understanding to my heart of how things happened and why they happened, if you will—the connecting of the dots. I do not have the answers to all things, but I do to a lot. I can see more clearly now the connection between the Patriot Guard Riders and Forever 22. I think one of the major connects with the Patriot Guard Riders is the fact that as Phillip's story was told, they would constantly encourage me to write about escorting Phillip home. My prayer is that I don't disappoint them. Being with the PGRs (as they are usually addressed during conversation and written correspondence) I do not think they know how much they have helped me in finally deciding to sit down and write this book. They have helped me understand more about the meaning of making a difference, as is conveyed in their slogan: "Standing for those who stood for us." It's folks like those of PGR who are there when you need support during those times you can't quite see the tree ahead of you for the forest. If you are a PGR member, thank you so much for your support and encouragement. You could be responsible in part for Forever 22.

I know I cannot even begin naming all of those who have made a difference. I will go through some of my fondest memories, and again, they are so many. Without a doubt, Jerry Turner and Joe Ace—they were my introduction to PGR, of all places in a hotel lobby in DC. Johnny Dee, I have an image of him kneeling beside Phillip's headstone that goes to the heart of why we do what we do. During that same time, there is the image of Penny, my wife, on the back of Big Sarge's bike. I am reminded of the times I was hanging out of Jerry's truck window shooting. Before I started taking the wall to events, I made as many missions as I could make. You guys have made a difference in my life.

The Texas Fallen Heroes Wall

October of 2010, we will find ourselves becoming involved with the Texas Fallen Heroes Memorial Wall. Since it is a traveling memorial, it's construction has to keep that fact in mind. Each panel is comprised of eighty 4x4 ceramic tiles on a plywood backing and a rich solid walnut trim. To date, the wall consist of fourteen individual panels. The first three are to honor WWII, Korean War, and Vietnam War veterans. Each panel bears information on the numbers killed in action and the number of wounded from each war. An introduction panel follows the three war panels. This panel introduces the KIA of the war in Afghanistan and the Iraq wars on terror. The dates on these panels are from the first KIA of Texas in 2002 to the current KIA of Texas in 2013. The panels are updated and repaired at the end and beginning of each year. When setup is complete on six tables with a table cover, it is thirty lineal feet of impressive honoring of our Texas fallen. In harmony with the mission I feel God has given me, this memorial makes a difference.

With a photo to accompany each name on an individual tile, each tile within that year becomes very special. Having my son's photo and name on the wall makes it very special to me, of course. Then the meaning of the traveling memorial reaches beyond that; it reaches that spot in the heart of those who stand in front of the wall. It is especially touching when a relative of the warrior on the wall points out their son or daughter, nephew or niece, maybe a cousin. A wife finds her husband, a mother her son, or a daughter locates her dad. A veteran finds a buddy with comments like "He took my place. I should have been on that mission. He died in my arms." I have heard the story a number of times from comrades. I have heard the pain, the taking blame that is not theirs to take. Survivor's guilt is a heavy load for someone so young to have to bear. I hear it in their hearts, as it weighs on them every day, not being able to get it out of their heads. My prayer, then, as a dad who has lost a son, is to be able to say to them with authority that it is a burden that is not theirs to carry. I want to reach out and let them know that we cannot live by what-ifs and if-I-had-onlys. Taking the blame that is not yours—what would your comrade say to that? Would you have done the same thing for your comrade? You know the reply is an unequivocal yes. It is no doubt the toll war has taken on us. We see and experience things that happen to human beings on both sides of the war that is so unimaginable that it terrorizes the mind and soul, sometimes beyond a lifetime. I think of the memorial wall as a healing wall. My mission with this wall is to make a difference.

If you stand in front of it and you do not know anyone personally, the memorial wall can educate you. When facing the names, and the photo above that name reminds you that the image you see could be your son or daughter, the neighbor's kid who possibly spent more time in your home than in his own. Maybe standing in front of that wall, you see the kids you taught in school or church. If you give your heart the time it needs, you will connect with the cost of your freedom. One time, I noticed a young girl at the opposite end of the wall. I could see that she was beginning to get emotional. I walked up to her and asked if she knew someone on the wall, and her response was "No sir." I told her what her heart just told me, that she understood the cost of her freedom, and she simply replied, "Yes, sir."

When we come to understand the price paid by so few for the remarkable freedoms we have, there should be a weight on our hearts in the form of honor, gratitude, and indebtedness. We can never repay the blank check our military men and women have written. The moment they gave their life on our behalf, the blank check was stamped "Debt paid in full." The debt we owe we can never repay, and there is no demand of a repayment, because the payment on our behalf was given freely and not as a loan. All that is required is honor and remembrance, which is our duty and responsibility. We acquire this without the option of participation as an obligation of respect and gratitude, anything less is nothing less than a shameful act of ingratitude and selfishness.

Each person I met and greeted while standing in honor of those on the wall is a tremendous blessing to my heart. As we walk through this part of what I have been doing with my time since 2010, I simply cannot imagine not being a part of the wall for the near future. The wall makes a difference to so many people in so many ways. Our schedule starts in April, as a rule, and ends the second Saturday of December with Wreaths Across America. During the course of about nine and a half months, we will set the wall up at close to sixty events. The wall has definite ties to Forever 22. The wall has become more than simply a traveling memorial. The wall offers a sense of remembrance for those who have loved ones on it as long as the wall moves from event to event.

A knowledge that they are not going to be forgotten because the wall is there making a difference in lives; therefore, those on the wall are making a difference. I think this is one of the biggest fears of the family and friends of the fallen. Displaying this awesome tribute to our fallen heroes is a part of my mission to honor the legacies of the men and women on the wall. I have been honored especially by having veterans visit the wall to find a buddy or someone they served with at some point. When I hear a serving warrior or a veteran say "He stood in for me, that should have been me on that wall," I can in turn share my story of Phillip and let them know that I truly understand their heart. I have shared time after time with warriors and veterans standing in front of the wall, and my heart has been humbled by the opportunity to make a difference in honor of my son and all of the sons and daughters on the wall. I have had the honor of sharing with the mothers and fathers of those whose images are on the wall. One other instance was that of a mother with her two young children kneeling in front of the wall as the mother pointed out their father. A wounded Special Forces veteran saw them, he knelt beside the children, and began to talk to them about how brave their daddy was. He would never be forgotten. This is a legacy built for those children. This is making a difference when he did not have to, or did he?

The two tile walls were the creation of Phil Darbone, who lived most of his life in Houston, Texas, and now lives in Louisiana. The creation of the ceramic tile wall came about when Phil buried his father who was a veteran. Out of his respect for his father's service and the service of others, he felt the heart call for the need to honor our present-day fallen heroes. Out of this passion, he created the ceramic tile wall with a photo and name of the fallen on individual four-inch tiles. His use of the tile was the result of considering the qualities of a number of options he could print an image on. None held the quality of printing on ceramic tile. In my opinion, Phil is a patriot, and this is his way of saying thank you to those young men and women who gave their all—that includes my son, who I am so proud to put on display that others might understand and connect with the cost of their freedom. So, to Phil and his family, from my heart goes a tremendous thank you for your patriotism.

American Exceptionalism

The dots connect. I first met this wounded warrior in Iraq at Camp Warhorse. Tell me God is not in our lives. He and I are friends, and he is a terrific mentor for other wounded warriors. He has created an organization that takes wounded warriors on fishing and hunting trips, and that gives them hope. Is not that what it's about—offering hope when there seems to be none? That is the mark of a warrior on a continuous mission. Buck Collins is a true American hero. Buck is more than that; you have been with me for a good while now that we have gotten to this part of the story. You know from your walk with me earlier that I tend to see the heart of a person; I tend to listen to the heart when I am listening to person who is speaking from the heart. God has blessed me, for sure. With Buck Collins, it is giving 110 percent. It is about making a difference in the face of heavy odds, that's what an exceptional American looks like making America exceptional.

I was once a soldier, and until my final sunset, making a difference is my mission. It is my goal. I will finish my mission as they have completed theirs as their final sunset came. As the vision of my mission becomes more defined, I am seeing that the vision to my mission is honoring the legacy of this nation's fallen heroes. Without them, we need to seriously ask, "Where and what would I be today?" We are on the path of our mission with a nwfound passion. That passion has to come from within the belly of the person the mission is given. No one else can have the passion for your mission that you must have. Others can have a passion for wanting to get involved because they agree with the premise of the mission based on the passion you show.

God has blessed me with so many good folks, one of them Phil Darbone. One of my earliest contacts was with an organization called Impact a Hero, who provides immediate and ongoing emotional and financial support for our severely wounded post–9/11 combat veterans and their families. I met Jim Hoelker, in 2008 when I was with the Patriot Guard Riders, providing a rolling tribute to the wounded from their hotel in Sugarland to Mercer Stadium just down the way. I was photographing the 5K run, and when it was over, Congressman Pete Olson, of District 22, introduced me to Jim as a Gold Star Dad. When I met Pete Olson in Friendswood, Texas, during a Fourth of July parade, he was then candidate Olson. When I met him, again at the Impact a Hero 5K run, he was Congressman Olson.

Penny and I attended our first gala and were seated at a table with the Patriot Guard Riders. From that point on, Impact a Hero has been one of my favorite organizations helping our wounded warriors and paying tribute to our fallen and their families. I remember meeting Jim Hoelker for lunch one day, and he presented me with an American flag that had flown in Afghanistan. I suppose what I would want folks to understand is that for the families of the fallen, after that KIA date, it is the actions of others who show their appreciation that perpetuate the memories of their fallen loved one and promotes their enduring legacy.

The following year, I would have the wall at the Sugarland Impact a Hero event. It would be at the event each year after that. I remember the second year we had the wall there, we set it up at Mercer Stadium early that morning, and after the event, we set it up on the mall plaza for the evening. There was one moment in time that was priceless. I had seen Casey Owens the year before, and he was an injured veteran who was wheelchair bound. When I saw Casey this time, I could not believe my eyes! He was walking toward the wall on his new prosthesis leg. My heart jumped for joy at what my eyes had the privilege to see. He walked to the wall, kneeled before it, and used his cell phone for light to find his buddies. It did not take long for the tears to come to his eyes once he located them. All I could do was let him know that I understood his heart because my son was on that wall. Whether he remembers, I do not know. I do know that the wall being there made a difference. That gives us a reason to continue to do what we can in an effort to make a difference.

We set the wall up at the Reliant Center last year for Impact a Hero's first event at that facility. Impact a Hero has grown that much in Houston. They simply overfilled the Sugarland Mercer Stadium and the hotel ballroom. The wall will be back at Reliant Center for this year's 5K run and gala. It is and always will be an honor to have the wall present at Impact a Hero. This year has a very special meaning to my family and me. Phillip will be Impact a Hero's inductee into their hall of heroes. What an honor.

I cannot find the words to describe my appreciation for Dick Lynch, founder of Impact a Hero. Dick has taken on as his God-given mission to do all that he can to support the heroes of the War on Terror. Folks, this is what patriotism is all about. A patriot does more than just wave a flag on Memorial Day, the Fourth of July, and Veterans Day, followed by a good ole time barbecue. Patriots get involved, giving of their time and resources out of a heartfelt appreciation and understanding of the cost of their freedom. Once again, let me express my thought: without the patriot, there would be no reason for any of us to serve in the military. There are so many more organizations, and I can best acknowledge them through my photos on my website.

The Watermelon Run for the Fallen

The Watermelon Run for the Fallen, held in Hempstead, Texas, has become an annual 5K fun run in honor of the fallen. It is with such spirit and integrity that each year it has grown by leaps and bounds. Hempstead Police Chief David Hartley is the force behind the run. The chief would not want me to say any more about him because he will tell you that it is not about him. I understand that and agree with him wholeheartedly, I agree that it is about our heroes and their families. It is about people being able to share and show their support and appreciation for their freedom that cost others and their families so much.

Chief Hartley lost his son, Army Staff Sergeant Jeffery L. Hartley, in Iraq on April 8, 2008. When I looked up the bio on Sergeant Jeffery L. Hartley, one comment about him stood out: his comrades could count on him. That, my friend, is what made him a hero. A hero is not something one sets out to become. It's something someone does, through an extraordinary set of circumstances, when one simply does what he knows is right without a second thought. A hero is born out of character, integrity, and an unwavering commitment to the mission. A hero makes a difference.

I remember last year Chief Hartley came up to me and asked how I was doing. I nonchalantly said, "Ah, OK." He put his big arm around my shoulder and said, "No, you are not OK." He was right, I admitted, but we learn to move forward. That is what this book is about, moving forward with our pain and memories, and, like the chief, finding a mission to make a difference. Chief Hartley was carrying on his son's legacy and that of my son, along with all the others represented by that day in August in Hempstead, Texas.

The Scott McIntosh Annual Charity Golf Tournament is another one of my favorite events. This event started in 2008. I was a guest at another charity tournament when I met Alex McIntosh, Scott's father at the clubhouse, and he had just finished golfing. We started a conversation that ended with Alex asking if we could bring the wall to the first annual tournament they were going to have in honor of his son Scott. I had the honor of meeting Alex and his family at another function just about a year prior. This event makes a difference. Do you see how God is connecting all these dots? I could not do this on my own, folks.

To make sure I get my facts straight, I again did a little research. I read an interview Alex did for the first golf tournament in honor of his son Scott. This is what he said when talking about the first tournament in 2008: "These soldiers, along with their families, display a devotion to duty and a willingness to sacrifice that cannot be put into words." What more needed to be said? They make a difference. I think we are beginning to get the picture. The words that touched my heart were "cannot be put into words." Remember when you first started this journey with me and I talked about my struggle to find the words?

One final event that finishes the year for the Texas Fallen Heroes Memorial Wall is Wreaths Across America-Houston. With a mission to

"Remember, Honor, and Teach," I cannot imagine a more appropriate way to end a year than this event at the Houston National Cemetery. The Houston event started in 2007

The director and his son were looking at a video about the Arlington wreath laying and commenting on the event here at the Houston National Cemetery. They placed their order for wreaths and called the cemetery to see when they could place them. They then found out that the Houston National Cemetery does not receive the live wreaths for all burial sites due to lack of funding.

The cemetery does receive seven wreaths (each representing one of the branches of service and the MIA/POWs) as all other national cemeteries do. The ceremony is held to place seven wreaths in front of the national cemetery.

The son, perplexed by this, claimed, "That's not fair." And later in the day, he simply stated, "Let's go get some wreaths." This was the beginning of a goal for not only one boy and his dad, but also for a family, friends, and an entire community. Now, over six years later, there is an entire city behind the event.

Is this not a reason for all of us to answer our calls to duty and make a difference? We have all of the examples we need and the many causes that wait for someone with the passion to take the mission on. I hope you are hearing the plea of my heart here on behalf of not just my son but also of all those who have served and are serving this great nation. Thank you, Scott and family. Thank you, Houston.

I will do about sixty events a year with the wall, and it is not within the purpose of this book to cover them all as great as they are, and with all of the special meaning they have that make them function. The focus of this book is on you, the reader. That you are able to walk through this story with me, find encouragement and inspiration, and come away with a burning passion to make a difference.

I think with the this chapter, we may be seeing with a bit more clarity where we are headed with this mission as the vision begins to come on board.

CHAPTER 17

The Texas Fallen Heroes Wall

October of 2010 we will find ourselves becoming involved with the Texas Fallen Heroes Memorial Wall. Since it is a traveling memorial, it is construction has to keep that fact in mind. Each panel is comprised of eighty 4x4 ceramic tile, on a plywood backing and a rich solid walnut trim. To date the wall consist of 14 individual panels, the first three are to honor WWII, Korean War and Vietnam, each panel bears information on the numbers Killed in Action and the numbers wounded from each war. An introduction panel follows the three war panels; this panel introduces the KIA of the war Afghanistan and Iraq wars on terror. The dates on these panels are from the first KIA of Texas in 2002 to the current KIA of Texas in 2013. The panels are update and repaired at the end and beginning of each year. When set up is complete on six tables with a table cover, it is thirty lineal feet of impressive honoring of our Texas fallen. In harmony with the mission I feel God has given me, this memorial makes a difference.

With a photo to accompany each name on an individual tile, each tile within that year becomes very special. Having my son's photo and name on the wall makes it very special to me, of course. Then then the meaning of the traveling memorial reaches beyond that; it reaches that spot in the heart of those who stand in front of the wall. It is especially touching when a relative of the warrior on the wall points out their son or daughter, nephew or niece, maybe a cousin. A wife finds her husband, a son or daughter locate their dad. A veteran finds a buddy, with comments like; he took my place, I should have been on that mission. He died in my arms; I have heard the story a number of times from comrades. I have heard the pain, the taking blame that is not theirs to take. Survivors guilty is a heavy load for someone so young to have to bear. I hear it in their hearts, as it weighs on them every day, not being able to get it out of their heads. Prayer then as a dad, who has lost a son to be able to say to them with authority it is a burden that is not theirs to carry. I want to reach out and let them know that we cannot live by what ifs and if I had only. Taking the blame that is not yours, what would your comrade say to that? Would you have done the same thing for your comrade? You know the reply is an unequivocal yes. It is no doubt the toll war has on us, we see and experience things that happen to human beings on both sides of the war that is so unimaginable that it terrorizes the mind and soul sometimes beyond a life time. I thing of the memorial wall as a healing wall, my mission with this wall is to make a difference.

When standing in front of it not knowing anyone personally the memorial wall that can educate. When facing the names and the photo above that name reminds you that the image you see could be your son or daughter, the neighbor kid who possibly spent more time in your home than his own. Maybe standing in front of that wall, you see the kids you taught in school or church. If you give, your heart the time it needs you will connect with the cost of your freedom. One time, I noticed a young girl at the opposite end of the wall; I could see that she was beginning to become emotional. I walked up to and asked if she knew someone on the wall, her response was "no sir" I told her what her heart just told me was that she understood the cost of her freedom; she simply replied, "Yes sir".

When we come to understand the price paid by so few for the remarkable freedoms, we enjoy. There should be a heaviness on our hearts in the form of honor, gratitude, and a debt we cannot repay, that we feel a need to demonstration. We can never repay the blank check our military men and women have written. The moment they gave their life on our behalf the blank check they signed on our behalf was stamped debt paid in full. The debt we owe, we can never repaid, and there is not requirement demands repayment, because the payment on our behalf was given freely and not given as a loan. All that is required is honor and remembrance that becomes our duty and responsibility.

We acquire this without option of participation as an obligation of respect and gratitude, anything less is nothing less than a shameful act to ingratitude and selfishness.

Each person I met and greet while standing in honor of those on the wall is a tremendous blessing to my heart. As we walk through this part of what I am doing with my time, I have doing this since 2010. I simply cannot imagine not be a part of the wall for the near future. The wall makes a difference to so many people in so many ways. Our schedule starts in April as a rule and ends the second Saturday of December with Wreaths Across America. During the course of about nine and a half months, we will set the wall up at close to sixty events. The wall has definite ties to what Forever 22. The wall has become more than simply a traveling memorial. The wall offers a sense of not being forgotten when it is displayed as often as is possible. For those who have loved ones on it a knowledge that they are not forgotten. I think this is one of the biggest fears of the family and friends of the "Fallen". For me displaying this awesome tribute to our "Fallen Heroes" is a part of my mission to honor the legacy of the men and women on the wall. I have been honored especially by having veterans visit the wall to find a buddy or someone they served with at some point. When I hear a serving warrior or a veteran say, "he stood in for me that should have been me on that wall". I can in turn share my story of Phillip with them and let them know that I truly understand their heart. It has been my distinct honor to share time after time with warriors and veterans standing in front of the wall. I have had the honor of sharing with mothers and fathers of those immortalized images on the wall. One other instance was that of a mother with her two young children kneeling in front of the wall as the mother pointed out their father. A wounded Special Forces veteran saw them, he knelt beside the children and began to talk to them about how brave their daddy was, and that what he did as a warrior will be remembered, as long as we remember and honor. This is legacy build for those children. It makes a difference and that goes to the heart of our mission. That is legacy preservation at work.

The dots connect, I first met this wounded Special Forces warrior in Iraq at Camp Warhorse, tell me God is not in our lives. He and I are friends and he is a terrific mentor for other wounded warriors. He has created an organization that takes wounded warriors on fishing trips, hunting trips and that gives them hope. Once again we see, making a difference, is not that what making a difference is about, offering hope when there seems to be none, making life not about yourself by rather about the difference you can make in the lives of others. That is a mark of a warrior on a continuous mission.

To the fallen, I pledge, as their final sunset has come, I will finish my mission as they have completed theirs. As we walk through this time, we see the mission a little more defined. I can see the vision of my mission as it becomes more vivid. I am seeing that the vision to my mission is the honoring of the legacy of this nation's fallen heroes. Without them, we need to seriously ask, "Where and what would I be today?"

I will do around sixty events each year with the Texas Fallen Heroes Memorial Wall, and my deepest appreciation goes out to the Military Order of the Purple Heart for their commitment to my son and all other military sons and daughters. I have no idea how long my mission will be, but I know that the mission of the wall will go on with or without me because it is the right thing to do. It makes a difference.

God has blessed me with so many good folks who have crossed my path. You just met one of the truest patriots there is—Phil Darbone, the creator of the Texas Fallen Heroes Wall. His story not only fits the theme of *Forever 22*, it is a story deeply imbued with the spirit of Forever 22.

The Texas wall was not the first creation of a memorial wall. A personal event sparked the creation of this memorial wall. Phil had a heart attack, and while he was in the hospital, taking care of the issue prompted some thinking that led to the question that when answered resulted in the desire to make a difference. While recovering, he thought about his little boy. The question in his heart was, how would he remember his dad?

After some time out of the hospital, the question was still unanswered. This goes to the heart of this book. He knew he needed to find that answer. Hence came God connecting the dots for Phil on a trip to DC's memorial wall. While visiting the Vietnam Memorial Wall, as he tells it to me, the lightbulb came on in his mind. The Vietnam Memorial Wall's heavy panels of stone were set in place, with the names of the fallen heroes etched onto each panel. The names on the wall were transferred from the etching to paper as the pencil passed over the name.

As Phil said, the lightbulb came on. He could create individual panels for the memorial. As he pondered the creation of the wall, it was no longer an option. He had to come up with the rest of the answers. What he came up with is a prime example of connecting the dots of the answers we are given. He would create a paneled memorial that could be mobile. Next, he would need to decide on the material to print the images of the fallen heroes and their names. He already had developed a database that was extensive and cross-referenced. He was in the business of making plaques that honored our fallen. The transfer of that concept to a ceramic tile mobile paneled wall was an easy step to the next issue solved. Phil tells me that he considered many mediums for the images that he could print. He considered everything from high-quality canvas to a wide range of other materials. None would equal that of printing on ceramic tile. Nothing else would give the feeling of individual honor as the individual tile that would belong to that fallen hero when in its place on the wall. I have heard this alluded to in so many ways from those who would say, "You know I just get the chills looking at this awesome wall."

God has connected the dots in my life, and this wall is certainly a part of it. The memorial wall has a connection to Forever 22 in making a difference. The wall is a part of my mission, a part of keeping the legacy of Phillip alive, as well as keeps the remembrance of all our fallen warriors alive in the hearts of patriots. From my heart goes a huge thank you to Phil Darbone and his family.

CHAPTER 18

The Making of a Hero

The making of a hero in these times is designed in the imaginations of Hollywood and other celebrities, such as sports figures, as a product of their own minds. When I think of heroes, I think of the comment made by a basketball star. During the course of an interview, when referred to as a hero, he responded unequivocally that he did not want to be a hero to young people. I developed a real appreciation and respect for him. His response and his reason made perfect sense. He pointed out that he did not fit the definition of a hero. That honor should belong to his dad or uncle or someone else not in the spotlight. He pointed out that if that person, out of the courage to live his everyday life, becomes the person that the young man looks up to and becomes his hero as an example of life, then that man is his hero. Heroes are not born, and they are not by design. They become heroes out of the character they exhibit while living their day-to-day lives.

When I think of our military heroes, I think of these types of qualities. Possession of these qualities that cause them to do the thing that makes them become a hero. Talk to a Medal of Honor recipient, and when you try to thank them for their heroism, they will most usually very quickly remind you that they are the hero, the men they could not save, or that the men they rescued are the heroes. They will remind you that they were simply doing their job. Sounds so very much like something Phillip would say while making a difference.

The making of a hero is not something we can plan for, as we never know who is going to be a hero at any given moment. Heroes are born out of the moment, unplanned reactions of selflessness to the needs of others. Heroes are born of the moments of "Oh, Jesus." That is the limit of conversation given prior to action.

We will walk through this part of the book I have saved for this point of the last chapters. I have a reason for waiting until now to write this chapter, because it is the most important part of the book. This chapter is that part of Forever 22 equation that falls on the right side of the equals sign. Forever 22 is a combination of dots that connect on the left side of the equals sign to become the sum total that becomes Forever 22. I think Phillip would have said, "Oh, good grief, Dad, why didn't you just say $2 + 2 = 4$?" He still makes a difference.

We have walked many miles together; I have said that several times in appreciation of your being with me through this. I have laid my head down so many times with the need of God's wisdom that it would be impossible to keep count. You have logged many hours of early mornings. I do not know where you are on the cups of joe. My record is in the hundreds of gallons most likely, and the hours spent pondering while sipping those gallons of joe.

The writing of this book has been encouraged by so many who have heard my story of escorting my marine home. People would say, "Carson, you need to write a book about this." So now I am close to having that done. When I first thought about it, I thought it was a good idea. The story of escorting Phillip home has become more than just about a dad and his son. My prayer is that it has become a story of encouragement, of inspiration, patriotism, and a renewed passion for American exceptionalism.

I chose to write in a way that you, my reader, could feel like you were walking, if not in my shoes, then at least beside me. It is said that if you want to know what a man feels, walk a mile in his shoes. I hope I have been able to create a written environment that has allowed you to do that.

I hope I have been able to demonstrate the need for a strong foundation of faith early on in life. We do not have to understand all in order for our faith to be solid, on which we will build our foundation of life on.

It was in my heart that the book was to be about a dad escorting his son home when he gave his life during a hostile action in Afghanistan. It is that and more, because I could not get to that point without telling you about how God made it possible. The possibility of escorting Phillip home from Ramstein, Germany, to Dover, then on to home in Houston, Texas, could only have happened by God's providence and the grace given to me. Forever 22 is beyond anything I can reach; it is perfectly within the reach of God, however.

As I sit here now with that handy cup of joe off to the right side of my keyboard, I am pondering my next words. What comes to mind is, let us, you and I, make a difference in life from this point forward. Let the dots of life continue to connect.

When I first sat down at the computer to start this walk through the recounting of escorting Phillip home, I struggled with two issues. Addressing these questions was necessary; I knew this in my heart before I could even consider stroking the keyboard to create the first sentence. I had to find an answer to the question, how do I find the words to describe what happened to my heart upon finding out that Phillip had been killed in Afghanistan? Then the question is, how do you find an adjective in the English language sufficient to describe the immeasurable depth of the pain felt when the hole left is immeasurable? How do I find a measurement that can accurately measure the width of the hole left in my heart? How do I find a set of words that can describe the distance of my sense of loss that is greater than the distance from the east to the west? This would be my place to be stuck so many times when I decided, OK, people are right. I need to do this. I could not get beyond those questions.

One day I was talking to a young man at a golf tournament about the book and my sticking points to a start. When he responded to the phrase "no words," he said, "That is your title." I thought about it, and it sounded right. However, when I sat down to write, that same obstacle was there. It was like running head-on into a brick wall. So I would abandon the effort.

Then one night, when I laid my head down, I thought of the need to start this book. I needed God's wisdom, for sure. Early the next morning, with a fresh cup of joe and some pondering time, I found in my heart the answer to that immovable wall. It was simple. I just needed God's wisdom. The answer, I realized, was within the question. It was simple. There were no words. I would never find the words to describe what my heart felt.

Then I turned my attention to my devotional of the day; being confirmed by the devotional was the answer to my prayer. Seems you and I have been there before. During that morning, my heart understood the true meaning of God being the only one who could reach to those depths of my heart that I cannot. Only God can walk the width of that sense of loss from the hole left in my heart from the storm that came to my shore. I could walk a lifetime and never walk far enough. Only God can measure that distance of loss that measures beyond east to west. The answer came when I laid my head down.

Now I was ready to tackle the next issue; only, I put "when I lay my head down" to work much sooner. My mornings are so important to the rest of my day. I was up early and in my cave, and by the time I sat down at my computer, with the fresh joe brewing, I had checked my e-mails, so my mind would not wander there during my pondering time. With each sip, just as we experienced it during our time in Iraq, the answer to my prayer begins to become clear. The story is centered certainly on escorting Phillip home. Without this, there would be no Forever 22. From the outset, I did not want to make this a book about God—not that I had a problem with God. I just had it in my mind that the title would demand a narrow focus on the event of getting Phillip home. Then with each sip of joe, I realized there was a broader narrative to the story.

You already know the answer: with a morning cup of joe and some pondering of the heart in communication with the spirit in me, the answer was obvious. I could not write this story without it being foremost about God. From the beginning to the end, you have seen how God reached back and far into my tomorrows to connect everything to the right moment in time.

So the making of the hero that Phillip would become is all about how God has worked in the lives of his mother, me, the rest of his family and friends, connecting the dots for what will be. God used parts of all of these lives in the making of Phillip. Once I realized this as a primary truth that would be central to all that I would do to get to the point God wanted me to be, then the story becomes about Phillip from the get-go and not me as it may have seemed at times early on. We all become secondary to God, and being secondary to God is exactly a great place to be.

About Phillip

He was brought into this world in 1983, born a Texan in Houston. His mother is a native Texan and I, his dad, am a Kentuckian who made it to Texas as fast as I could, which took a short twenty-seven years. Phillip would be the middle boy, born between his older brother Aaron and his younger sister Sara. He would also be younger that his two half-sisters, Kimberly and Dawn. From the beginning, I was a blessed dad.

Growing up, Phillip was extremely shy through high school. When he was but a small lad, he would never be found anywhere away from the house more than an arm's length from either of my legs. I felt for him, as I was very shy growing up. It took the army and Vietnam for me to overcome my shyness. Though I felt for him, I also knew he would overcome this.

When I think of memories, one of my favorites from a time when he was around five years old, was when he would crawl up onto my lap and go to sleep. I can savor those memories today as being priceless. I am reminded today of one of my mother's favorite hymns as she would sit and rock one of my younger brothers or sister to sleep. As that old heavy oak rocker would do its magic to the sound of mother singing "Precious Memories," imagine is exactly what that moment is to me today.

Each child is a unique creation of God, on loan to us as parents. It is for that reason, and because of that reason, that you love one no more or less than the other. Anything other than that would not sit well with nor would it be right with God, and it is not what being a mom or a dad is about. At this point, my eyes get blurry, my heart swells a bit, and then it lets me know that all is well with my soul.

I can see clearly now how growing up with his brother and sisters was as much a part of who he became as designed by God. The shoes fit the other feet too—he helped them become who they are today. This point goes to what you and I learned through our walk in Iraq. We are to make a difference in each other's lives. That goes for friends who would come to know him as the kid who would either sit or stand with those long arms folded across his chest, with that smirky little smile and few words. The few words would become sort of his trademark among his peers and those who would get to know him. They would become as E. F. Hutton's words. When he did speak, people paid attention.

A look from those penetrating eyes would send a message that was unmistakable communiqué; it was clear you did not want to go there without ever hearing a word spoken. His best buddy loves to tell the story of Phillip and a girl at school who had captured his heart. She at the time was dating a college freshman. Will Bowers, Phillip's best friend through their last two years of high school, tells about the time they were in the cafeteria. Now Phillip never ate lunch at school, but he would go with Will to the cafeteria. Well, as Will tells it, one day Phillip was being himself, sitting there quietly, with those arms folded, while others around him ate. When the girl of his dreams walked in with her college boy to sit down for lunch, Phillip just sat there with his arms folded. The way Will tells it, "I just see Phillip dressing this guy down without ever saying a word or making expression directed at him. The guy, according to Will, went to the principal's office crying because Phillip looked at him. His buddies would testify to his ability to dress someone down without a word, using only what they saw in his eyes.

Will would tell us that there were times when all Phillip had to do was lay a hand on his shoulder and he would know not to do whatever he was thinking of doing. At other times, Phillip would simply look at him and say, "That's stupid."

There are so many neat stories about Phillip, like the one time he talked his buddies into pulling into a parking lot. When questioned why he wanted to be there, he looked up at one of those tall parking lot light poles and said, "To see if I can climb it." He did, and a policeman came by to find out what the guys were up to. When he looked to see Phillip perched on top of the pole, the police officer said, "Son, can you come down?" Phillip answered, "Not a problem." Now where have you heard that before? Once he was back on the ground, he was asked why he did it, and his answer was to see if he could.

Phillip had close to a photographic memory. Will loves to tell the story of their chemistry class. How the teacher truly believed Phillip was cheating. The teacher decided he was going to catch Phillip in the act of cheating, so when the test started, he stood right behind Phillip. Phillip sat there for a bit with those arms folded, before he finally picked up his pencil to finish the test ahead of everyone else. When he turned his paper in with just the answers, without showing his work, the teacher immediately started checking his answers. Phillip aced the test, and that was the end of the teacher's suspicions. He did not turn in homework most of the time. We ran into that problem when he was in junior high school. We received a call from the school for a conference with his reading teacher. Now we could not figure out what in the world the problem might be. Phillip simply did not get into trouble. He was too shy still at this point. The first thing the teacher did was assure us that Phillip was not in trouble. He simply wanted to know why he did not turn in homework. He told us that Phillip by far was the best reader in the class, his comprehension was way above his grade level, and he aced his entire test, but he would not turn in homework. The only thing that made sense was that he felt it was a waste of time. I had no idea he was not turning in homework. That was the first order of the time after getting out of school: homework before anything else.

During the summer months, Phillip would spend most of his time with me on jobs, as I was self-employed and had the luxury of being able to do that because at that time, most of my jobs I did alone or with one or two helpers. He and I became close. I took Aaron along for a number of years until I decided he could make his own mind up about going. That simply was not his bailiwick. That is a part of what helped us to mature into who we become. It didn't mean in any sense that I thought less of Aaron and more of Phillip. My heart could not go there. It simply meant that Phillip spent more time with me.

There are so many stories, as is the case with most families and their kids. There was the time Will's parents needed to replace a portion of their sidewalk in front of their house. It was going to cost a fair chunk of money to break the section out and replace it. Phillip looked at it and determined he and Will could do the replacement job. So Phillip asked if he could borrow the tools needed; of course he could. He and Will set about breaking out the old concrete with a sixteen-pound sledgehammer. They prepped the ground and set the forms. Phillip had worked with me on concrete jobs so he knew what he was doing. Phillip measured a figured the amount of concrete they needed. They had their mesh cut and ready to drop in place before they poured. They had only one problem, and that was a tree root running out into the middle of the sidewalk. That root was the source of the problem, to begin with. Phillip, after thinking about it a bit, said, "Not a problem. I'll call Dad."

When I showed up, I took an axe out of the van and handed it to them. They cut the root to just outside where the form would go. All else was good. The next day, they poured the concrete and stuck with it until the troweling was finished. This story means so much to me because Phillip knew he could count on me for the answer. That is so central to everything about Forever 22—counting on God for the answers. Being the best you can be, not being afraid to help and do for others. It was those traits that helped Phillip become who he was and who he would become. I sincerely believe that heroes are not born; they are made as they answer their call to duty.

As the kids grew in stature, they also grew in character, and that would determine who they would become as adults. Phillip's sister would be so much like Phillip later on in life. Her teacher called her a free spirit. Aaron was more on the philosophical side

Phillip would graduate one of eight from Grace Community Christian School in 2000. His high school friends and classmates would remember him for his gift of listening to a friend's heart without judgment; they could know that he was a true friend.

Phillip the Young Man to Become a Marine

Sometime during his high school years, Phillip developed a liking of knives and guns. He was not obsessed with them, but he liked gun and knife magazines. I had bought him and his brother an SKS rifle when they were in their early teens. Gun safety came as a natural to both boys. When we would go camping,we would also take the rifles. Those were such good times. Those are the memories you hang on to when everything else can be lost.

Phillip's character would continue to develop. I can see now that everything he did from the time he was a little guy to the time he was killed in Afghanistan led to him being the marine he became. He could have gone to college and would have been more than capable of doing whatever he wanted. That just was not for him at that time. Aaron and I had a conversation the other day, and he told me that he and Phillip talked about that. He said Phillip said he was considering the marines then and college afterward. I tried to teach my kids to think for themselves. Do not do anything simply because someone else is doing it, even if it is a good thing. Phillip was in control of his own actions. He made a difference.

He chose not to drink because it was his choice not to and not because of some external pressure not to. He appeared tough as nails on the outside, but he had the softest heart on the inside. Children at church loved Phillip, and the younger youth looked up to him. I think a lot of the respect came because they could see a rare quality in Phillip. His quietness was probably at the top of the list, followed by his willingness to listen, his ability to do for you without making you feel you owed something in return, and many more attributes. When I think about Phillip, I think about the stories I have heard over the past nine years. I hear of so many stories of young men and women who were willing to set themselves aside for the good of others. What they are willing to give for the good of our nation and the principles this nation stands for. Who else would you rather see take up the defense of such a precious commodity than the best. American exceptionalism at its highest, and they make a difference.

I remember when he first started going to the Austin, Texas, area on weekends with friends to rock climb. I would lie in bed and hope that he would be OK. He had never had training in rock climbing. After a few times, God put my heart at ease, and I realized that it was not Phillip I needed to be concerned about—it was the guys with him. That did not need to be a concern either because they had Phillip at their backs, another quality of a good warrior.

These would be the types of character and qualities that his buddies came to appreciate about Phillip. I was going through some of his things and came across the brass grenade casing, and it had an envelope wrapped around it, secured with a rubber band. This was about a year after Phillip was gone. I opened it up and started reading it. The letter was from a sergeant of another platoon who described how his task was to take some men up a mountainside for a recon mission. Phillip was not in Sal's platoon, but Sal was able to choose who he wanted to go with him. He chose Phillip because he had heard about how good Phillip was. They made their way up the mountainside OK; however, the recon took longer than anticipated. Once they had the information they were after, they needed to get back down the mountainside to link up with their unit. The problem they had was if they went back down the way they came, they would not be in time to link up with the rest of the guys. Now what are they going to do? Leadership and confidence is a premium need in times like these.

Phillip said, "We are going down the other side of the mountain."

Sal was not going to have any part of that because Phillip was not a rock or mountain climber. Then Phillip simply convinced him that he and the rest of the team could do it. The question was how. Phillip told Sal he would talk them through it, and they would make it. The letter expressed how much he appreciated Phillip.

I could go on and on, but I can feel Phillip with those folded arms, that smirky smile, and a soft, "Oh, good grief, Dad." Are you not glad that we have such young men and women as gatekeepers of our freedom?

Now it is time to understand that the dots connect once again in our lives. There were many dots that were simply specks along the way and for the most part were never really seen. When time became right according to God's plan, those seemingly small and sometimes unseen dots connected to make huge sum in life.

It is for all the reasons in the things I write about throughout this book that this story first is truly about God and His presence in our lives, from the first breath we take. This story is not about me; it is about how God used the life he gave me. It is a story about Phillip—the boy, the young man, and the United States Marine. It is a story about the legacy Phillip has left behind for you, the reader. His legacy is one that, above all, invites and encourages you to strengthen your faith. A legacy that encourages you to finish your mission against your final sunset as they have finished theirs. We have in our warriors from the beginning of this nation to the heroes of today, examples of courage to live by. We have a reason today to "stand in honor" and "remember in prayer" those who stood in our place. Let us allow God to connect the dots of life and be the person God created us to be.

CHAPTER 19

SECOND TRIP TO IRAQ

We will find ourselves coming up on two years since we left Iraq. I cannot quite put my fingers on what I am feeling after being home for almost two years. I cannot quite understand the unrest in my soul. It was not that I was unhappy with anything. It was more of a something-missing feeling. Could it be that being overseas, being in somewhat of a dangerous environment had gotten into my blood? I do not really think so, as I am not a person persuaded by emotions like that. I had heard it many times said that working in these spots had to be in your blood. I suppose that is true, to a degree. No, my feeling as I take a closer look at it had more to do with the nature of not having finished something. Have you ever been there? These are the times that make knowing which direction to take seem impossible. Not wanting to make a choice out of by gosh and by gum reasoning, decisions under these circumstances are really tough, but you know one fact for sure: you have to sort of grit your teeth at times and bite the bullet, knowing that God is with you, and do it. That is the one neat thing that we have come to appreciate and understand more of during the writing this book. God has never abandoned us during our walk together, nor will He abandon us now. He may say, "Boy, what in the world were you thinking?" but He would not give up on us and leave us out in the cold by ourselves.

To this point, you have walked with me through some of the things I have managed to get myself involved in, and for that, I am grateful, and for them as well, because I realize now that they helped nudge my thinking in the direction I needed it to go. I suppose this is one of those examples in real life and in real time where the apostle Paul is encouraging us to be content in whatever state we find ourselves. That state is subject to change when we least expect it. If we do not stop sitting on our keisters waiting for life to be brought to us, then sometimes we are gently pushed into something or a direction that ends up being a blessing without realizing it at the time. I definitely believe God causes the paths of people to cross without any real reason for them to do so otherwise, and at the time, we can only suppose God has a reason. I suppose you could attribute this to pure happenstance. I do not think so

By the end of the year, I did not know what I was feeling. The compounding fact that the unknown feeling, further complicated by the sense that I needed to be doing something, made it imperative that I needed God's wisdom. I needed to start thinking about replenishing the bank account; that was not the main reason for what was gnawing at my heart because money, I have learned, can almost always be made one way or another. I did not find myself financially at a crisis point as of yet. However, what I had in the bank would not last forever without the assistance of some income. Toward the middle of the year in 2008, I took a job working for a home center store, the wages were fine for the income I needed to add to the money I already had; hence, I needed to find a job. There were several problems I encountered—the biggest one being that my knees had become so worn out at this point that even on a part-time basis, the long periods of standing on the concrete floor absolutely did a number on them. At this point, I had two situations that needed attention; my knees could not handle the concrete, and my mind could not handle the boredom during slow times. Make believe busy work and me as partners have never ginned and gotten along. We will find ourselves running headlong into being off mission. We were not making a difference.

It was during this time, though, that I thought a lot about Phillip. He would have been ready to go out and either build something or tear it down. That would have probably been a more successful attempt at earning what I needed than working in the environment I found myself. I had clear images of him. I could see him standing in heaven looking down on me with those long arms of his folded over his chest and with the smirky little smile of his, he would say, "Oh, good grief, Dad." He probably would not have believed I took the job in the first place. It was so out of character for me. I know he would be thinking of something different. The longer I stay on the job, the more I disliked it. The job simply was not where I was supposed to be, and I knew it. For each time I would walk around doing make-believe work, my mind would go back to Iraq. Finally, I concluded that was what I needed to do. We have not talked about when I lay my head down in some time; well, it was time to get back to what we know works, and that is counting on God's wisdom. Going back to Iraq had less to do about money than it did with completing a mission. I cannot remember how long I worked, maybe six months. It seemed like it would never end. I did not hate it; however, by the same token, I did not like it. I did not feel like the job was beneath me in any sense of the word. I just simply did not feel I was where I needed to be.

I would lay my head down and wake up to an early cup of joe and sip on it while I pondered my situation. I knew in my heart that I was on the right track, so I went online and filled out an application. KBR did not have a carpentry foreman's job opening but they did not have carpentry openings. I was not particularly interested in having to be in charge anyhow.

I remember I was driving the feeder off Beltway 8 when I got the call from the KBR HR department. From the sound of his voice, I knew I had the job. We talked a bit to get some preliminaries out of the way, and he told me he would get back with me. He called back, and I would get a packet with instruction for what to do before going to the processing center.

The packet arrived with the instruction of preprocessing information. The process had changed a lot. However, I made it through everything I needed to do. I was to start processing on December 5, and that was fine with me. I really did not want to go back to Iraq before the sporting clays tournament was over. I was not prepared to forgo the job for the tournament, however. When December 5 came, there was a delay in the start time due to a storm that had done some serious damage in the area of the processing center, which caused a delay of about three weeks or more. Their schedule was bumping up against the Christmas holidays and the New Year. My new processing time would be about the fifth of January now. It seemed I was still not going to be able to make the sporting clays tournament. The new processing time was now down to three weeks. I started the processing sometime around the middle of January. All was going well until it came time for the blood pressure test again. You guess it, my blood pressure was high, and at that point, I was on medical hold. I have three weeks to get to my doctor to get the blood pressure under control. I needed to have my blood pressure checked three days in a row by the doctor and get a release from him. This would put my return to the processing center sometime into February. I would make the sporting clays event after all.

I passed the medical exam and now had two weeks of processing, I had to stay at the hotel in the area, and that was OK with me. Have you had to drive through Houston traffic going to work and return home? It is miserable. With the processing completed, there was a week of waiting for transportation out of the country. This put me into March for a departure time to Iraq. I was fine with all of this.

I was satisfied in my soul that I had made the right decision. With each night, I laid my head down, and the next morning with my cup of joe and time of pondering. I knew the reason I needed to go back to Iraq was to find that uncompleted part of the mission.

The time I spent at Dubai then on to Camp Speicher gave me a lot of lone time with God. My thoughts began to turn to Phillip and his legacy. The question was, what could I do? I had no real influence, and I did not have the assets to start anything on my own. This would definitely have to be a God thing. He is probably thinking, *Really*. I believe God allows us to go in directions sometimes that maybe we should not have gone. I suppose being the wisest of fathers He knows that sometimes we have to simply live and learn.

Those underlying thoughts and questions that put me back in Iraq were not a troublesome thing when they popped into my mind; rather, they served as a reminder to me that I was again on a mission. This mission was clearer than the first trip to Iraq. I knew my mission had something to do with Phillip, that the end of understanding the second trip, I was in a fog without a clue right now.

Are you ready to join me with this part of the story in progress? We will be at Camp Speicher for about three months and then sent to the carpentry shop at Camp Warrior in Kirkuk, Iraq. I would eventually end up in the newly created construction department. I was beginning to feel like the child no one wanted. There was a different feel to being in Iraq this time. The few months at Camp Speicher has a strange feel to it; maybe part of that feeling was seeing people fired and sent home for not wearing their KBR ball caps. Most of the time, these were people who were interested in doing their jobs. They were people who cared about doing their jobs. This made no sense to me at all. These things took place almost on a daily basis. Carried out by overzealous safety and security people who most likely had no clue as to how to do a real job. I did not try to figure it out. I just knew that God had me there for a reason, and my job was to do the best of my ability anything less would be a lack of integrity on my part, and God for sure would not be happy with that.

God would bless my time at Camp Warrior; I wanted to do my best while on the job. Laying my head down was as much a part of my life's routine at this point as early mornings with my cups of joe and pondering time. These three items were my partners in crime, so to speak. They certainly stood by me and served me well when all else seemed to escape me. As we are about to discover, this trip to Iraq will be on a much different playing field than the first thirty-three months. We will also find God just as capable and ready to be with us as we walk through this time in Iraq. On this trip, we have making a difference as our reference to the mission.

My Mission with the Military

For the first three months at the carpentry shop, things did not go so well. The foreman did not like me. He had this notion that I was there to take his job. Nothing could have been farther from the truth. However, when we are insecure in our position because we really do not know our job, then the truth really does not matter until it's realized in the heart. This man really thought I was there to take his job. I had no desire to take his job. I am so grateful for the trust I have in God; I never have a need to worry about someone taking a job that God gives me.

I was pleasantly surprised by the number of people who knew me or knew about the work I'd done at Camp Warhorse or Camp Speicher as "the cameraman," and that did not sit too well with him at all. When I laid my head down each night, God would work on my heart. Early the next morning, with that fresh cup of joe and my pondering time, the answers I sought for the day would surface, ready for action.

As my time went forward at Camp Warrior, I would find myself making new friends on the military side. The contact would mostly occur as I did my job for KBR, but all else I did on my own time. I received an e-mail from a battalion commander of a unit; someone had told him that I might be able to help him. He needed a memorial photo for one of his fallen warriors and wanted to know if I could help. When I thought about the young warrior and I thought about Phillip, God gave me the answer. I would use the photo of the sunset and guard tower I took at Warhorse shortly after being in Iraq with a photo of the fallen soldier. I e-mailed the commander back with my idea and asked that he send me a photo of the young warrior if he liked the idea. He did, and I created a composite of the guard tower and sunset with Sergeant Leroy O. Webster superimposed on it.

The commander invited me to attend the service. I was the only KBR civilian there. I had let my camp manager know that I was working on the photo for the unit on my off time. He did not have a problem with that. Then when I asked my supervisor for time off to go to the memorial service, he told me he would have to get permission for that to happen. It would be OK to take time to attend the memorial service. In addition, it was made clear that I was to take this time off my time sheet

It was during that memorial service that I saw a passion for our fallen, our wounded, and our veterans. With the click of each shutter release of the Nikon around my neck, I could feel the imprinted image firmly pressed onto the pages of my heart. As I watched the service, my mind would fill with thoughts of Phillip. They were so real, and the dynamics of the images in my mind made me feel as though he was standing there beside me taking it all in. These can be very special moments, depending on how we choose to let them make a difference in what we decide to do next. We can choose to allow the pain caused in our hearts put us down or, on the other hand, we can overcome the pain and make a difference for the very reason the pain is there. We will choose the latter because that is the side we will find God is on. It was when the service had concluded and the warriors filed by the warriors cross with a wreath on one side and the memorial photo to the other side. As they stood in front of the memorial items, they would offer a prayer, a moment of silent respect. Some simply touched the dog tags hanging from the rifle grip of the M16 that was a part of the soldier's cross. While others simply paused for a moment and yet others would leave a token at the foot of the soldier's cross, the emotions varied from warrior to warrior.

It was so hard to concentrate while fighting back my own remembrances swelling with the force of a storm bringing them up to the top of my heart from so deep within. I could feel the physical reaction of my heart to the pain within. My eyes turned to focus on the soldiers and others as they made their way to a line where Colonel Cook was at the head. Colonel Cook's XO, being next in line, and then the command sergeant major of the battalion. Others from the command were in the line to shake hands in silence or with a few words of respect as the soldiers filed in by one by one. I remember in particular watching the battalion commander's face, I had only seen this look once before; it was the square-jawed look of a soldier in a lot of emotional pain, and this was his way of keeping the emotions in check. I had seen this look on General Peter Pace's face at a Time of Remembrance ceremony in DC. I could feel the colonel's pain as it identified with the pain that was in my own heart at that moment.

When the memorial service concluded, it struck me as odd that no one from KBR attended a memorial service for a fallen warrior. I learned later that the camp manager had rubbed the military the wrong way. He did not have respect for the military, I found out. That point became clear as I was leaving the building and our paths crossed. He wanted to know what I was doing there, I told him I had permission to be there and made sure I made a point of the fact that I was off the clock and on my own time. Justice has a way of working itself into our lives. He was relieved of his position and sent to Camp Speicher and then sent home. I am not in the least way suggesting that this happened to him because of me. I am certain of the fact that when we make life all about ourselves, the natural order of things tend come for a visit.

I had the honor of creating two more memorial photos for two other warriors killed from the same unit. My time spent with the military allowed me to feel like I was making a difference. We were on a mission.

Memorial Wall at Kirkuk

I think the most significant event of this second trip would have to be the memorial wall built at the Kirkuk airstrip. The distinguished visitors pad (DVP) was being readied for use when it was decided to name it in honor of fallen warrior Sergeant Leroy O. Webster.

Now enters CW2 Mike Ebinal with his mission to build a memorial wall that honors those fallen heroes of Iraq. It is neat to see how God can use all situations to his good and to glorify Him at the end of the day. My boss sent me on this assignment just to get me out of his hair. He did not particularly like me because he thought I was after his job. In reality, I could want anything less. Therefore, he sent me on this task of meeting CW2 Ebinal to find out what he had in mind and what we could do to assist him. The thought in my boss's mind was that it was a dead end, but it would get me out of his hair.

That day was the beginning of a new phase of our mission. A huge undertaking for the military, it would require joint army and air force efforts to make this memorial project work. We will never be able to forget that afternoon. Again, as the reader of this story, it is still great that you can be a part of this as it unfolds. As the warrant officer laid out his vision of how he saw the memorial wall, I followed him. I not only followed what he envisioned as the finished project, I could see it completed.

I cannot recall the exact order of our conversation, but he told me he was a six-year marine who then joined the army in order to get helicopter pilot training. We talked about his family, and he showed me a photo of his daughter. It was not hard to see that she was the apple of his eye. He was anxious to get home on R&R to see her. It moved my heart to tell him about Phillip, that I was eight years in the army in Vietnam from 1967 to 1968, how I supposed he thought he had to be tougher than dad. At the end of our conversation, there was no doubt about the friendship. Before we left the proposed site of the memorial, I told him that I thought it was an awesome idea and that I could see it finished. Remember, I told you that God had bestowed the blessing upon me of being able to see things finished. Well, I could see this wall finished and the entire honor it would bring to those whose names would appear on the wall.

A few weeks later, my boss told me that I was to go to the site and see how things were going. I needed to meet the foreman of the heavy equipment department there along with the warrant officer. I had already been dropping by to check the site out. The layout was explained to the heavy equipment foreman, and he said it was not a problem setting the concrete panels in place. The meeting was short. Now to make it happen, all Warrant Officer Ebinal had to do was submit the work request.

I went back to the office and told my boss of the results of the meeting, and he let me know that he did not believe it was going to happen. Well, my boss did not understand many things, one of them being the mind of a soldier;. He was an air force brat growing up, but he understood nothing of what it meant to be a warrior. He also did not understand the working of God in the hearts of his people. It was in my heart, and I could see the project finished. It would happen, and it did, indeed.

David handed me the work order and asked that I be there with my camera and check on the project. The big crane arrived on location and was set in place with the outriggers extended to stabilize it during the operation to lift the concrete walls from the flatbeds as they were pulled into place to be offloaded. This was a sight to behold, and music to my ears when I heard the sound of the 18-wheelers with their flatbeds loaded with concrete barrier walls approaching the site. There was joy in my heart and a bit of sweet satisfaction that came with being right. When on God's mission, it does not mean that He takes away the human part involved; it simply means that He will work with what He has. My heart was so blessed as I watched the trucks pull into position to be unloaded by the crane. I think this crane was a ninety-ton. The project unfolded with each concrete wall set in place, with each empty truck moving out of the way for the next wall to be offloaded.

I would enjoy meeting and sharing with Warrant Officer Ebinal. He and I talked about painting the wall. I told him I would like to get volunteers from KBR to paint it, and he agreed to that. I was able to get volunteers to help with the paint project to of the memorial. I was careful to seek the approval of my boss and the camp manager. I think it took us about two weeks to get it completed. We are talking about ten-foot-tall by ten-foot-wide, both sides, times twenty-eight. That ends up being twenty-eight thousand square feet of concrete to be painted by guys who had already put in a twelve-hour day in the sun, as they were tradesmen. I could not get any office types to volunteer; they were the losers of a blessing for their selfishness. Need to call it like it is. The guys whose names would appear on the wall gave their lives. What can I say? I had to be careful that I did not allow myself to become bitter.

Laying my head down would provide me with God's wisdom to walk in His light on this issue.

After sharing with him my experience of escorting Phillip home, we would talk about family, and he was about to take leave to go back to Fort Hood, Texas. He showed me of photo of his youngest daughter. She was no doubt the apple of her daddy's eye. Those were such terrific times, making a difference.

The dots that would connect from this project and others would not become evident as to how they connected to Forever 22. All I knew at the time was I worked according to the wisdom God provided me and done by the grace He would give me. I had a job to do and a mission to accomplish—that was my concern at the time. It was August, and all the individual walls were painted by KBR patriots who volunteered their time after twelve hours in the hot sun. Respect and appreciation for these men live in my heart and memory to this day.

The fact is, I would learn later on that the introduction wall to the memorial would tell the story of how the story of a dad escorting his son home after being killed in Afghanistan made a difference as to whether the wall was built. Warrant Officer Ebinal told me later when I caught up with him at Fort Hood, Texas, that on that day we met, for the first time he was prepared to go back to his boss and tell him the project simply could not be done. However, he said after hearing Phillip's story and that I could see the project completed, he had to try it.

The point here is that those who give their lives can still make a difference in the hearts of those who enjoy the benefits of their sacrifice. This was another tick in the marching on toward that intended mark. For Phillip's legacy and of all of those whose names appear on that memorial wall. God had truly blessed my soul.

Even though I had to leave before the project was finished, my heart was so proud of all the KBR employees who gave of their time after a long day to help, and all of the army and air force warriors who volunteered their time. Go to my website to see the start-to-finish photos of this unbelievable sight.

It was August, and I had not taken an R&R as of that time. It was time for me to go home. I was turning in my toolbox as a part of my clearing camp process. I was at a counter with my toolbox in hand when the clerk behind the counter asked me to put it up on top so he could take inventory of what was inside. Well, as I am fond of telling people,

I think I just got old at that point in Iraq. I heard a pop, and I felt the pain from my right shoulder. I finished the process, and by the time I made my way back to the operations area, I knew I was hurt. I had no idea how and to what degree I had hurt my shoulder, so I turned in my paperwork and then decided I needed to go to the medic. I did not expect any treatment at the clinic. The medic probably would not know what to do, nor could he even if he did know. I just needed the fact that I injured my shoulder documented.

When I entered the clinic, there was only one on duty. He was in his office with the lights out, watching a video. I knew this guy would not have a clue as to what to do, as he continued to watch his video. Without looking up, he asked if I could move my arm. I could. His conclusion, again without looking up, was that since I could move my arm, all was fine at the time of this genius assessment. I knew to turn and walk out was the better part of being prudent at the time.

That night, I really needed the power I found in laying my head down. My shoulder bothered me throughout the night. The next morning, I had my morning cups of joe and pondering time. I needed God's wisdom here to keep me above the fray.

Luggage went through security and was loaded onto the truck. I took a quick look at my shoulder, and it was beginning to show signs of bruising from the internal bleeding. I decided to make another visit to the medic. I was hoping the medic I knew would be on duty. When I got to her office, she was at her desk, with the lights on I might add. I would have her to look at it. As I talked to her about the shoulder, the medic from the day before heard the conversation and decided that he had better cover his behind from his lack of actions the day before.

He was quick to say that I had been in, and he would take care of it. When I rolled my T-shirt sleeve up out of the way, he decided to put a heat pad on it. This was the wrong thing to do; but it was not going to do any harm, so I didn't say anything. What would be the point? He saw the bruising, and at this point, it was about three inches long and maybe two inches wide. After an hour, he decided that maybe I needed to see a doctor. We got into a vehicle and went to the crash unit where a doctor looked at my shoulder and pressed around a bit. He determined that the shoulder was not likely dislocated but badly torn. There was nothing at this time that the army doctor from the cash unit could do.

By the time I got to Camp Liberty in Baghdad, at the time of roll call the next morning I looked at my shoulder and saw that it was bruised from the elbow up to the shoulder and across half of my chest. I decided I needed to check in with the medics at Camp Liberty as soon as roll call was finished. They filed a report that involved security and safety not only from Camp Liberty but also Camp Warrior and Camp Speicher. From that point, my R&R status was changed to medical. The medics at Camp Liberty wanted to fuss over me for waiting so long, until they understood that I went to the medic at Camp Warrior. That is when things took on a completely new nature. I have nothing but praise for the medics at Camp Liberty, and I would be on the next flight out for sure.

I was set to see a doctor at the Canadian Specialist Hospital in Dubai when I got there. The results of the MRI showed four badly torn shoulder muscles. It was quite an experience; life could be worse, but it was not, so I would go with the flow.

Radio Show from Camp Warrior

I had the opportunity to do a radio show from Kirkuk. It all started when someone sent me an e-mail that told the story of a mother whose son was in the burn unit at San Antonio, home of the Brooks Army Medical Center. She went on a radio station out of Florida called GI Radio. For her son's birthday, she simply wanted people to send him some birthday cards. I went online and found the contact information to the radio station. There are those times that God moves your heart to take action, and you simply have to do it. I wanted to get in touch with this mother so I could send her son some cards from Iraq. I received a return e-mail, with as much information as they had to give. It also came with an invitation to be interviewed by the talk show host, Tom Graver. I sent back an acknowledgment of the e-mail and with an answer of yes. That was the beginning of about seventeen shows. After that, I would take my lunch hour late on that day and stand out in the middle of the desert to make my mobile phone call to Florida. I had about twenty minutes just after 0700 hours eastern standard time. I had no idea what I was doing, but it was easy to talk from my heart about our warriors, our veterans, and the fallen. I made my last radio show on my way out of Baghdad. I was on my way home to get my shoulder patched up. God blesses us in so many ways.

My second trip to Iraq was a fast and short seven months, but God managed to bless me in so many ways. I am not sure I left with a better idea of where God wanted me. I did leave with the fact that there was still a mission for us to be about, and that mission would not be finished until God decided it was finished. That is really all we need to know in order to move on.

CHAPTER 20

At the End of the Day

You and I are about to walk that last mile together after so many miles. I feel like I can know a little bit about you if you are reading this last chapter. By virtue of the fact that sticking with me to this point tells me some things as to your nature because you have walked this far with me. You can tell a lot about a person by what they are willing to read. There is nothing physic about what can be reasonably deduced.

As we walk through the last couple of chapters written, I think I discovered the reason for our second trip to Iraq. If you will remember, we really did not achieve much of anything during our time there as far as the job was concerned. As we settled in at Camp Warrior, it seemed to me that the people who worked there had no idea who they were there to support. I think if I could go back and put that toolbox up on the counter in a different way I would do it. I have good mobility with my injured shoulder, and I only have pain from the injury when I try to lift too much too often. I cannot hold a tool like a screw gun straight out in front of me; it simply will not happen. If my shooting sessions are too long, the shoulder starts to bother me. I can deal with that. I do not believe God caused my injury in order to teach me a lesson, as some believe when accidents happen. I do believe; however, that God strengthens us through circumstances and gives us the grace to overcome most situations.

I think the last trip to Iraq was necessary for me to come full circle and find my niche in life. I think I learned from the last trip that things are not always as they seem to be. I learned that when God has your back, you are never alone, and you are never left out in the cold. Making a difference is not always at the moment the most profitable thing; however, at the end of the day, it becomes the most profitable thing you could have done. We have been in this spot before: When at the end, before you turn the lights out on the day, take the time to take a quick glance back and walk away knowing that all is well with your soul.

Finding where we belong can sometimes be so elusive and at the same time be right in front of us. At this point, I would like to narrow my thoughts to finding meaning, direction, reason to belong, and how to find where to fit in now. Especially from the heart and mind of a dad who lost his son. I can only speak for myself and only from my heart. I will tell other Gold Star families I can hear their hearts and I can understand a lot of what they are feeling, but what I cannot do is tell them how to remedy the particular set of emotions they are dealing with at the time. Even though I have walked in their shoes, I have had to walk that lonesome valley on my own—not alone, mind you. That walk is different for each person who has to walk it.

Earlier in this book, I talked about walking that valley. The one thing I do know about that valley is that I do not have to keep on walking it. I know the only reason I would continue to walk it would be if I thought in some way my son might be there. I know in my heart that he is not. You might wonder how I can know that. That good and fair question deserves more than an empty "Just because I do." I know this to be true because God has my heart first off. Then because that is real, I can know that God is not in that valley. He was there and walked it with me when I had to walk it the first and only time. I am certain of this in my heart; therefore, why would I want to go back to such a dark place knowing what I'm searching for is not there? I prefer to be where God is with me, and that puts me where my son is, because his spirit is with God.

When I Lay My Head Down

I have been home from my last trip to Iraq for five years come August. Good grief, how time flies. It has taken a lot of air travel to get me to this point. In addition, as you know, to many cups of joe for those early morning pondering sessions. It has taken almost nine years for me to get to this point in life.

Writing this book has not lacked strong urging on the behalf of those who have heard Phillip's story. I could make any number of excuses, but the most valid excuse has been dealt with, that being how to describe what I feel in my heart. Then the only other valid reason dealt with is whether or not to make this a book about God. You have been with me on this walk—what do you think? Could God be left out?

I am not sure if I could have done anything differently, and I have come to the point God would have wanted me to be for the time being. In my search, the question is, have I made a difference? You can answer that. Those I have dealt with can probably answer that, or at least to some degree. I know in my heart that I had come to many forks in the road, and while God had a light before my feet, it was only there for me to take one step at a time. There was no sign posted at my feet or anywhere I could see it, and the light made sure I could see the next step I took when I was at that fork in the road, and I took it.

I would find the answers after I would "lay my head down" at the end of each day. Wake up the next morning ready to build on the day before. If the day before was a wash for me, then I would have twice as much to do in this new day. I have been developing a routine that has paid off for me for some time now. I am by no means where I would like to be, or where God would have me be.

I would learn more about the concept of when I lay my head down, not a problem, and a new concept of when I have purpose in my heart. The lesson of a purpose in my heart has taught me that all thought processing—incoming or outgoing—is filtered through our hearts, just as our blood is pumped in and out of it. The heart is central to physical life, and it is most certainly central to the spiritual. I do not know where your spiritual beliefs lie; I can only tell you how I see it without telling you how the cow ate the cabbage.

I learned from my time in Iraq to be more organized than I have ever been in my life. Once home, it seems I forgot most of what I learned. Since I have honestly engaged myself in writing this book, a lot of that wants to come home. It has taken starting with already built-in routines, if you will, like getting up early, my morning cups of joe, followed by reading my e-mails. Those things were the bedrock of my developing routine. I would then add to those established routines others one at a time.

At the end of the day, when I wrote the paragraph just above this one, I now have a habit of looking back on my day before turning the lights out in my man cave; and when I turned the key in the lock, I knew all was well with my soul. That has become such a relief for me at the end of each day. Before I lay my head down for the night, my mind hears the small voice from deep within my heart: "Make a difference."

Up early this morning with, "This is the day Lord hath made; I will rejoice and be glad in it." Comes to my mind as I walk from the house to my man cave, the first thing to do is to make a fresh pot of joe. Then I check the e-mails. God taught my heart about wasting time, and that was one of the biggest waste of time I had to get a handle on. I think we all have those things that take up our time, and we know it does. That is why we do it as a quasi-excuse for not doing what we need to do. The tool God put in my heart was the memories I have of Phillip. You might wonder, how does that connect to wasting time? The connection in my heart between Phillip and wasting time is that when I think of Phillip now, I think of Forever 22 and the mission it has set in motion for me. I am then reminded of "Make a difference." How can I do that and waste my time on the Internet? Now the excuse is taken away. When I exit the e-mail search, I do so with a grateful heart, understanding that God has a mission for me. If you are like me, and I suspect I am not alone, grab that cup of joe, or whatever you grab a cup full of, and take some time to ponder your situation. I talk about dealing with the pain of losing a son because that is the hardest thing in my world to deal with. Then I remember my son. I remember that what he did took courage, it took putting others ahead of himself, and it took having the will to answer his call in life. Then I can see him with those folded arms and that smirky smile, followed by "Oh, good grief, Dad." After that, how can I allow myself time to be wasted away with whatever I may come up with for an excuse to not do what my mission in life requires of me? The answer is I cannot.

Continue to Move Forward

At the end of the day, I ask myself, *Have I moved forward today?* If I answer honestly and the answer is no, then I need an honest answer as to why not. Upon a closer examination, and not to my surprise, I will be able to conclude that I let "stuff" get in the way most of the time. *Stuff* was one of Phillip's favorite words to use when he did not want to define whatever was at hand for him. I have found that there is a lot of undefined "stuff" that keeps us from ever leaving the starting line.

On those days that I can, with honesty, say today was a good day, then I need to take a close look at what made it a good day. I need to continue doing that and adding to that which makes a good day. The determination I have of how I will deal with good and bad days comes from my heart and not my surroundings. I choose to allow the memories of my son and my family to be a part of my life worthy of doing my best. When I choose to move forward with this in mind, Phillip makes as much of a difference as each member of the family does, friends included.

To live life, you have to get involved in it. Philip got involved with life early on. It is fair to understand that no one can feel the depth of your sorrows. I have learned that while that is true of anyone on this earth, God can, and is the only one who can. For there to be a blessing, we have to reach beyond ourselves to where God is, and he will do what is impossible for us to do and reach that point for us.

Now at this point, you might be wondering again what all of this has to do with Phillip and Forever 22. It has everything to do with Phillip and Forever 22. As I opened my heart and mind to whatever direction God would have me go, whatever door God opens, I will step through it.

Time with the Patriot Guard Riders

I do not know if I could ever thank them adequately enough for their support knowing I was a Gold Star Dad. Their appreciation for the sacrifice Phillip had given, I will always be short on words to tell them what that meant to my heart. With my cameras around my neck, the

Patriot Guard missions would take me to a variety of places. I would meet some of the best American patriots around.

One of my fondest and most fun memories is hanging out of the passenger side window of Jerry Turner, a.k.a. Water Boy, with my camera clicking away. I can still see the lead bike with Phillip's Never Forget flag, a stark reminder of the duty to never forget the cost of our freedom.

I think one of the most valuable assists from my time with the Patriot Guard Riders is the opportunity they gave my heart to see the bigger picture. It is not about one's self; it is about the mission and the reasons that mission exists. The time spent with the Patriot Guard Riders allowed my heart to find the vision I so desperately needed to continue the mission I was given. I can say I have that vision and mission today. I do not get to go on near as many missions as I used to, but that does not mean they are any less in my heart and on my mind.

The Texas Honor Ride

My first exposure to the Texas Honor Ride came toward mid-September 2007 at a cowboy church in Conroe, Texas. They were having their last fundraiser of the year before leaving Houston for their annual ride to the Brooks Army Medical Center (BAMC), in San Antonio, Texas. These guys and gals don't know how much they helped me through this time. The Texas Honor Ride has a special place in my heart because it was their event that led me to the WWII 6th Cav group that became a favorite of the sporting clays tournament. That same event introduced me to Rick Harris and the Vietnam-era Huey that served in Vietnam. With that Huey, I would discover that Phillip's best friend in high school worked as a volunteer with the foundation the Huey belonged. Still ahead of me, opening doors so the dots can continue to connect, you can see how God is. The Huey would be a huge favorite at the sporting clays tournament four of the five years of the tournament's existence, donating funds to the wounded warrior's homebuilding organization, Homes for our Troops.

Most of all, they gave my heart the chance to understand a fact that would become a big part of my life when I set up the Texas Fallen Heroes memorial wall. That fact is what they are doing for the wounded warriors and their families is the best way to honor those comrades of theirs who have made the ultimate sacrifice. I have the honor of making sure this is a statement that those involved in the event hear and know from my heart. Texas Honor Ride, my heart thanks you with more gratefulness than words are available to express it. I especially salute Johnny Dee.

CHAPTER 21

MOVING FORWARD

As I write these last two chapters, a lot of thoughts run through my heart, and then are sent to my mind for action. I look back to the first few times I told of escorting Phillip home, people almost immediately would let me know they thought I should write a book about it. There were those times when I knew people were right. However, as I look back now, my heart simply was not ready at that point. Each time I decided to sit down to write, my thoughts could never get beyond trying to find the words to describe what was in my heart. Then there was the second hurdle to cross: I needed to deal with choosing the focus of the story. There was no doubt in my mind that the book would be about escorting Phillip home. From the beginning, I had this narrow vision of what the book should focus on. I did not want this book to be about me or my time spent in Iraq. Then because of the narrow scope I had set for the story of the book, I did not want it to become a religious type of book either.

When I did start sitting in front of the computer with my fingers ready to tap out the first sentence, I ran into a brick wall head-on, not being able to get the first word on the document page. With the first, reminiscence out of my memory databank being how I got to the point of applying for a job with KBR. Then my thoughts were flooded with the struggle I had with doing things my way and finally settling on the fact that only God's way could lift me out of the mess I was in at the time. Then I began to understand that without a story about God, a story that connected my being in Iraq, there would have never been a story about escorting Phillip home.

The purpose of this chapter is not to recount the entire story. It is about the truly exceptional Americans that my son has the distinct honor of being in their company. It is my prayer that after you have put this book down, you will have already been inspired to do things God's way. I hope you can find the courage to walk that valley because no one can walk it for you. But understanding this: you do not have to walk it alone.

We are all created with a calling engineered into our life's program system. What we do with that calling is entirely up to us when we realize that it is there. While I recognize that the environment we are born into, by no choice of our own, has an effect on our lives as they develop, it does not determine who God created us to become in this life. I truly believe that at some point, everyone understands there is a calling on their life, and that at that point, there is no one or nothing that can stop them from responding to that calling.

From my own experience, I can tell you that I knew God was real when I was but a lad. I did not need His physical appearance before my eyes to believe what I knew to be a fact in my heart. I heard a sermon by a Houston pastor not too many days ago that made what I believe much clearer than I have ever heard it explained. He explained what happens to the Christian at the time of death. What happens to him at that point and beyond seemed once again to be one of those times that God gave me the answer I needed for the time I needed it.

As you have walked this far with me, you might remember when I found out I had lost Phillip. Remember on the flight from Iraq to Germany, which was a time that my faith served me so well. I was able to stand on that solid foundation and face the storm that had come to my shore. I knew in my heart at that point what I believed, why I believed it, and, most importantly, it was a part of my solid foundation. God caused my heart to think about those who had gone through this lonesome valley and had to walk it on their own. I wondered, on that flight, how in the world anyone could talk such a walk without knowing God was real. How could they do this without knowing the fact that He walked that valley with him or her, not for them, but because the pain was still just as horrible? It was within that context of thinking that I realized how blessed my soul was to firmly believe that when the body, the temple of the soul, no longer has a physical life, it is at that point and in less than an instant of a moment that the soul is present with the Lord for a believer. With that firmly in my heart, I knew that I was on a mission to take the temple of Phillip's soul home to lay to rest. That made my mission impossible, very possible.

It is on the matter of the soul that departs the body at the time of death that I would like to make, not a correction but, rather, a clarification. We have so many times heard the phrase "body, mind, and soul." In fact, this phrase is in the motto of the YMCA. It is a part of the founder's belief that the body is the temple of the soul, and considering that, the care of it is as a temple of a holy entity. What God has moved my heart to set a little more clearly is that the mind and the body are the physical parts of the person that houses the soul, and for the Christian, the Holy Spirit. This next point is crucial to the understanding of what makes the difference in all of humankind and the Christian. That difference is that when God created Adam, he breathed into Adam a soul that no other part of His creation possesses. What happens next for the believer is totally a matter of humbling the soul and accepting the gift that Christ died for to give us. That gift allows us to be present with the Lord at the time of death. Knowing this, again, made the mission impossible, very possible. The Holy Spirit takes the soul to heaven.

As I started from the first chapter and moved forward, style was not as important for me to achieve as the mission I found myself, and I would focus on that mission from the time I realized I was on it. Is that not neat of God? Oh, by the way, you are on a mission, since you are going to be there anyhow. God knows exact who we are and how we are; do you believe for one minute if God were to let us know that we were going to have a mission in addition to twelve hours, seven days a week, five months at a time in sandy 125-degree-weather that we decide, "Thank you, but no thanks." I think our tendency would have been to wallow in the mud right where we are.

See, that is why we need to, when we lay our heads down, ask for His wisdom. If He is that wise in dealing with our worthless hides, then can you imagine what it would be like for those who go against us? I would not want to be in their shoes or boots at all.

God reached a way back in my life to connect dots that I had almost forgotten or did not think would be worth an iota of good at any point. However, He kind of started with the grateful heart given me when

I was born, for as poor as we grew up, one had to be grateful for the intangibles because the tangibles just were not there. Then He moved forward through my high school years and then to Vietnam. It is just amazing how much He knew and cared about me back then.

When I felt as though I had made enough wrong decisions, that conclusion brilliantly arrived at when I knew by the evidence of a lifetime of doing it my way, I threw my hands up in the air and surrender a humble heart to God. Guess what, He was right there. We decided I could no longer do it my way. In writing this book, I learned an important concept that I hope I can pass on to you now that our walk is finished. That is that no matter how desperate we get, no matter how hard we try, and no matter how far we think we can reach, God has to meet us right where we are. If we were capable of reaching, Him then we mostly like would think we did not need Him—at least not at that point.

That lonesome valley, that valley of the shadow of death that I had to walk on my own because no one could walk it for me—I did not have to walk it alone. Through the pages of that chapter, you walked it with me; you walked it with God and Phillip. My heart knows for sure and is grateful for the knowledge that there is no need for us to stay in that valley or ever go back to it. We will find no one there but ourselves with the pain and sorrows of our heart.

In writing this book, I have discovered that sometimes the vision of the mission does not come outright. Sometimes we just have to keep moving forward before we can see far enough down the road to understand what is going on and how the cow ate the cabbage. I have a much clearer vision today than I did in May of 2004. One theme throughout this story is making a difference.

We cannot make a difference unless, like our warriors, we are moving toward the sound of the guns firing. We cannot make a difference from the couch in front of the television. I learned a long time ago that all of my fixin'-tos still sit idle waiting for that around-to-it. All the dots connect—the little dots of making a difference and the bigger dots of making a difference; they all make a huge difference on the other side of the equations. The sum of the parts equals the whole, which is where we want to be at the end of the day when we turn the lights out.

At the end of the day, when you turn the lights out to your world, where will God find you? It is my hope that after I lay my head down, get up the next morning with my cup of joe, and pondering, God will have given me another book to share with you. I would look forward to walking with you again.

CHAPTER 22

Making a Difference to Final Sunsets

Now at the end of the day when I lay my head down, I simply pray for God's wisdom for the next day, I have been doing this for a long time now. Over the last few years, it has become more meaningful. The use of the phase has become a part of my daily routine. Just as I have learned other concepts over time and a couple of new ones in recent time.

Phillip was always learning, and I think I have come to recognize that trait in his brother and sisters. I also think I have learned to pay much closer attention not just to my own family but I have also learned the importance of paying closer attention to those around me. In doing so, the question becomes, how can you make a difference when every minute of the day is all about you and your needs? The answer is that you most likely make very little difference in your own life, much less in that of someone else's.

As I think about the chapters I have written, I realize that as we walked through this story, there were times my heart would feel that pain that only God could reach. I also realize that in writing a story, I have learned so much. I have realized things that I simply have missed for a long time. God has taught my heart through writing this book. Most of all, it has given me a better look at the vision for the mission you and I started out on from the beginning.

I have the vision in perspective, and now I can carry forward on that mission against my final sunset in life. Realizing fully that we do not retire from life until God retires us. Making a difference has been a thread of dots in my life from the beginning. Phillip's legacy has opened my heart and eyes to that mission.

Phillip, like everyone else who either gave their lives or have given that pound of flesh and bone, so to speak, in the fight to preserve our freedom, had no idea what it would cost him. People like him certainly knew that the possibilities existed. They had no way of knowing how far over that line they would be required to go. From this, we can draw examples of many things of which courage comes to mind first, commitment to what they started, inspiration for doing what is right and good.

When I think of Phillip, it is hard for me to think of him in terms of just him. I think this is in part because I realized shortly after we buried him that my heart understood the concept that he no longer belonged just to me, his father; rather, belonged to a group of heroes who now belong to a nation.

Looking at that thought and realizing that it has truth in it helps with the process of moving forward. Without rehashing a position, I would just like to remind you that I feel there is a great chasm between moving on and moving forward. Mostly because of the connotation, the differences of the use the two words inferred in their meanings.

For those who are trying to move on, as outsiders looking in refer to it, it also implies that you have to leave something behind or forget something in order to make that move on time possible. It is for this reason that for those who have walked that mile in my shoes, I will encourage them to move forward when their time comes. The biggest and most significance thing in this thinking is that you can neither simply leave behind nor forget what has caused you to be in the spot you are in now. I believe that by the grace of God, you can move forward with your pain and with those memories. If you were capable of leaving the pain behind and forget the memories that cause that pain, then what happened was not the big a deal, simply put.

Having established that, it is for that reason I considered some time ago that folks were right—I needed to write about this. It also had not happened overnight due to the amount of urging early on. The amount of time has everything to do with the depth of the pain I could not sit down and describe adequately with even an exhaustive vocabulary. The words simply were not there.

In your walk with me, you know that many nights of laying my head down went into that simple request for wisdom beyond anything I possessed. You also know that I would consume many cups of joe for me to get to this point. Then, likewise, you know that there were untold numbers of hours pondering the days that followed with those cups of joe.

The point is that at the end of the day, starting with that early morning phone call on what started as a normal day of "This is the day the Lord hath made; I will rejoice and be glad in it" was followed by thoughts of how blessed I was on my way to call home. I think the point I want to make as clear as possible is that you can be on top of the mountain with all going your way; in fact, life can be going better than it ever has. Then in an instant, as we have walked through that instant, things can change your entire world.

At the end of the day, for this part of our discussion, it is my sincere desire that if you have made this walk with me and you do not have a solid foundation under your life, then this book is for you to realize you need to start building that foundation before a storm catches you unaware. This is I think the first installment, if you will, of Phillips legacy to you and so many others.

You have walked with me from the start of *Forever 22*, when I had come to the end of doing it my way. Start with where you are and build each day with each night of when you lay your head down. Get up early, enough to give yourself time with God. It is your choice on the cup of joe. I am still having those cups of joe, and give your heart that pondering of the day. Let your answered prayers be revealed to you.

I just realized when using the title *Forever 22*: do not spend excessive time looking back because in the end, a lot time will have been spent where you can do nothing anything about. I have a lot of times during the day where the memories will be brought forward to remind me of Phillip and as I press on forward, they help me keep the vision and mission firmly planted as my standard bearer, making a difference. It would be such nonprofitable consumption of time for me to invest in what Phillip could have done, maybe would have done. This is how I would rather spend my time in remembrance of Phillip. He was twenty-two years old when he made that ultimate sacrifice. He will, therefore, *forever* be twenty-two. It is that point that he will forever remain and it is that point that he was making a difference. I will pick up his cause, and he will continue to make a difference because I will be his standard bearer.

I needed to try explaining what is in my heart at this point. After some time of pondering, with my cup of joe to the right of my keyboard, I think I have a handle on what is on my heart. Remember when I expressed the fact that Phillip did not give his life in expectation that my life would end also. That is a fact that is on my heart a lot as I have had a chance to think about many different things in the process of writing this book. It is not a fact that is a burden in any sense of the word. It is, as I listen to the hearts of others, a point that I have come to realize as a part of my mission: a part of Phillip is continuing to make a difference in life. Especially when I consider what people have said about the seemingly little qualities that added up making him who he was as they applied to those individuals. Out of this realization comes a simple understanding. In the end, it is the connecting of all of the dots that makes the difference. Some spectacularly grand vision that is a grandiose version at oneself does not make a difference in the lives of others.

With that, I am led to the next item that is on my heart. We have to deal with the facts that we have at hand. I deal with the fact every day that Phillip is no longer here. The question is, do I miss him. You bet I do, but I also have the rest of my family, and they not only need me, but they also deserve me as husband and dad to continue to be that to that final sunset of my own. They deserve all that I am capable of and can give them. I cannot do that while I allow myself to wander around that lonesome valley. Especially, if I understand there is nothing for me to find there. I will find Phillip in being the best husband and dad I can be. If I do not want that echoing, "Oh good grief, Dad" to be present in my thoughts constantly, then I know what I have to do and what I have to be.

I have a very grateful heart for those things that hold memories of Phillip; however, at the end of the day, that was not Phillip. If Phillip's memorial is to live on, then it has to be about making a difference, because he was ever here. As I move around Texas with the memorial wall, I know that Phillip's spirit is with me. I also know that with me in that spirit are his brother and sisters, because they mattered so much to him. It becomes a family effort; it becomes a Texas effort as the grateful hearts of Texas are inspired to do what they can to make a difference. It is from the grateful heart that comes as a part of the nation he and his comrades have fought and died because of their service.

It is with great hope that as a nation we cannot look upon the price with which our freedom, with liberties to the pursuit of happiness will never be looked on as something due to us. I am a realist and understand there are those who live at the expense of those who have paid the price and whose families continue to pay the price. I understand those folks think it is everyone else's duty to defend their perceived right. At the same time, I know that there are many patriotic Americans out there. I know that America is still exceptional because God makes her. I know the prevailing thought about God being absent in America, I submit to you that He is more alive than the critics would have you believe. Is there a bigger need for God, absolutely?

Thank you for walking this long journey with me. I hope you have found something from your walk to take away with you. I am looking forward to writing some more. I would like to write about American exceptionalism because I truly believe it is. It is in my heart to write, with the hope of making a difference about some of the concepts I have come to know that have worked an awesome changed in my life. It is about making a difference. Then there is a more in-depth story about working in Iraq. It has so many great challenges, times that only God could have come through with the answer. Those are my inspirational, encouraging, and motivational aspirations.

I think my next book will be an inspiring fiction about a boy who had to leave the Appalachia Mountains at twelve to survive on his own when he was forced to leave his home in the hills. Down From the Hills, is already in the works. I hope you will be looking for it. You can keep up with it on my website.

Edwards Brothers Malloy
Thorofare, NJ USA
February 17, 2015